The **MP3**

and Internet
Audio Handbook

Your Guide to the Digital Music Revolution!

Bruce Fries
with Marty Fries

The MP3 and Internet Audio Handbook

TeamCom Books

P.O. Box 1251
Burtonsville, MD 20866
www.TeamComBooks.com
301-847-7600, 301-847-7638 (fax)

Credits

Editor: Karen Porterfield
Cover Design: Michael Lynch
Illustrations: Christine Finn and Bruce Fries
Contributing Writers: James Barrett, Rithy Chhuan, Brian Maeng, Karen Porterfield, Ann Rolfes, and Joe Rolfes

Notice of Rights

Cataloging-in-Publication Data

Fries, Bruce

The MP3 and Internet audio handbook : your guide to the digital music revolution! / Bruce Fries with Marty Fries. – 1st ed.

p. cm.

Includes bibliographical references and index.

LCCN: 99-94978
ISBN: 1-928791-10-7

1. MP3. 2. Music–Computer programs. 3. Internet radio broadcasting. 4. Music–Computer network resources. 5. MP3 players. I. Fries, Marty. II. Title.

ML74.4.M6F75 2000   780'.285

Printed and bound in the United States of America   9 8 7 6 5 4 3 2 1

Dedication

To my grandmother, Nellie Collins, for whom I promised myself that I'd publish a book she'd live to see, even though she may not be able to read it because of her poor eyesight.

Acknowledgements

Thanks to all of my friends and relatives who supported me, and thanks to all of the people who provided input to help make this book better than I possibly could have on my own.

Special thanks to the following people who provided valuable feedback on the manuscript: Gabriel Bouvigne, Bill Calder, Peg Calder, Scott Cannon, Steve Conzett, Tom Critchfield, Barbara Fries, Robin Gross, Rob Jolles, Bob Kohn, Chris Kroells, Matt Oppenheim, Jean Nicolle, Scott Sibley, Derek Sivers, Amy Stevens and Larry Thomas. And thanks to all the people on the message boards at MP3.com who regularly shared their knowledge of MP3 and digital audio with me and other users.

This book was truly a team effort, and I want to make sure proper credit is given to each contributor. My coauthor Marty Fries wrote the following chapters: *Connecting Your PC to Your Stereo, A Digital Audio Primer, Hard Disk Recording*, and *Recording Your Own CDs*. Ann Rolfes and Joe Rolfes performed the research for and wrote most of the *Digital Music and Copyright Law* chapter and many of the Web site descriptions in Appendix A. Karen Porterfield did much of the research and writing for the *Music on the Web* and *Internet Radio* chapters, in addition to acting as Editor for the book.

Screen shots in this book were provided courtesy of the following parties: Adaptec, Mediascience, Microsoft, MP3.com, MusicMatch, Nullsoft, RealNetworks, Rolling Stone Network, Spinner.com, Syntrillium, vTuner.com and Xing Technologies.

Contents

List of Tables

List of Figures

Preface

Like many people, I listen to a wide variety of music and I like to have good music playing when I entertain. But radio stations don't always play the songs I like, and many of the CDs I own only have one or two good songs. As a result, I end up spending a lot of time swapping CDs and making tapes with mixes of my favorite music.

Recording tapes from records and CDs, even with good equipment, is always time-consuming. It takes at least an hour's worth of my time (usually more) for every hour's worth of music I record. And if I screw up and set the wrong level, or if I decide on a different order of songs, I often have to re-record the entire tape.

It's a lot of work to keep even a moderate size music collection organized. It seems like each CD rack or case eventually fills up, which means more racks and cases, which means searching through multiple racks and cases just to find one CD. As soon as I get one rack alphabetized, I inevitably purchase a few more "must-have" albums and have to rearrange the whole collection to fit these in.

A few years ago, I purposely stopped alphabetizing my CDs (some of my friends thought the alphabetizing was a symptom of anal retentiveness). But that made it even harder to find things. I had a lot of compilation tapes with music from different bands, but the sound quality was deteriorating and I didn't have time to record new ones. Because of all the hassles of dealing with tapes and CDs and the limited selection of local radio stations, I just didn't listen to music as much as I would have liked to.

After years of searching for a better way, including looking into large capacity CD changers, hi-fi VCRs and digital audio tapes, I finally found a solution in the form of MP3 and my personal computer. I was on the verge of spending a few hundred dollars on a CD changer and DJ mixer when I learned about MP3. Thanks to MP3, I now have a much more powerful solution and I only spent about $75 (for a new CD-ROM drive and some shareware). This solution is so powerful that I sometimes refer to it as the "Holy Grail" of home recording.

Now, I can play any song with a click of the mouse and spend five or ten minutes making playlists for parties instead of several hours making tapes. I can record CDs with up to 12 hours of high quality music and download playlists to a portable player that can store five hours of music on a card the size of a matchbook. I can listen to Internet radio stations programmed to my musical tastes, and if I hear a song I like, I can purchase it on the spot and download it to my PC.

I was so impressed with these new-found capabilities that I decided to write a book and teach others about the benefits of downloadable music and streaming audio. I wanted to make it easy for anyone to get started and avoid the months of research and trial and error I went through, finding the best products and figuring out the best ways to make everything work.

This book isn't just about digital music technology: It's also about a revolution that is reshaping the music industry and putting more power into the hands of consumers, musicians and independent record labels. You can become an active participant in this revolution by supporting open standards like MP3 and by resisting efforts to impose encrypted formats and restrictive licensing policies.

So come join the revolution, and take control of your music, whatever your reason—whether you're a music lover and like the ease and flexibility of MP3; whether you're a musician and like the idea of 50% royalties and direct access to your fans; or whether you're a true revolutionary and want to reduce the control that the major record labels have over most of the music we listen to.

Best wishes, and welcome to the Digital Music Revolution.

Bruce Fries

Bruce Fries
Silver Spring, Maryland

Introduction

Downloadable music formats like MP3 and streaming audio on the Internet are revolutionizing the way music is distributed and consumed. With these technologies, consumers have more convenient access to a wider variety of music and more control over how they listen to it. Musicians have increased access to fans and more options for distributing their music. Independent record labels have a better way to promote and distribute music to a wider audience. And the major record labels have a serious threat to their dominance of the industry.

What Is MP3?

MP3 (technically, MPEG Audio Layer-III) is a standard format for compressing digital audio. MP3 squeezes audio files to about one tenth of their original size, while maintaining close to CD quality. Songs in MP3 format can be downloaded from the Internet, created from prerecorded music, or recorded from scratch. MP3 files can be played on personal computers, Walkman-style portable players (like the Rio) or one of the new generation of dual-mode MP3/audio CD players. Another common use of MP3 is for audio books and Internet radio.

What Is MPEG?

MPEG stands for Moving Picture Experts Group. The MPEG committee works under the direction of the International Standards Organization (ISO) and establishes standards for encoding audio and video in digital format, and for interactive graphics applications. MP3 is just a small part of the MPEG family of standards. Thanks to MPEG, we also have standards for technologies like DVD (Digital Versatile Disc) and DirecTV.

Why Are So Many People Excited About MP3?

The main benefit of MP3 is its high level of compression, which makes for smaller files and faster downloads. With MP3, you can store more than 12 hours of high-quality music on a single CD, versus the standard 74 minutes.

With the matchbook-sized memory cards used by portable MP3 players, you can fit the equivalent of a dozen CDs in your wallet. (I verified this by putting some SmartMedia cards in my own wallet.)

MP3 compression allows you to use your computer as a digital jukebox that can hold thousands of CD-quality songs. You can quickly find and play any song with a click of a mouse and never have to worry about tapes wearing out or records getting scratched. Instead of spending hours making tapes or programming a CD changer, you can compile customized playlists in minutes.

Figure 1 - Capacity of an Audio CD vs. an MP3 CD

Audio CD   MP3 CD

Compression also makes it practical to download music from the Internet, where you can access thousands of songs from artists all over the world. With MP3, you can download a four-minute song in less than 15 minutes (with a 33.6 kbps modem), compared to more than 3 hours for the same song in CD audio format. Now you can sample a wide variety of music from the comfort of your home and find some great music from independent artists you might not otherwise be exposed to.

MP3 opens up a whole new range of possibilities for musicians. If you are an independent or emerging artist, MP3 and the Internet give you a low cost way to promote your music worldwide and keep in touch with fans. You can sign with one of the new Internet record labels, retain the copyrights to your music, and keep a much larger share of the revenue.

Downloadable music and streaming audio are rapidly growing in popularity, but widespread acceptance has been limited by the fact that these are relatively new technologies, and there is a shortage of people who understand them. There's also a lot of hype and contradictory information coming from many different sources. There's confusion about terminology, debates about sound quality, and concern about the ease with which unauthorized copies can be produced and distributed.

The goal of *The MP3 and Internet Audio Handbook* is to cut through all the hype and provide you with easy-to-understand information, practical advice and step-by-step instructions to help you begin using these technologies right away, without time-consuming trial and error.

About This Book

This book is structured to appeal to several types of readers, so some sections will naturally be more relevant to your interests than others will. You should simply skip over any sections that don't interest you.

Due to space and time constraints, most of the examples in this book are based on IBM PC compatible systems running Windows 95/98. Later editions will include more information pertaining to other systems.

Following are descriptions of each chapter.

Part 1: Digital Music and the Internet

Chapter 1. The Digital Music Revolution discusses why MP3 and digital music on the Internet are causing so much excitement and how they are revolutionizing the way music is marketed and distributed.

Chapter 2. Music on the Web describes how to find, sample and purchase music via the World Wide Web. This chapter explains the basics of downloadable music and streaming audio, and discusses music search engines and music piracy. Included are descriptions of popular online music sites.

Chapter 3. Internet Radio discusses the advantages of Internet radio over traditional broadcast radio, along with the factors that affect sound quality and availability. Included are descriptions of programs for listening to streaming audio, listings of popular Internet radio stations, along with information on streaming MP3 and webcasting licensing.

Chapter 4. Digital Music Distribution describes the new generation of Internet record labels and provides an overview of secure music distribution systems, including the Secure Digital Music Initiative (SDMI) and future systems.

Chapter 5. Digital Music and Copyright Law covers what consumers need to know about legal issues related to digital music on personal computers and the Internet. Issues related to the legality of ripping and downloadable music are covered, along with information on statutory licenses for webcasting and summaries of key U.S. copyright laws.

Part 2: Turning Your PC into a CD-Quality Jukebox

Chapter 6. Getting Started with MP3 provides an overview of what you need to get started with digital music, including hardware and software requirements, methods of obtaining, organizing and playing music, and recommended system configurations.

Chapter 7. Choosing the Right Software discusses the software needed to play digital music on a personal computer. Popular software, including audio players, multimedia players, all-in-one programs and DJ mixer programs are covered.

Chapter 8. Choosing the Right Hardware explains the hardware requirements for working with digital music on personal computers, including processor and memory requirements, peripheral interfaces, CD-ROM drives, CD recorders, speakers, sound cards and USB audio devices. This chapter also covers portable players, memory cards, MP3/audio CD players and MP3-compatible car stereos.

Chapter 9. Organizing and Playing Music teaches you how to organize and play downloadable music on your computer. This chapter also covers accessing the CDDB, adjusting playback volume, options for storing digital music, file type associations, working with playlists, and useful features like skins, plug-ins and remote controls.

Chapter 10. Connecting Your PC to Your Stereo explains the best ways to connect your computer to a stereo or home entertainment system. Connection fundamentals, sound card and stereo receiver inputs and outputs, analog and digital connections and wireless audio transmitters are all covered.

Part 3: Understanding Digital Audio

Chapter 11. A Digital Audio Primer explains the basics of sound and provides an overview of digital audio technologies. Sampling, resolution, dynamic range, signal-to-noise ratio and bit-rates are covered, along with the advantages of digital audio. File size and bandwidth requirements and various forms of compression are also discussed.

Chapter 12. Digital Audio Formats explains digital audio file structures, compression codecs and streaming audio. Also included are descriptions of common digital audio formats and streaming audio systems.

Chapter 13. MPEG Audio provides technical details on MPEG Audio and explains how MP3 relates to other MPEG standards. Information on MPEG standards, layers, encoding methods, bit-rates, embedded data (ID3 tags) and sound quality is included.

Part 4: Recording Audio on Your PC

Chapter 14. Hard Disk Recording teaches you how to use your computer as a digital recording device. Recording from analog sources, direct digital recording, sound card mixing functions, noise reduction, vinyl and tape preservation and recording software are all covered.

Chapter 15. Digital Audio Extraction explains how to extract digital audio from CDs. Ripping software, CD-ROM drive compatibility, the ripping process and jitter correction are discussed. Tips for successful ripping, factors that affect ripping speed, verifying quality of ripped files and analog ripping are also covered.

Chapter 16. Making Your Own MP3 Files explains how to create MP3 files from uncompressed audio and how to record directly to MP3. Encoding software, constant versus variable bit-rates, selecting the best bit-rate, and verifying results are all covered.

Chapter 17. Editing Sound Files covers how to clean up sound files before and after converting them to MP3. Normalization, trimming silence, noise removal, adding fade-ins and fade-outs, and optimizing audio for the Web are all explained. Utilities for directly editing MP3 files and batch processing WAV files are also covered.

Chapter 18. Recording Your Own CDs teaches you how to use a CD recorder to create standard audio CDs and data format MP3 CDs. CD construction, CD-R and CD-RW formats, CD standards and file systems, recording options and media types are explained, along with strategies for ensuring error-free results.

Part 5: Step-by-Step Tutorials

Chapter 19. Basic Tasks provides step-by-step tutorials for downloading files, installing software, playing music and modifying file type associations.

Chapter 20. Software Tutorials provides step-by-step instructions for common tasks in AudioCatalyst, Easy CD Creator, Cool Edit, MusicMatch Jukebox, RealJukebox and Winamp.

Appendices

Appendix A. Interesting Web Sites provides descriptions of interesting music-related Web sites. Included are listings of online music stores, Internet radio sites, Internet record labels, artist resources, music news, MP3 information, home recording and pro audio, music licensing and industry associations.

Appendix B. What and Where to Buy lists hardware and software for working with digital audio on personal computers, including prices and where to buy. Also included are listings of speakers, cables and audio interfaces.

Appendix C. Recommended Reading lists books recommended by the author for readers who want to sharpen their basic computer skills or want to learn more about the technologies covered in this book.

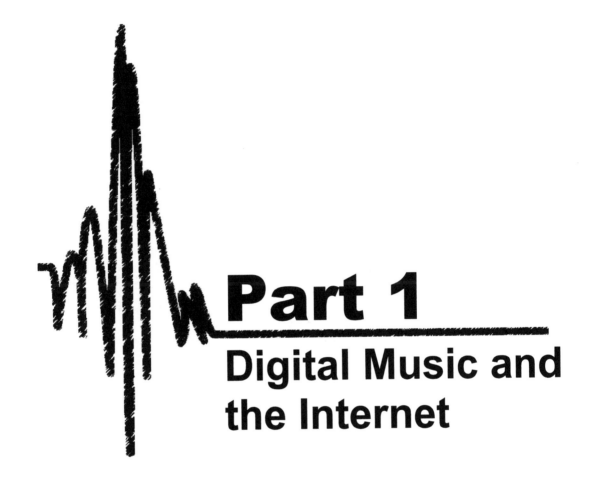

Part 1

Digital Music and the Internet

Chapter 1

The Digital Music Revolution

A revolution is underway in the music industry that is having a greater impact than when compact discs displaced vinyl records in the early 1980s. This revolution is driven by improvements in technologies for compressing digital audio that make it practical to distribute music over the Internet and turn personal computers into digital jukeboxes that can hold thousands of songs.

The Digital Music Revolution is already having a widespread impact on many industries. New business models are rapidly evolving and placing established businesses under increasing pressure. It will be years before the full effects are seen, but even at this early stage, many people are benefiting from opportunities created as the digital music industry takes shape.

A key reason why this revolution is moving so rapidly is the universal nature of music. Music plays an important role in our lives, affecting our moods and making us feel connected to the rest of the world. But finding music to suit our personal tastes requires a lot of time and effort. This is why we have record labels and radio stations: They act as filters for the music we hear and save us the trouble of sifting through thousands of songs every year.

The problem with this state of affairs is that most of what we listen to, and when we listen to it, is decided by the record labels and radio stations. Individual consumers have little say in this process other than their ability to vote with their wallet and the dial on their radio. One of the reasons why so many people make tapes is so they can listen to the kind of music they like, whenever they want to. Unfortunately, even with the latest equipment, recording tapes is a time-consuming and unforgiving process.

MP3 has changed all of this, virtually overnight. With MP3, you no longer have to worry about tapes wearing out or have to search through multiple boxes or racks to find one song. You no longer have to program a CD changer or change tapes during parties. You don't have to spend hours recording new tapes every time you decide on a different order of songs. And you don't have to buy an entire album when you only like one or two songs.

Thanks to the Internet, you no longer have to rely on local radio stations to listen to music you like, and you don't have to worry about albums being out of stock at the local record store. You have access to a much wider selection of music, and you can listen to radio stations that play music based on direct input from listeners.

Besides benefiting consumers, the Digital Music Revolution also gives musicians more control over their music. Thanks to MP3 and the Internet, bands that don't have contracts with a record company now have access to a worldwide distribution channel that offers them a much higher profit potential. With Internet distribution, much of the overhead disappears. In fact, Internet record labels typically offer royalties of 50%, compared to the 12%-15% typically offered by the major labels.

The economics of Internet music distribution are so compelling that even major artists are choosing to distribute their music through the Internet. Some bands are going a step further and setting up Web sites to sell music and merchandise directly to their fans. Even if only a small percentage of their fans are online, this approach can generate much greater profits because the costs are so low.

Of course, artists who opt to go it alone won't be able to benefit from the marketing and distribution resources of a label. But by working with an independent label that offers Internet distribution, artists can have the best of both worlds: help with producing and promoting their music, and the increased profits and visibility provided by the Internet.

It's important to remember that MP3 is just one of many factors in this revolution. What makes this revolution so powerful is the convergence of MP3 with other factors, such as the increased processing power and storage capacity of personal computers, the widespread availability of music on the Internet, and the growing dissatisfaction among musicians with the status quo at major record labels.

MP3 happened to be the format that was best positioned when the other factors converged. The fact that MP3 is an open standard and has a tremendous amount of grassroots support has helped it become the de facto standard for downloadable music. Extensive media coverage has also helped MP3 gain more mind share among consumers than any of the competing formats.

MP3 has come to represent more than just a technology: It's become a symbol of the Digital Music Revolution, representing freedom, flexibility and empowerment. An MP3 subculture has even evolved with millions of users who hang out in the chat rooms and message boards of hundreds of MP3 sites scattered around the Internet. These users exchange information and advice, debate key issues and closely follow developments in the industry.

A key factor early in the Digital Music Revolution was the development of Winamp, a popular program for playing digital audio on PCs. Winamp was the first full-featured program for playing music in MP3 format. Winamp was developed by Justin Frankel in April 1997, shortly after he dropped out of the University of Utah. Winamp quickly surpassed other players in popularity because of its advanced features like equalizer presets and support for third party plug-ins and skins. In June 1999, Justin's company, Nullsoft, was acquired by America Online (AOL) for approximately $80 million in stock—not bad for a 20-year-old.

The spark that made the revolution front-page news was the lawsuit filed by the RIAA (Recording Industry Association of America) and the AARC (Alliance of Artists and Recording Companies) to prevent Diamond Multimedia (now S3, Inc.) from selling its Rio portable MP3 player. Before the Rio, MP3 users were limited to listening to MP3 files on their computers. But the Rio provided a way to make MP3 portable and, therefore, more appealing to mainstream consumers. Suddenly, MP3 was a serious threat to the recording industry, which had previously not paid much attention to it.

The RIAA is concerned about MP3 because its small file size and lack of security measures make it easy for people to illegally reproduce and distribute copyrighted music. College students with fast Internet connections quickly found out that with MP3 they could download hundreds of songs in less time than it would take to make a trip to the local record store. This kind of piracy is difficult to prevent because the music is just digital bits, and not physical media like tapes and CDs. On the Internet, a single copy of a file can grow to thousands of copies in minutes.

The RIAA argued that the Rio was a digital recording device covered by the Audio Home Recording Act of 1992. A provision of this law requires consumer digital recording devices to incorporate the Serial Copy Management

System (SCMS), to prevent the proliferation of multiple generations of perfect digital copies. The RIAA also maintained that the Rio was used primarily to play pirated music downloaded from the Internet.

In June 1999, the U.S. Court of Appeals ruled unanimously in favor of Diamond Multimedia, accepting its argument that the Rio was a computer peripheral and not subject to the SCMS requirement. The court also ruled that the Doctrine of Fair Use (see Chapter 5) allows consumers to "space-shift" music by copying it to another device, similar to their right to "time-shift" video recordings. The right to time-shift was established in the case of Sony versus Universal City Studios in 1984 (464 U.S. 417), which concerned the sale of videocassette recorders in the United States.

Diamond Multimedia not only won the lawsuit; they also received massive amounts of free publicity, which helped increase the demand for the Rio to the point where they were producing more than 10,000 of them per week. The ruling in favor of Diamond Multimedia was also a victory for consumers and consumer electronics manufacturers. But the battle over consumer's fair use rights is far from over, and will likely require further legislation.

The popularity of MP3 provided a wake-up call to the recording industry and to companies promoting proprietary digital audio formats. Because of the potential for piracy provided by open formats like MP3, the recording industry is attempting to establish a "secure" digital music format before they start releasing downloadable music by major artists.

Millions of people are already using MP3, so any secure format will need to have compelling advantages to convince them to switch. Even if new formats are sanctioned by the recording industry, consumers can still choose to convert songs from CDs (which are unencrypted) to MP3. Or they can use a sound card and a simple piece of software to convert encrypted music to MP3 (or other unencrypted format).

Even with secure formats, piracy will always be a threat. As fast as the industry comes up with security measures, hackers will find ways to crack them. But an even larger threat to the major record labels is the advent of Internet-based labels, and artists leaving the fold to sell their music directly to fans.

This change is driven by economics and a growing dissatisfaction among many artists with the policies of the major labels. Internet music distribution causes packaging and distribution costs to drop to almost nothing, making it possible for just about anyone to set up an online music store or record label. There's not much the industry can do to prevent the rapid shift to independent Internet labels other than embracing Internet music distribution and sharing a larger percentage of the profits with the artists.

It's important to remember that technologies like MP3 and the Internet are only enablers. The Digital Music Revolution is really about empowering consumers and musicians. Technology will drive much of the change, but the most significant changes will come once mainstream consumers start using computers and portable MP3 players in place of records, tapes and CDs, and when major artists begin switching to Internet labels once their contracts with the major labels have expired.

Ultimately, these changes will result in lower prices for consumers, more royalty dollars for musicians, and more profits for independent record labels. These advantages should more than offset any increases in music piracy by bootleggers, or by consumers who now can easily swap digital music files via chat rooms, e-mail and diskettes.

As with any revolution, there will be winners and losers. In the case of digital music, there will be far more winners than losers. The biggest potential losers are the major record labels and retail record stores. If they don't quickly transition to doing business over the Web, they'll quickly lose a big chunk of market share to the new generation of Internet record labels and downloadable music sites like EMusic.com and MP3.com, and to online music retailers like Amazon.com and CDNOW.

The use of digital music on personal computers and the Internet will continue to grow rapidly, but it will not replace conventional methods of distribution any time soon. Just as customers of Internet malls and Internet banking will still be able to visit their local mall or bank branch, Internet music distribution is likely to be a complementary market force rather than a replacement for traditional markets. The results will be difficult to predict, but consumers and independent musicians will certainly be among the winners.

Chapter 2

Music on the Web

The Internet is the perfect medium for delivering products like music that can be represented by digital bits. Online music stores have been selling music in the form of records, tapes and CDs for several years. But now, with audio compression technologies like MP3, they can sell downloadable music and eliminate the costs associated with physical goods.

On the Web, a single company can play the roles of record label, music distributor and retailer. This type of "vertical integration" can translate to both lower prices for consumers and higher profits for the store. Setting up an online music store requires a fraction of the investment of a "brick and mortar" store, and dozens of new online music sites are opening for business every day.

Online music stores typically offer a much wider variety of music, lower prices and greater convenience than traditional record stores. You can shop from the convenience of your home, and at most sites you can listen to sample clips of songs before making a purchase. When you shop for music via the Web, you have access to almost every album in existence. Albums are rarely out of stock, unlike retail record stores where many potential customers leave without making a purchase because the albums they want are sold out.

Online Music Formats

On the Web, you'll find music in three forms: music stored on physical media (like records, tapes and CDs); music in the form of files that can be downloaded to a computer; and music that you can listen to as it's "streamed" over the Internet (similar to the way you listen to AM and FM radio).

The Internet or the Web?

The Internet is a network of networks that extends to all parts of the globe. A network is a group of devices (computers, servers, printers, etc.) that are connected with each other in a way that they can communicate and share data. The Internet has many parts that are defined by communication protocols. Internet protocols include those for e-mail, file transfer, the World Wide Web and streaming audio.

The World Wide Web is the graphical part of the Internet that you access through a Web browser, like Netscape Navigator or Microsoft Internet Explorer. The Web exists primarily in the form of HTML (Hypertext Markup Language) documents that are stored on (or generated by) Web servers. These documents are transmitted via HTTP (Hypertext Transfer Protocol) to your browser, which interprets the HTML and displays it. Your browser also communicates input from you to the Web server. Individual HTML documents are called Web pages. Groups of Web pages are called Web sites.

Records, Tapes and CDs

Many Web music stores sell music in the form of physical media, such as records, tapes and CDs. This is really just another form of mail order— whatever you purchase must be shipped to you. These types of sites will continue to exist as long as consumers prefer to receive music on physical media. (Many people prefer a packaged product, even if they must pay more for it.) And even if the industry switches over entirely to MP3 (or other compressed format), much of the music is likely to be delivered on CDs or similar physical media.

One advance that involves the delivery of digital music on physical media is the ability to purchase songs from different artists and have them burned onto a custom CD. Sites like CDNOW and MusicMaker.com offer this service for music from a limited number of artists. There has been some resistance to the delivery of music on custom CDs from both artists and labels. It turns out that some artists are refusing to let their music share the same CD with other artists. Also, record labels make a lot of money selling CDs that contain only a few good songs. Allowing music to be sold by the song could seriously reduce their profits.

Downloadable Music

Downloadable music is simply music in the form of a computer file that you can download from a Web or FTP (File Transfer Protocol) site and play on a PC, portable digital audio player like the Rio, or a CD player with an appropriate decoder chip. MP3 is well suited for downloadable music because its high level of compression reduces download times, while preserving sound quality.

A key advantage of downloadable music is that you no longer have to purchase an entire album when you just want one or two songs. Downloadable music also makes it easy for you to sample and purchase music from the comfort of your home.

Downloadable music gives independent bands a low-cost method of distributing and promoting their music. To gain exposure, many artists are now offering full-length promotional songs that can be downloaded for free, in the hopes that if you like the song, you'll purchase other music by them.

The number of sites offering downloadable music is growing rapidly, and once the recording industry's SDMI (Secure Digital Music Initiative) standards have been implemented, you'll be able to purchase almost any song or album this way. Even at this early stage, you can find many good (and legal) songs in downloadable format. Most sites price their songs between $1 and $2 each, depending on the popularity of the artist.

See Chapter 19, *Basic Tasks*, for instructions on downloading and playing MP3 files.

Figure 2 - Downloadable Music

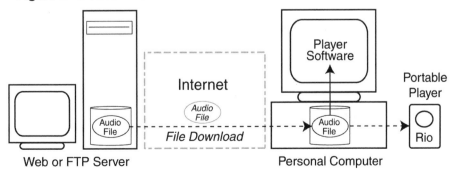

Are Downloaded MP3 Files Legal?

Just because you find an MP3 file and download it for free doesn't necessarily mean that it's a legal copy. It's only legal if the copyright holder has explicitly authorized that song to be freely downloaded (see Chapter 5, *Digital Music and Copyright Law*).

Streaming Audio

Streaming audio enables you to listen to digital music without having to wait for the entire file to download. Streaming audio is used by many online music stores to play short clips from songs so customers can listen to samples before they buy. This is a great way to sample music from new bands. Streaming audio also allows you to use your PC to listen to Internet radio stations (see Chapter 3, *Internet Radio*).

Steaming audio works by transmitting chunks of music to a buffer (temporary storage area) in your PC. A few seconds are needed to fill the buffer before the song starts playing, but once it's filled, it allows the music to play continuously even if the Internet connection is temporarily disrupted. If the connection is disrupted for too long, the buffer will empty, and you'll hear gaps in the sound.

Most downloadable formats can also be streamed, but the quality will usually be worse than a downloaded file because it's limited by the speed of your Internet connection. One advantage of downloadable music, compared to streaming audio, is that the speed of your connection affects only the download time, but not the sound quality.

Figure 3 - Streaming Audio

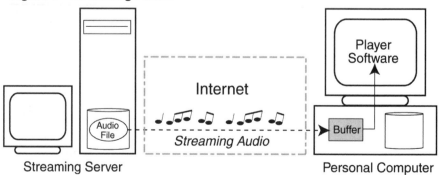

Streaming Server   Personal Computer

Finding Music

On the Internet, hundreds of thousands of songs are spread across thousands of music sites, so finding a specific song can be difficult. Many of the smaller sites specialize in just a few genres or in music from emerging artists. Many of the larger sites have catalogs with hundreds of thousands of songs from dozens of music genres (categories). The better sites organize their music by artist and genre and provide tools for navigating the site and searching for music.

You can spend a lot of time browsing, searching and sampling songs before you find any you like. But if you persist, you will find many excellent songs by lesser-known artists and a growing number of major artists. I've found dozens of great songs this way. Many of these were promotional songs that were available for free. In other cases, I paid a dollar or so per song, and, in a couple of cases, I liked the music so much I purchased the CD.

Following is a listing of a few popular online music sites. See Appendix A, *Interesting Web Sites*, for additional listings.

CD Baby (*www.cdbaby.com*) For some great music (mostly in CD format) by emerging artists, visit CDbaby.com. The music sold on CDbaby.com covers dozens of genres and is personally selected by CD Baby's founder, Derek Sivers.

CDNOW (*www.cdnow.com*) CDNOW is currently one of the largest music retailers on the Web. CDNOW's site has a wide selection of music in record, tape, CD and MiniDisc formats, along with a growing catalog of downloadable music.

EMusic (*www.emusic.com*) EMusic is both an Internet record label and music distributor. EMusic has a good selection of downloadable music from both lesser-known groups, and from better-known artists, like Frank Black and the Catholics and They Might Be Giants.

MP3.com (*www.mp3.com*) MP3.com offers a wide variety of music in both CD and MP3 formats, from thousands of emerging artists. MP3.com is also a great resource for MP3-related news and information on the latest MP3 hardware and software.

Optimizing Downloads

GetRight ($17.50) from Headlight software (*www.getright.com*) is a handy download manager and scheduler program. With GetRight you can queue up multiple MP3 files and schedule them to automatically download at night or while you're away. TweakDUN ($15) from Patterson Design Systems (*www.pattersondesigns.com*) is a utility program for Windows that can increase modem download speeds up to 30% by eliminating fragmentation of data packets.

MP3 Search Engines

A few sites have created search engines for finding MP3 and other types of multimedia files. You type in the name of the artist or song, and the engine searches the Internet for files that match. Lycos, a major Internet portal, has even devoted a section of its site to an MP3 search engine. Scour is another good search engine that can be used to find MP3 and other types of multimedia files.

AudioGalaxy

AudioGalaxy (*www.audiogalaxy.com*) hosts Web pages for bands and features a search engine for MP3 files. The search engine provides ratings for site availability and speed. FTP sites are scanned every 15 minutes to verify their status. AudioGalaxy also provides reviews of featured artists and labels, links to downloadable software, as well as a chat room for communicating with other users.

Napster

Napster (*www.napster.com*) is an MP3 file sharing service that maintains a central directory of shared MP3 files that exist on individual user's computers. Users search by song title or artist name and Napster displays links to matching files on the computers of other users. Each link lists the file's resolution and size, and the speed of the user's Internet connection. The first user then selects and downloads the MP3 file directly from the other user's computer.

Napster has generated a firestorm of controversy and a number of lawsuits from the recording industry and individual artists who are concerned about their music being copied without their consent. Napster does not store or transmit the MP3 files; but it does facilitate the sharing of copyrighted music on an unprecedented scale. As of this writing, Napster does not charge for the service or pay royalties to the copyright holders of the music that is shared.

> **Download Problems?**
>
> You may experience problems when you try to download files found by MP3 search engines. This often happens because many MP3 servers are run by amateurs and have limited capacity and availability.

The key attraction of Napster is that it provides a single source where you can find almost any song by any artist. The fact that it's free is an added bonus. But it may not be around for long—at least not in its current form. There is a good chance the courts will force Napster to shut down or block trading of songs by most major artists (which will eliminate its attraction for many users).

Other distributed file sharing services, such as Gnutella and Freenet, have no central server that can be shut down, no company to sue, and no management team to negotiate with. But they are much more difficult to use than Napster.

Scour

Scour (*www.scour.net*) is a search engine that can find MP3 files, videos, images, and other types of audio and multimedia files. The Scour Web site has listings for other sites where you can download music, listen to Internet radio or even see what's playing on TV. Scour's site also has a comprehensive guide to Internet radio stations.

To download MP3 files from Scour, you first must install the Scour Media Agent, which manages file downloads and stores them in the folder of your choice. When you search for MP3s, remember to use the advanced search option, then select MP3 as the media type to search for. After that, all you need to do is enter the artist and/or song name.

Music Piracy

It's important to remember that although the Internet is still a largely unregulated and unpoliced frontier, copyright laws are just as applicable to music obtained via the Internet as they are to music purchased through a retail store. Currently, many MP3 files of songs by major artists are illegal copies, and downloading them makes another copy, which is still illegal, even if the site charges no money for it. (See Chapter 5, *Digital Music and Copyright Law*.)

Most big name artists have sold the rights to their music to a major recording label, and many big labels have not yet approved distribution of their music in unsecure, downloadable formats like MP3 because of concerns about piracy. However, a few of the more enlightened labels are beginning

MP3 Fakery

During your searches for new MP3 sites, don't be surprised if you happen upon fake ads that launch a succession of annoying pop-up ads for adult sites when you click on them. Many fly-by-night sites have no qualms about accepting these kinds of advertisements.

to post promotional songs in open formats like MP3, and a few of the major labels are beginning to test the waters by offering songs in proprietary formats like Liquid Audio and WMA.

If you do a lot of surfing, in addition to visiting popular MP3 sites, you may stumble upon obscure Web and FTP music sites run by amateurs. Many of these sites contain pirated music. But even if you could find every song you wanted, you'll quickly find that the hassle of downloading songs from these sites isn't worth it.

Many of these "amateur" sites have limited accessibility because their servers can only handle a small number of users (e.g., 5) at once. To avoid detection by the RIAA and other authorities, some of these servers are up only during certain hours of the day. Many FTP sites also have a download ratio, meaning that you are required to upload a certain number of files in exchange for the files you download.

Legitimate downloadable music sites, such as EMusic.com and MP3.com, offer high reliability and go to great lengths to ensure that any music available on their sites is properly licensed. Table 1 lists some of the better-known online music sites. See Appendix A, *Interesting Web Sites*, for more listings.

Table 1 - Popular Online Music Sites

Web Site	Address
AMP3.com	*www.amp3.com*
CDNOW	*www.cdnow.com*
CD Baby	*www.cdbaby.com*
CDuctive	*www.cductive.com*
EMusic.com	*www.emusic.com*
MP3.com	*www.mp3.com*
Rioport.com	*www.rioport.com*

Chapter 3

Internet Radio

Broadcast radio hasn't changed much over the last few decades—it's always been a one-way medium. The program manager (and occasionally the DJ) determines the type of programming, including which songs are played and how often they are played. For the listener, it's a "take it or leave it" proposition. If you like what a station is playing, you listen to it; if you don't like it, then you either have to suffer through it or turn the dial until you find something better.

Because traditional radio is not an interactive medium, there is little feedback from listeners. In theory, listeners ultimately determine what music a station plays and how often. But listener feedback is indirect and slow through the existing rating systems. And the ratings systems are driven more by business considerations than by the preferences of individual listeners.

A common complaint about broadcast radio is that stations do little to help listeners identify songs. (How often have you heard a song on the radio and wanted to know the name of the song or artist, but the DJ never announced either one?) Other complaints include excessive amounts of commercials and a limited number of local stations to choose from.

Internet radio eliminates many of the shortcomings of broadcast radio because it's delivered through the Web—an inherently interactive medium. Internet radio offers multiple stations per site and allows interactive feedback so each listener can directly influence programming.

Internet radio also gives you access to a far wider variety of stations and programming than traditional broadcast radio. Radio sites on the Web can have dozens of stations featuring uninterrupted music, comedy, sports and talk shows, news, special events and many other types of programming.

Internet radio isn't limited by geography like broadcast radio is. In fact, Internet radio is often used to extend the reach of regular broadcast stations. If you're traveling out of the broadcast area of your favorite home station, you may still be able to listen to it if they also transmit their programming over the Internet.

Another advantage of Internet radio over broadcast radio is its availability in buildings where radio reception is poor or regular radio isn't an option. As long as you have an Internet connection, you can tune in and listen anytime.

Most Internet stations display the name of the song and the artist the entire time the song is playing, and some stations can also display album graphics, credits, and lyrics, along with links to the artist's Web site. If you hear a song you like, many stations provide a link so you can purchase the song or album on the spot.

Some sites, like Live365.com and Radio Sonicnet, even allow you to set up a personal radio station, which you customize by selecting the artists and the types of music you want to hear. Once your radio station is set up, you can tune in and listen to music customized to your tastes. You can also make your station available to other listeners.

Major players like America Online and Rolling Stone Magazine are getting involved in Internet radio. AOL's Spinner.com Web site offers over 100 stations and a selection of more than 150,000 songs. Rolling Stone Radio features stations that play music selected by rock stars, such as David Bowie, and other celebrities. Many of these larger sites also offer music charts, industry news and other types of music-related content.

Many broadcast radio stations now have Web sites, and many rebroadcast their regular programming via the Internet. Sites such as Broadcast.com act as aggregators (collectors and distributors) of streaming media programming and Web content for both traditional radio stations and Internet-only radio stations. Some stations even archive their shows on their Web site, so you can listen later if you missed the broadcast.

Internet radio sites can generate advertising revenue with both announcement-type commercials and banner ads. In this respect, the economic model of Internet radio is similar to broadcast radio. But Internet radio sites can expand on this model to earn commissions on products sold through their sites. Some sites even offer premium subscription services, similar to cable and satellite TV.

Most Internet-only radio sites feature banner ads, but few have commercial announcements that interrupt the programming. Aggregator sites that rebroadcast programming from traditional radio stations usually include the commercials along with the programming. Many of these sites also play a short commercial when you first connect. Some services like vTuner offer commercial-free listening only if you purchase their "plus" software.

Due to the requirement for an Internet connection, Internet radio isn't yet as portable as broadcast radio. But within the next few years, hand-held PCs will be able to double as portable radios. (Hand-held PCs already offer wireless Internet access, and several models, including the Cassiopeia and HP Jornada, include sound capability and software to play MP3 files.)

Sound Quality

The main factor limiting Internet radio is bandwidth. Dual channel ISDN (128 kbps) is the minimum needed for high-quality stereo music, but the majority of users have much slower connections (typically 28.8 kbps modems). Voice quality is usually fine at slower connection speeds, but music quality is barely acceptable with a connection slower than 56 kbps.

Other fast Internet connections such as DSL, cable modems, and satellite links provide enough bandwidth for CD-quality audio. However, even with unlimited bandwidth, network congestion can cause problems during peak usage periods. These problems will eventually be solved, but it could be years before the majority of Internet users have access to fast connections.

Another problem, even bigger than the connection speed of individual users, is that most streaming audio (and video) on the Internet is transmitted in a unicast mode—which is extremely inefficient. With unicast, each listener (or viewer) receives a separate stream. A station that has 500 users connected will send 500 copies of the same stream.

Even if all users had fast Internet connections, the Internet currently could handle only a few million simultaneous listeners with unicast transmissions. There is nowhere near enough server capacity and bandwidth to support tens of millions of listeners or viewers like network radio and network television can.

Eventually, the Internet will become multicast enabled, and a single stream will be able to be shared by multiple users. Only then will Internet radio be able to compete on the scale of traditional broadcast media. By the time that point is reached, the traditional radio and television networks will have had a chance to transition much of their programming to Internet.

Digital Radio

Digital audio technologies like MP3 are a key part of Internet radio because they help squeeze more sound through slower Internet connections. But digital technology can also be used in other forms of radio as well to improve the sound quality and transmit related information along with the music. Broadcast networks already use MP2 (similar to MP3) to transmit audio signals to their affiliate stations.

Eventually, all forms of radio will go digital. Cable and satellite TV systems already offer multiple music channels and have the capability to display text and video with music. Some systems, such as DMX (Digital Music Express), already offer digital transmission over cable and may eventually offer true interactivity.

Traditional broadcast radio stations can use digital transmission to offer improved sound quality and display song titles and artist names along with the audio. Portable digital radios featuring a small display to show text and graphics will become commonplace within the next few years, and portable satellite and cellular radio services that allow a station to "follow" you as you drive across the continent will also become available.

Internet radio is available now, and, thanks to the high degree of interactivity provided by the Web, it opens the door to a whole new world that broadcast, cable and satellite radio can't. Eventually cable and satellite services will offer interactivity or even merge with Web TV and Internet radio. Until these media converge, consumers will be faced with a bewildering array of delivery mechanisms for audio and video content.

Figure 4 - Media Overload

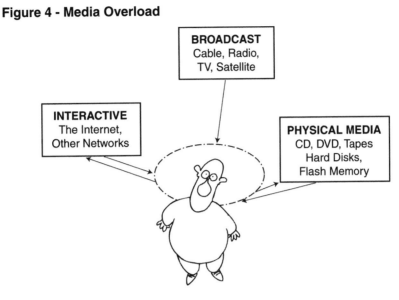

Listening to Internet Radio

To listen to Internet radio, you need software that can play streaming audio. Streaming audio is a subset of streaming media (audio, video and text, etc.) and comes in several formats, so you may need to install more than one program.

Many players, such as the RealPlayer and the Windows Media Player, support multiple formats, including streaming MP3. The fact that there are multiple formats and players for streaming audio can be confusing. Fortunately, most sites include links for you to download any software required to listen to them.

At the very least, you should install the latest versions of the RealPlayer, Windows Media Player and at least one of the full-featured MP3 players, such as Sonique or Winamp. These programs will allow you to listen to the majority of Internet radio sites.

Most players can be downloaded for free, although there are a few, such as the Plus version of the RealPlayer, that you must purchase. Fortunately, the free version of the RealPlayer offers everything most users need. The Windows Media Player is included with Microsoft Windows. Sonique and Winamp are both freeware.

Many of the larger radio sites, such as Spinner.com and Rolling Stone Radio, require you to install their own "tuners." Both of these sites use RealAudio, and you'll need to install the RealPlayer along with their own software. Many of the larger sites also require you to register before you can download their software, and some require you to login each time you listen.

vTuner

vTuner (*www.vtuner.com*) is a program, based on the RealPlayer, which provides an easy way to find and listen to thousands of stations (radio, television, Webcam, and others) from all over the world. The free version of vTuner categorizes stations by type and geographic location and provides browsing and searching capabilities. vTuner Plus ($29.99) adds station scanning, playback scheduling, station ratings based on quality and reliability, and replaceable "skins." The Plus version also lets you avoid listening to advertisements.

vTuner Main Screen

Table 2 lists some of the more popular streaming media player software that can be used to listen to Internet radio.

Table 2 - Streaming Media Players

Player	Streaming Formats	Web Site
QuickTime	QuickTime, MP3 and others	*www.quicktime.com*
RealPlayer	RealAudio, MP3 and others	*www.realaudio.com*
Sonicbox iM Tuner	MP3, RealAudio and WMA	*www.sonicbox.com*
Spinner	RealAudio	*www.spinner.com*
vTuner	RealAudio	*www.vtuner.com*
Winamp	MP3 and others	*www.winamp.com*
Winplay	Encrypted MP3	*www.radiomoi.com*
Windows Media Player	WMA, MP3 and others	*www.microsoft.com/windows/ windowsmedia*

Popular Radio Web Sites

A sampling of popular Internet radio sites follows. Many more sites are available but aren't covered here due to space limitations. (For more listings, see the Internet Radio section of Appendix A, *Interesting Web Sites*.)

iCAST

iCAST (*www.icast.com*) offers a wide range of entertainment content, including downloadable music, Internet radio, movies and Web TV. Music channels include genres such as alternative rock, blues, classical, hip-hop, jazz, latin, metal and reggae.

iCAST also provides links to dozens of independent Icecast (streaming MP3) stations with programming that ranges from various genres of music to comedy and talk shows with offerings such as Rush Limbaugh and animal noises. (See if you can tell the difference between the latter two.)

The iCASTER player handles both music and video and provides a nice graphical interface for locating stations from around the world. It also supports skins and includes a chat window and playlist organizer.

The iCASTER is based on the Windows Media Player, which must be installed before the iCASTER program is installed. An MP3 player like Winamp or Sonique is required for listening to the Icecast streams.

> **Sonicbox**
>
> Sonicbox's iM Tuning Service TM allows you to easily tune into any station on the Web (including iM broadband-optimized stations) and create playlists of your favorite stations. The iRhythm TM hardware allows you to wirelessly control and transmit Internet audio from your PC to your home stereo system. The iRhythm base station connects to your PC via a USB port and transmits audio to one or more receivers, using 900 MHz wireless technology. The iRhythm also includes a remote control that allows you to change stations and adjust the volume while away from your PC.

Radio Sonicnet

At Radio Sonicnet (*www.radio.sonicnet.com*) you can listen to music from the site's own stations, listen to other people's customized radio stations, or even create your own personal radio station. You can also buy a CD on the spot if you like a song.

To listen to music, choose a station and click on the speaker icon or the **Listen Now** link. The Radio Sonicnet tuner will load and, after a few seconds, a song will start playing. The tuner will then display the title and artist name. To stop a song that's playing, click on the **Pause** button above the song title. You can click on the **Skip** button to go forward to the next song, but you can't go back to the previous song because of current webcasting laws.

Click on the **Artist** link to learn more about that artist. You will see additional links for news, interviews, reviews and links to other sites for that artist. You can also subscribe to an e-mail list to automatically receive the latest information about that artist.

To create your own customized radio station, click the **Create My Station** button. Then choose the music genres (Blues, Jazz, Rock, etc.) to include. You then rank the genres depending on how frequently you want that type of music to be played. To listen to your station, click the **My Radio.Sonicnet Station** button on the main page.

You can edit the station by clicking the **Edit My Station** button and rating the list of artists and/or genres according to how often you want that type of music to be played. Webcasting laws prevent the station from displaying the complete list of artists at once, but you can refresh the page to display additional artists.

Sonicbox iM Tuner

You can rate any song by clicking on the **Less/More** button while the song is playing. This influences how often music by that artist will play on your station in the future. If you hate the song and never want to hear songs by that artist again, select **0**. If you love the song and want to hear more music by that artist, select **5**. Otherwise, select a rating somewhere in between.

You can create links to your station and post them on other Web sites or e-mail them to your friends. Click **CREATE A LINK** for the HTML code required for the link. Cut and paste the HTML from the appropriate box to your e-mail message or to the HTML code for your Web page.

To listen to Radio Sonicnet, you need the Windows Media Player.

RadioMoi

RadioMoi (*www.radiomoi.com*) provides access to thousands of songs, an Interactive Music Library that lets you play DJ and create your own shows, and an Interactive Jukebox that lets you select songs to be played on demand (only a portion of the songs are approved for interactive access). Channels (RadioMoi calls them shows) include an array of music, comedy and celebrity interviews.

RadioMoi was the first webcaster to sign an agreement with the RIAA and to be licensed under the Digital Millennium Copyright Act. This license allows RadioMoi to stream copyrighted sound recordings and requires them to make royalty payments. RadioMoi also provides links to artist and record label Web sites and lets listeners purchase albums on the spot.

Radio Moi uses an encrypted form of MP3. To listen to audio, you must use Winplay (the free RadioMoi player). If you have other MP3 players, such as Winamp, installed you may need to change the application associated with the .M3U file type. Otherwise, your MP3 player may attempt to play the RadioMoi channel—which it can't because of the encryption. (See Chapter 9, *Organizing and Playing Music*, for information on file type associations.)

Spinner

Spinner (*www.spinner.com*) is owned by America Online and offers access to more than 150,000 songs across 100+ music channels, grouped by genre, with programmable presets. You can rate any song that's played, access artist information, and, if you want, purchase the CD. Currently, Spinner doesn't allow you to set up your own station.

To listen to Spinner on a Windows system, you'll need to install their stand-alone player. If you're on a Mac or Unix system, Spinner offers a player that runs in conjunction with your Web browser. You'll also need to install the RealPlayer.

Tunes Radio

Tunes Radio (*www.tunes.com*) offers a diverse selection of music in many different genres, including blues, country, hip hop, jazz and rock.

The Tunes Radio channels are located on the left side of the player. Only some of them show, so you'll need to use the up and down arrow keys on the player to scroll through them. Click on the name of a channel to play it. After several seconds, the song will begin to play, and the song title and artist name will be displayed.

You can rate any song while it's playing by clicking on one of the check-boxes labeled 1-5. If you like the music, you can click on a link that will take you to a page where you can purchase the album.

To listen to Tunes Radio, you need the Windows Media Player.

Streaming MP3

Streaming MP3 has rapidly become the choice for amateur webcasters worldwide. Now, anyone with a PC and an Internet connection can inexpensively stream music to listeners throughout the world, using SHOUTcast or Icecast streaming MP3 software.

Spinner Plus Tuner

SHOUTcast

Nullsoft's SHOUTcast (*www.shoutcast.com*) provides users with a simple way to stream MP3 music to listeners all over the world. SHOUTcast servers can submit their description and status back to the main SHOUTcast server directory, which allows listeners to locate SHOUTcast servers without knowing their IP addresses.

Icecast

Icecast (*www.icecast.org*) is an open source streaming MP3 server, similar to SHOUTcast. It is available for free, including the source code. Because it is open source, useful modifications and additions by users are incorporated back into the main code for the benefit of all users.

RadioSpy

RadioSpy (*www.radiospy.com*) helps you find SHOUTcast servers and listen to webcasters from all over the world. RadioSpy lists the available SHOUTcast servers and identifies them by music genre and type of programming. When you choose a server, RadioSpy connects you to the server's audio stream and the Web page of the station. When you connect to a SHOUTcast server, you can also chat with the DJ or other users who are listening to the same music. You'll need an MP3 player, such as Winamp or Sonique, to use RadioSpy.

Webcasting Licensing

Internet radio stations can give listeners a high degree of control over the music they hear, but the music industry seems to fear that giving listeners too much control will reduce music sales. Their reasoning seems to be that if people could choose to listen to any song at any time, there would be little incentive for anyone to actually purchase music.

While the recording industry was slow to recognize the potential of downloadable music, it was quicker to recognize the potential (and threat) of Internet radio and lobbied to have laws enacted to protect its interests. The Digital Millennium Copyright Act (sponsored by the recording industry) addresses the issue of webcasting by providing statutory (provided for by law) licenses for webcasters who meet certain conditions. (See Chapter 5, *Digital Music and Copyright Law*, for the requirements for statutory webcasting licenses.)

Some Internet radio sites exist that webcast music illegally, but many webcasters want to be "legal" and are obtaining or have obtained the licensing required. Amateur webcasters are popularizing streaming audio, just like grass roots support and the Internet popularized MP3. But the recording industry is bent on ensuring that proper royalties are paid whenever copyrighted music is played and that music streamed over the Internet doesn't cut in to music sales.

In addition to licensing fees, webcasters are subject to several significant restrictions. For example, while Internet radio listeners can select the songs they want to hear, it is illegal for webcasters to allow them to select a particular song to play instantly, unless the song has been specifically authorized for interactive distribution. Even though listeners can create personalized stations, the site's DJ must rotate the playlists and determine when each song is played.

Webcasters are concerned that these types of restrictions will inhibit their ability to play the music that listeners want to hear, and make it financially unfeasible to operate a radio site. Internet radio is evolving rapidly, and more legislation may be required as it matures. Eventually, more standards and laws will be established and Internet radio will become a major component of our media, just like broadcast radio and television. Until then, it's still a bit like the Wild Wild West.

Chapter 4

Digital Music Distribution

Digital music consists of electronic bits and can be distributed via phone lines, cable systems, satellite transmission and networks like the Internet, eliminating the need for packaging, warehousing and shipping. Currently, most digital music is delivered on physical media in the form of CDs, but the Internet is rapidly becoming the delivery medium of choice for many artists and labels.

Internet music distribution is a boon to independent artists because it enables them to increase their visibility and keep a much larger share of the profits. Internet distribution is also a great opportunity for independent record labels and any of the major labels that are flexible enough to adapt to this new model.

Many major artists, such as the Beastie Boys, Public Enemy and Tori Amos, are already taking advantage of Internet music distribution. More major artists and labels are beginning to support this method of distribution, now that SDMI standards have been established.

Internet Record Labels

Over the past few years, a new generation of Internet record labels has appeared and is establishing a new business model for music distribution. Internet labels can help independent artists quickly gain exposure to potential fans worldwide. Many Internet labels also double as online music stores and sell music in downloadable formats like MP3 and on physical media like CDs. Most Internet labels also create and host Web pages for artists or include links to the artist's own site.

Internet labels typically split the revenue from music sales with the artist on a 50/50 basis. This business model is similar to the Advantage program that Amazon.com offers independent authors and small publishers. Some sites offer arrangements that include sharing advertising revenue in place of a percentage of sales. Several of the leading Internet record labels are described below. (See Appendix A, *Interesting Web Sites*, for additional listings.)

AMP3.com

AMP3.com is an Internet record label that sells downloadable music and pays artists up to 50 cents every time one of their songs is downloaded. Sponsors pay anywhere from 10 to 20 cents per download to place ads at the beginning of songs. Consumers have the option of downloading songs for free or purchasing the songs with the ads removed.

EMusic.com

EMusic (formerly GoodNoise) is one of the better known Internet record labels and music distributors. Through relationships with artists and license agreements with leading independent record labels, EMusic offers a wide variety of downloadable music in MP3 format. EMusic also offers other sites a percentage of sales that result from customers who use the site's link to EMusic.com.

Garageband.com

Garageband.com is a true Internet label and a great downloadable music site for fans of independent music. Garageband.com is one of the few sites that actually signs bands to recording contracts. Contracts are typically worth $250,000 and are awarded based on the input of site visitors.

MP3.com

MP3.com's Digital Automatic Music (D.A.M.) system lets any artist sign-up to have their album produced and sold by MP3.com. Artists on MP3.com get exposure to over 6 million listeners per month, with no sign-up cost or monthly fee. The artist simply receives 50% of the price of every CD sold. If the artist gets a record deal with a label, they can cancel the contract with MP3.com without obligation.

SpinRecords.com

SpinRecords.com is a resource for emerging artists and their fans. The site is dedicated to the independent and underground music scenes and provides all types of services as an independent label to unsigned artists and bands. Visitors can download music, share information on the message boards and purchase products from the spinstore. There is also a section for local music, with information on clubs and concerts in major cities.

New Stars Wanted

If you're an independent artist or musician in a new band, you can upload your music to RollingStone.com and have your music heard by the industry's most influential critics. Rolling Stone editors will listen to the original MP3 tracks you upload, and each month they review and rate the 10 most promising songs. You can also post your band's bio, photos, lyrics, tour schedules and track the number of downloads your music receives.

Secure Music Distribution

Many record companies are hesitant to release music in open formats like MP3 because of the potential for piracy. As a result, several companies have developed secure music distribution systems designed to track downloads and prevent unauthorized copying.

Watermarking

Virtually all secure music distribution systems use some form of watermarking to help identify the source of pirated music and protect the rights of copyright holders. Watermarking transparently embeds copyright and licensing information in the music data. (Additional information such as lyrics, album graphics and promotional material can also be added to the file.) The files are then registered with a digital rights management server that tracks the number of copies sold and the amounts of royalties due.

Encryption

Most secure music distribution systems use some form of encryption to protect the music from unauthorized use. Some of these systems assign the user a personal key or passport, which can only unlock songs purchased by that user. Others require a separate key for each song. In each case, the consumer must use a software or hardware player supported by the system.

Encryption presents several problems. The biggest is that consumers are choosing digital formats like MP3 because of the freedom, flexibility and convenience they offer. People who purchase downloadable music want to be able to play it on any of their computers or portable players, without having to worry about entering a key. Encryption will prevent this flexibility, unless all manufacturers of hardware and software for playing downloadable music agree on the same standard and develop a system that is completely transparent to the consumer.

Consumers have a legitimate need for music in unencrypted formats, such as MP3. Many people have made large investments, over many years, in "unsecured" music in the form of records, tapes and CDs. In the future, if consumers have no choice but to purchase music in an encrypted format, they will not be able to use the hardware and software of their choice to play all of their music.

Consumers who choose to use a PC to store and play their music have a reasonable expectation to be able to "format-shift" music (convert it to another format) so they can exercise their right of "fair use." (See Chapter 5, *Digital Music and Copyright Law*, for more information on the Doctrine of Fair Use.)

Developers of proprietary formats and audio encryption schemes seem to forget that the audio needs to be unencrypted before anyone can listen to it. When a digital signal reaches the D/A converter in a sound card, it is in a raw, unencrypted format. In fact, two software utilities—Total Recorder and Audiojacker—can be used to capture digital audio signals from any player and store them as unencrypted WAV files. The WAV files can then be easily converted to MP3 (or other format).

Of course, makers of these software packages aren't trying to encourage illegal duplication of music. Their software just makes it easier to record from any source, including the programs that play "secure" music. Make no mistake, it is illegal to unencrypt a song and then distribute it without the copyright owner's consent.

Some "secure" systems allow you to burn one copy of each song to a standard audio CD. But there is nothing to prevent you from extracting the audio from that CD into an unencrypted format that you can use anywhere. All encryption will do is make it more difficult for you to use the music. Encryption will not prevent a determined person from unencrypting and copying music, and it certainly is not going to stop bootleggers from pirating it.

The Secure Digital Music Initiative

The Recording Industry's Secure Digital Music Initiative is an ambitious effort dedicated to the development of technical specifications for securing music across all digital delivery platforms. SDMI was formed in December 1998 and consists of over 100 companies from the recording, consumer electronics and computer industries.

A key goal of SDMI is to protect the interests of music copyright holders by developing a system to mark recorded music with rights management data that can be recognized by all audio devices. The first SDMI specification was adopted in June 1999 and will be implemented in two phases.

Players that support the Phase I specification will be able to play music in most current formats, including SDMI and open formats like MP3. Phase II of SDMI will establish a secure format, which uses watermarking technology to embed copyright and licensing information in the music. Phase II compliant players will be able to detect and reject unauthorized uses of music that was created in the secure format. Phase II devices will also be able to play older songs in unsecured formats like MP3 without any restrictions.

The Portable Devices Specification's proposed default usage rule would allow users to make no more than four (4) usable copies of a recording, of which three (3) may be transferred to other SDMI-compliant devices. In order to make more copies, the original source must be recopied producing again 4 usable copies[1].

Privacy Issues

Many people have concerns about their privacy being violated by copy protection schemes that collect and/or embed unique identifiers through watermarking. Robin Gross, a staff attorney for the Electronic Frontier Foundation, voiced the following concerns:

"The Electronic Frontier Foundation is concerned about consumers being required to submit personally identifying information in order to access a song. The idea is to require such information of people because it creates a record of who is authorized to access that particular copy of a recording. But a consumer would not want to give personally identifiable information about themselves in case the copy is ever used in ways that the copyright holder has not authorized. That's alienating for the consumer."

"Also, databases of who has access to what songs present a potential to seriously compromise an individual's privacy expectations in unintended ways. Even though companies may have no desire to use the information they collect, once it exists there are numerous ways the data could be used that the consumer, or even the company, will neither expect nor desire. For example, law enforcement could easily subpoena an artist for records of who has

---

[1] Source: SDMI Web site (*www.sdmi.org*)

downloaded songs. The ability to read, listen, associate, and think anonymously is part of a strong First Amendment tradition in this country that protects people who share dissenting, unpopular, or controversial ideas."

The issues of privacy and inconvenience that secure music distribution systems present to consumers will be the biggest factors that prevent widespread market acceptance. It's one thing to require consumers to register a $100 software package, but to require them to register and enter personal information for a $1 or $2 song, and keep track of a key, is a lot to ask of someone who is used to just inserting a tape or CD and pressing play.

Future Distribution Methods

Eventually, digital music distribution systems will evolve to be as much a part of the music industry as Postal, UPS and FedEx shipments are today. Some of these systems will offer consumers more flexible options for purchasing music. Options may include music subscription services, where you pay a flat monthly fee to listen to an unlimited amount of music, and micropayments, where your account is charged a small amount each time you listen to a song.

Some "rent-to-own" systems will allow you to listen to a song a fixed number of times for a small fee and purchase more "listens" when you reach the limit. Once you have paid for more than a specified number of listens, you "own" the song. Other systems may let you download and listen to any song for free for a limited period (week, month, etc.), after which you must purchase a key to be able to listen to the song. With a "super distribution" system, you can e-mail copies of songs to friends, who will only be able to listen to them for a "demo" period unless they purchase a special key.

It's difficult to predict which systems will catch on with consumers and just as hard to predict whether or not enough manufacturers will agree on any one system to make it economically viable. Meanwhile, you still have more options than ever before to find, purchase and listen to music. And you always have the right to "vote" with your wallet if any "secure" systems are imposed that add inconvenience to your music experience.

Chapter 5

Digital Music and Copyright Law

The freewheeling nature of the Internet, combined with compressed digital audio formats like MP3 that can be easily copied, has led to an epidemic of copyright infringement. However, digital music on computers and the Internet is protected by the same laws that protect music on records, tapes and CDs, along with several laws that focus specifically on digital music.

Rights of Copyright Holders

Copyright law establishes rights for both copyright holders and for purchasers of copyrighted works.

A copyright holder has five exclusive rights:

- **Reproduction:** The right to copy, duplicate, transcribe or imitate the work in a fixed form.
- **Modification:** The right to modify the work or create a new work based on an existing work.
- **Distribution:** The right to distribute copies of the work to the public by sale, lease, rental or loan.
- **Public Performance:** The right to recite, perform or play the work in a public place or transmit it to the public.
- **Public Display:** The right to show a copy of the work in a public place or transmit it to the public.

Anyone who violates any of these exclusive rights is considered an infringer and is subject to civil and criminal penalties.

Copyright laws also uphold certain rights for purchasers of published works but invoke limitations on the use and reproduction of those works. For example, if you've purchased a CD, you may legally make a recording of it onto tape for use in your car, or for your boom box at the beach (no sense getting sand scratches on your original CD). You can record as many copies as you like, but only if the copies are for your own private, noncommercial use.

> **U.S. Copyright Law - Title 17 of the U.S. Code**
> **Section 106. Exclusive rights in copyrighted works**
>
> "Subject to sections 107 through 120, the owner of copyright under this title has the exclusive rights to do and to authorize any of the following:
> (1) to reproduce the copyrighted work in copies or phonorecords;
> (2) to prepare derivative works based upon the copyrighted work;
> (3) to distribute copies or phonorecords of the copyrighted work to the public by sale or other transfer of ownership, or by rental, lease, or lending;
> .
> .
> (6) in the case of sound recordings, to perform the copyrighted work publicly by means of a digital audio transmission."

Similarly, you may purchase and download an MP3 file and copy it onto your Rio player, as long as you don't resell or give away any copies of that file.

Copyright protection arises automatically when an original work (song, book, etc.) is fixed in a tangible medium (tape, paper, etc.) of expression. No registration is required, but you must register before you can file a copyright infringement suit.

The term of a copyright varies depending on when the work was created, who created it and when it was first distributed commercially. For works created after January 1, 1978, the term is the life of the author plus 50 years. The term for works made for hire is 75 years from the date the work was first published (distributed commercially) or 100 years from the date of creation, whichever expires first.

A common legal myth is that a work needs to have a copyright notice to be protected. This is no longer true. For works created on or after March 1, 1989, the copyright notice is optional. Another common myth is that it's okay to distribute copyrighted material without permission as long as you don't charge for it. It doesn't matter whether you charge for it or not. If you distribute unauthorized copies, it's still copyright infringement. Some people assume that it's OK to use copyrighted material without permission if their use would help to promote the work. It doesn't matter; permission is still required.

Copyright Law and Consumers

Many people either don't think about copyright laws or they make assumptions—such as these laws apply only to business use of copyrighted material, or they target only bootleggers and blatant pirates. Copyright laws apply to everyone, and they not only protect the rights of artists and creators of intellectual property, they also protect consumers and manufacturers. The following hypothetical case studies illustrate how copyright laws can affect users of digital audio formats such as MP3.

Case #1: Ripping CDs

Robert is a diehard Kiss fan. He owns every Kiss CD ever recorded and wants to listen to Kiss at work. So he ripped his Kiss CDs (copied them to his hard disk) and converted them to MP3 format, and then brought them to work to annoy his co-workers. Beth, who works in the cubicle next to Robert, likes jazz. She tried to turn off the noise from next door by telling Robert that his MP3 files were illegal.

Robert told Beth that since he purchased the CDs, he could copy them and use them however he pleased, as long as the copies were for his own use. Beth did some research and showed Robert a page from the RIAA's Web site that maintains that ripping songs from prerecorded CDs is illegal. Robert, afraid he was in hot water, retained the law firm of Dewey Cheatum and Howe. After billing him $400, they advised him not to worry. They told him that since the MP3 files were for his own use, he was protected by the Audio Home Recording Act. Who is right—the RIAA or Robert's lawyers?

> **Audio Home Recording Act - October 1992**
>
> **Section 1008. Prohibition on certain infringement actions**
>
> "No action may be brought under this title alleging infringement of copyright based on the manufacture, importation or distribution of a digital audio recording device, a digital audio recording medium, an analog recording device, or an analog recording medium, or based on the noncommercial use by a consumer of such a device or medium for making digital musical recordings or analog musical recordings."

Audio Home Recording Act

The Audio Home Recording Act represents a historic compromise between the consumer electronics and recording industries. As part of this compromise, digital audio recording systems for consumers must include a device that prevents multiple-generation copies.

In exchange for this protection, U.S. manufacturers and importers must pay royalties of $1 to $8 per digital recording device. Two-thirds of these royalties go to the Sound Recording Fund, which allocates small percentages for nonfeatured artists and backup musicians. The other third goes to the Musical Works Fund and is split 50/50 between songwriters and music publishers.

The legality of ripping depends on the interpretation of several laws. The Audio Home Recording Act protects consumers who use digital or analog audio recording devices to make copies of prerecorded music, as long as the copies are for noncommercial use. But, because computers are not considered recording devices, as defined by the Audio Home Recording Act, Robert is not protected by this law when he rips his CDs.

The drafters of the Audio Home Recording Act didn't realize or consider that personal computers would ever be used to record and play high-quality digital audio. They also did not foresee the impact of the Internet on the recording and broadcasting industries. Several bills related to these technologies have been enacted to update the law. (See the end of this chapter for a summary of key copyright laws.)

Even though ripping is not specifically addressed by current laws, it turns out that Robert does have the right to rip his own CDs, according to Bob Kohn, co-author of the leading treatise on music licensing, *Kohn On Music Licensing* (Aspen Law & Business 1999). Kohn maintains that making an MP3 copy from your CD for your own personal use is clearly permitted by Congress.

In 1971, when enacting legislation that protected sound recordings under the Copyright Act, Congress stated, "It is not the intention of [Congress] to restrain the home recording, from broadcasts or from tapes or records, of recorded performances, where the home recording is for private use and with no purpose of reproducing or otherwise capitalizing commercially on it. This practice is common and unrestrained today, and record producers and performers would be in no different position from that of the owners of copyright in recorded musical compositions over the past 20 years."

It is therefore clear, according to Kohn, that Congress believed that the Doctrine of Fair Use, which is now embodied in Section 107 of the Copyright Act, protects audio home recording from copyright liability as long as the MP3 file is for your own, noncommercial use and you do not distribute copies of it to anyone else.

The ruling, in June 1999, by the U.S. Court of Appeals in the RIAA vs. Diamond Multimedia lawsuit over the Rio portable MP3 player makes it even clearer that Doctrine of Fair Use allows consumers to "space-shift" and "format-shift" music by ripping it to their hard disk and converting it to MP3.

So Robert's MP3 files are perfectly legal, (although for a different reason than he was told by his lawyers), as long as he purchased (and still possesses) the original CDs. However, he may not sell or give copies away, or use the copies for any commercial purposes.

Case #2: "I'm just giving a copy of the song to a friend; I'm not selling it!"

Justin purchased a CD recording of *Grease Monkeys* by the Bad Mechanics. His friend Bill also liked the album, so Justin burned a copy of it onto a CDR and gave it to Bill so he can listen to it while he works on his car.

Justin is generous, but he's committed copyright infringement by violating the Bad Mechanics' copyright on *Grease Monkeys*. Since he bought the original CD, he can copy it as many times as he likes for his own use. What he can't do is give or sell copies of any of the songs from *Grease Monkeys* to his friend Bill or anyone else.

The First Sale Doctrine of the 1976 U.S. Copyright Act allows someone who purchases a recording to then sell or otherwise dispose of that recording. But a person who sells or gives away a recording may not keep, sell or give away any other copies. In other words, if only one copy of a recording was purchased, then only one person should possess it and any copies made from it.

> **U.S. Copyright Law - Title 17 of the U.S. Code**
>
> **Section 109. Limitations on exclusive rights: Effect of transfer of particular copy or phonorecord**
>
> "(a) Notwithstanding the provisions of section 106(3), the owner of a particular copy or phonorecord lawfully made under this title, or any person authorized by such owner, is entitled, without the authority of the copyright owner, to sell or otherwise dispose of the possession of that copy or phonorecord."

Case #3: Free downloads of Top-40 songs?

Becky loves to download MP3 files off the Internet. One day, while surfing for new music, Becky found the site EmPeeFree.com, which offered free downloads of Celine Dion's *My Heart Will Go On*. Since Becky saw the movie Titanic 10 times, she knew she "had to have" the song. Becky downloaded My Heart, only to find the copyright police knocking on her door the next day. Where did she go wrong?

Becky has unknowingly violated the law by downloading pirated music. Since Becky has no intention of distributing or selling the song, she probably won't get a visit from the copyright police. But she still has the moral responsibility to avoid copying pirated files in the first place. The site offering pirated copies of *My Heart Will Go On* is also in violation of the DMCA (and other copyright laws) and is likely to face legal action from the RIAA on behalf of the copyright holders.

The U.S. Copyright Act of 1976 states that song owners have exclusive rights on copying and distributing their music. They may permit copying and distribution but are entitled to royalties for that permission. A more recent law is the Digital Millennium Copyright Act (DMCA), passed in 1998. The DMCA states that without permission from a song's owner, it is illegal to make copyrighted music available online for distribution.

Typically, songs are covered by two copyrights. The first is for the actual notes and lyrics, or what is referred to as the *musical work*. Usually, copyrights on musical works are owned by the artist and his or her publicist. The second copyright is for the artist's interpretation of the musical work and the actual recording, referred to as the *sound recording*.

Copyrights on sound recordings are typically the property of the record label (e.g., EMI, Warner Brothers). To offer downloads of copyrighted music, a Web site must have licenses for both the musical work (performance licenses) and the sound recording (mechanical licenses).

Currently, much of the online music in MP3 format by major artists is distributed without permission by unlicensed sites that allow unlimited downloading. However, many independent artists, who are not bound by recording contracts, welcome the opportunity to distribute their songs online in hopes of attracting an audience.

Case #4: Is it legal to download any songs for free?

Jim is the ultimate computer geek. He's spent long hours ripping music from CDs and downloading MP3 files from the net. Recognizing these technological talents, his friend Mike asks him to create a CD using some free promotional MP3 songs he downloaded from BadNoize.com.

Jim's computer skills are excellent, but he's musically challenged, and he churns out a CD that can only be described as painful. Still, he feels he's done Mike a service and charges him for the cost of a blank CD. Mike, upon listening to the CD and hearing songs like *Bite My Toenails* by the Bunion Peelers, wishes the CD was still blank.

Jim has displayed extremely poor taste, both in his choice of music and in charging Mike for the cost of the CD. Still, he's broken no laws. *Bite My Toenails* is essentially shareware, free for anyone to download and distribute in hopes of making The Bunion Peelers a household name.

The Bunion Peelers own all copyrights on their songs—probably because no record company will sign them. But the group has declared their music to be public domain so it can be freely distributed to reach more listeners like Jim and Mike.

Sites offering the Bunion Peelers, or any music downloads, should—but are not required to—post a disclosure of the artist's permission to distribute. Such a disclosure adds legitimacy to the site and helps consumers make educated decisions about which songs may be downloaded legally.

Many Web sites offer free downloads of promotional music authorized by the copyright holders. But just because an artist offers free downloads of a song, it doesn't necessarily mean that the music is in the public domain. Music is only in the public domain if the copyright has expired, or if the copyright holder has explicitly declared the music to be public domain.

Public Domain

The term public domain refers to intellectual property (music, software, text, etc.) that may be freely copied, distributed or performed. Intellectual property becomes public domain when the copyright expires or the copyright owner (not always the creator of the work) explicitly declares that the work is public domain.

Case #5: Trading MP3 downloads

The downloads are flying at the Hedon IST (Hedon Institute of Science and Technology). The hottest rage on campus is the competitive MP3 download contest. Students get a point for each MP3 file they download and two points each time a music file is downloaded off their own site.

Students are cutting classes to amass points and, coincidentally, to get some of their favorite music for free. With everyone swapping MP3 files, the students have virtually eliminated the need to buy CDs.

Some of the Hedon IST pre-law students believe that the MP3 download contest is legal since the Audio Home Recording Act of 1992 protects consumers' rights to copy songs for noncommercial purposes. Since bragging rights are the only prizes involved with their competition, the students have no qualms about trading the MP3 files.

These Hedon IST students have cut too many classes and misinterpreted the Audio Home Recording Act. Now they are music pirates and are violating several copyright laws.

```
Audio Home Recording Act
Section 1006. Entitlement to royalty payments
"(a) Interested copyright parties
The royalty payments … shall … be distributed to any inter-
ested copyright party--
(1) whose musical work or sound recording has been--
(A) embodied in a digital musical recording or an analog mu-
sical recording lawfully made under this title that has been
distributed, and
(B) distributed in the form of digital musical recordings or
analog musical recordings or disseminated to the public in
transmissions,…"
```

Although they do not directly profit from the MP3 download contest, the contestants are eliminating the need for students at the school to purchase CDs. By copying and trading their music, the students are committing copyright infringement and depriving the artists of their rightful royalties.

The contestants are also violating the No Electronic Theft Act, which was an amendment to U.S. Copyright Law (Title 17 of the U.S. Code). The NET Act redefines the term "financial gain" to include the receipt of anything of value, including the receipt of other copyrighted works. In other words, the copyrighted songs traded during swap meets have commercial value. Students obtaining free copies of these copyrighted works are realizing a financial gain, and therefore are in violation of the NET Act.

The NET Act also sets penalties for willfully infringing a copyright: (1) for purposes of commercial advantage or private financial gain; or (2) by reproducing or distributing, including by electronic means, during any 180-day period, one or more copies of one or more copyrighted works with a total retail value of more than $1,000.

```
No Electronic Theft (NET) Act - Amendment to Title 17
of the U.S. Code (U.S. Copyright Act)
Section. 2. Criminal Infringement of copyrights

(a) DEFINITION OF FINANCIAL GAIN-
"The term 'financial gain' includes receipt, or expectation
of receipt, of anything of value, including the receipt of
other copyrighted works."

(b) CRIMINAL OFFENSES-
"(a) CRIMINAL INFRINGEMENT- Any person who infringes a copy-
right willfully either--
(1) for purposes of commercial advantage or private finan-
cial gain; or
(2) by the reproduction or distribution, including by elec-
tronic means, during any 180-day period, of 1 or more copies
or phonorecords of 1 or more copyrighted works, which have a
total retail value of more than $1,000,
shall be punished as provided under section 2319 of title
18, United States Code."
```

```
U.S. Copyright Law - Title 17 of the U.S. Code
Section 107. Limitations on exclusive rights: Fair use
"In determining whether the use made of a work in any par-
ticular case is a fair use the factors to be considered
shall include --
(1) the purpose and character of the use, including whether
such use is of a commercial nature or is for nonprofit edu-
cational purposes;
(2) the nature of the copyrighted work;
(3) the amount and substantiality of the portion used in
relation to the copyrighted work as a whole; and
(4) the effect of the use upon the potential market for or
value of the copyrighted work.
The fact that a work is unpublished shall not itself bar a
finding of fair use if such finding is made upon considera-
tion of all the above factors."
```

The Hedon IST students are also violating the Doctrine of Fair Use. By offering free song downloads and eliminating the need for fellow students to purchase CDs or MP3 files, their contest is affecting the market potential of the music.

Case #6: Downloadable music and Webcasting

Allison wants to distribute music online. She started her own Web site and makes over 100 new music downloads available to visitors each month. Allison only distributes music by independent musicians and doesn't charge anything for downloads.

U.S. Copyright Law allows for distribution of copyrighted music—but only with the song owner's permission. The Digital Millennium Copyright Act, states that without permission from the copyright owner, it is illegal to make music available online for unlimited distribution.

To distribute most popular music, Allison would have to contact each copyright holder individually for licensing rights. Instead, she's chosen to offer only free downloads of fringe artists, like the Bunion Peelers, who encourage open distribution and don't require payment.

Some sites, like EMusic.com, have the exclusive rights to sell the recordings offered on its Web site, so Allison could not offer any of these recordings without contacting EMusic. However, EMusic would welcome Allison's linking to the EMusic.com Web site and will pay Allison a percentage of sales that result from customers using her link to the site.

What if Allison the webcaster wants to stream her favorite songs instead of offering them as downloads?

Webcasting (streaming audio) is used by Internet radio sites to transmit music and other types of audio over the Internet. Hundreds of Internet radio sites offer listeners a taste of every type of music available.

According to the Digital Performance Rights in Sound Recording Act of 1995, music copyright owners may authorize and be compensated for the digital transmission and distribution of their copyrighted work. Some artists and labels may be more flexible than others when it comes to allowing downloads and streaming of their music.

Like professional disc jockeys, Internet radio broadcasters must have permission to duplicate or transmit sound recordings. This requirement is mandated by the 1976 Copyright Act. Luckily, for webcasters and music fans alike, the Digital Millennium Copyright Act allows webcasters to obtain a statutory license for Internet broadcasts.

A statutory license is one provided by law instead of by individual copyright owners. With a statutory license, webcasters can stream all the music they want without acquiring separate licenses for each song. However, even with a statutory license, webcasters must still pay royalties on the songs they broadcast.

If Allison wants to become a licensed broadcaster and feels she can meet the criteria for a statutory license, she should contact the U.S. Copyright Office at the following address to request a statutory license:

> Library of Congress, Copyright Office
> Licensing Division
> 101 Independence Avenue, S.E.
> Washington, D.C. 20557-6400

If Allison does not meet the criteria required for a statutory license, she must obtain licenses from each copyright owner for any sound recordings she wants to broadcast. Currently, there's no organization that grants blanket licenses to webcasters who do not qualify for a statutory license. Therefore, Allison will have to contact each copyright owner individually or risk infringement liability.

Below is a list of the criteria webcasters must meet to qualify for a statutory license.

Webcasting Criteria

According to the Recording Industry Association of America (RIAA), webcasters must meet the following criteria. These limitations are in place to discourage listeners from downloading or copying music files for free and thereby limiting the market potential of the songs.

Sound recording performance complement: A webcaster may not play in any three-hour period more than three songs from a particular album, including no more than two consecutively, or four songs by a particular artist or from a boxed set, including no more than three consecutively.

Prior announcements not permitted: Advance song or artist playlists generally may not be published. However, webcasters may announce the names of a few artists to promote the type of music played on the site or channel. If an artist's name is announced, the webcaster may not specify the time that artist's song will be played.

Archived, looped and repeated programming: Programs that are performed continuously, automatically starting over when finished, may not be less than three hours in duration. Merely changing one or two songs does not meet this condition. Additional parameters for these types of programming are set by the license.

Obligation to identify song, artist and album: Beginning in October 1999, when performing a sound recording, a webcaster must identify the sound recording, the album and the featured artist.

Other conditions: In addition to the above, webcasters must meet other conditions such as accommodating technical measures, taking steps not to induce copying and not transmitting bootlegs.

Source: RIAA Web site (*www.riaa.com*)

Case #7: Professional DJ using MP3 files instead of CDs

DJ Dan is one of the most popular DJs in New York City. He's spent years building his business and his music collection and now owns over 1,000 CDs. Unfortunately, Dan has developed disc problems in his back and is restricted from heavy lifting. He's read about ripping CDs and plans to convert the best hits of his CD collection to MP3 files. With his collection in MP3 format, Dan can easily tote his most popular songs on a lightweight laptop computer. Dan's doctor will be happy, but what about his lawyer?

DJ Dan knows about the Audio Home Recording Act of 1992 and believes that since he purchased his CDs there's no problem with copying them into MP3 format. However, as stated in Cases #1 and #2, the AHRA only applies to copies made with certain types of recording equipment and not to copies made with a computer. Some people believe that Dan would be covered under the Doctrine of Fair Use because he owns the CDs and is not distributing copies to anyone else.

If DJ Dan goes a step further and burns the MP3 files on to a CD-R, he may run afoul of the RIAA for not obtaining a mechanical license, even if the CDs are for his own use. But this may also be considered fair use. The RIAA has not gone after individuals like Dan in the past, so we may never find the answer to this unless some Dan or some other DJ gets caught using MP3s burned on to CD-Rs and is sued for infringement.

Case #8: Professional DJ playing at a local catering hall

DJ Dan is celebrating because he just signed a five-month contract with a local catering hall. The facility hosts "all-you-can-eat" shrimp feasts through the spring and summer and wants Dan to provide entertainment. Dan is thrilled with the contract but isn't sure whether he or the catering hall has the responsibility to obtain licensing for the music he plays. What are the responsibilities of the DJ and the catering hall?

U.S. Copyright Law (Title 17, U.S. Code) allows businesses to broadcast music but requires permission to provide copyrighted music in any format (live, reproduced on tape or CD, or broadcast, etc.) in any type of hall, restaurant, bar, elevator or other public area. The same law also places the burden of responsibility for obtaining permission for use of copyrighted music on the owner/proprietor of the establishment.

> **U.S. Copyright Law - Title 17 of the U.S. Code**
> **Section 115. Scope of exclusive rights in nondramatic musical works: Compulsory license for making and distributing phonorecords**
>
> "a) Availability and Scope of Compulsory License.
> When phonorecords of a nondramatic musical work have been distributed to the public in the United States under the authority of the copyright owner, any other person, including those who make phonorecords or digital phonorecord deliveries, may, by complying with the provisions of this section, obtain a compulsory license to make and distribute phonorecords of the work. A person may obtain a compulsory license only if his or her primary purpose in making phonorecords is to distribute them to the public for private use, including by means of a digital phonorecord delivery."

Any time DJ Dan plays a song while in the catering hall, he is giving a public "performance" of that song. U.S. Copyright Law restricts the use of copyrighted music in public performances to individuals or businesses with proper licenses. The catering hall is responsible for obtaining permission to "broadcast" songs within their establishment.

Either the owner or DJ Dan must obtain permission for every song he plays. They could either contact each song artist and publisher individually or obtain blanket music performance agreements from the performance rights societies that collect royalties for owners of music copyrights.

The three performance rights societies in the United States are:

- **ASCAP** (American Society of Composers, Authors and Publishers) *www.ascap.com*
- **BMI** (Broadcast Music, Inc.) *www.bmi.com*
- **SESAC, Inc.** *www.sesac.com*

These organizations provide licensing rights for recording artists and publishers that own copyrights on songs. Portions of the fees collected from DJs and businesses go to artists and publishers in the form of royalties. Another site to visit for related information is the NMPA (National Music Publishers' Association, Inc.) & Harry Fox Agency site at *www.nmpa.org*.

Case #9: Amateur DJ playing music at a friend's party

Greg Brady has the most sought-after collection of TV theme songs and 70's hits in town. He's spent years collecting compilation CDs and browsing the racks at the local record store for vintage classics. Recently, he's added to his 70's collection by downloading tunes over the Internet. Greg's friend Jan is hosting a 70's revival party and wants him to provide music for the party.

Greg has acted as "DJ" at a few other parties in the past, so he's comfortable with introducing the songs, taking requests and hosting music trivia contests. He dusts off his canary-yellow leisure suit and platform shoes, grabs his music collection and his Mr. Microphone, and heads for the party. Does Greg have to worry about copyright laws since he's only playing music at a friend's free, private party?

Greg may be the "official" DJ for the party, but since he's not giving a public "performance," he is not violating any copyright laws. If he wants to be safe, he could obtain blanket music performance agreements from each of the performance rights societies that represent the copyright holders of the music he plays, but these agreements are only necessary for public performances, and in many cases the establishment already has them in place.

Case #10: Restaurant playing music from its own stereo system

George owns a Mexican restaurant/bar called WindBreakers Burrito Bar. His place isn't big enough for a band, but he keeps the place hopping with his own CD collection and stereo system. Every Saturday night, WindBreakers is packed for a late-night disco dance party. What licensing precautions should George take to ensure that the music keeps playing at Windbreakers?

Like the catering hall and DJ mentioned in Cases #8 and #9, George needs a Music Performance Agreement to broadcast music in his place of business. The Digital Performance Rights in Sound Recording Act of 1995 allows for business owners to broadcast copyrighted music in, or in the immediate vicinity of, their place of business. This permission, however, must be granted by the copyright owners or agents. Blanket Music Performance Agreements from performance rights societies are the easiest way to obtain that permission.

> **U.S. Copyright Law - Title 17 of the U.S. Code**
> **Section 114. Limitations on Exclusive Rights**
>
> "(A) Any person who wishes to perform a sound recording pub-
> licly by means of a nonexempt subscription transmission un-
> der this subsection may do so without infringing the exclu-
> sive right of the copyright owner of the sound recording
> (i) by complying with such notice requirements as the Li-
> brarian of Congress shall prescribe by regulation and by
> paying royalty fees in accordance with this subsection; or
> (ii) if such royalty fees have not been set, by agreeing to
> pay such royalty fees as shall be determined in accordance
> with this subsection."

U.S. Copyright Laws

The case studies in this chapter are just a few examples of people copying or broadcasting music owned by other people. . If you plan to play copyrighted music in public, broadcast it or make copies in any format, keep the following laws in mind:

U.S. Copyright Act, Title 17

The Copyright Act states that song owners have exclusive rights on copying and distributing their music. They may permit copying and distribution but are entitled to royalties for that permission. This law limits public performance and broadcasting of copyrighted music by consumers, professional DJs and businesses.

First Sale Doctrine

The First Sale Doctrine is a portion of the U.S. Copyright Act: Anyone who purchases a recording may then sell or otherwise dispose of that recording. However, the seller may not keep, sell or give away any other copies. In other words, if only one copy of a recording was purchased, then only one person should possess the original and any copies.

Audio Home Recording Act

The Audio Home Recording Act of 1992 allows consumers to record music for private, noncommercial use. If you're making money by playing or distributing copyrighted music, you must have permission, in the form of licensing, from the owner or owner's agent.

WIPO

The World Intellectual Property Organization (WIPO) negotiates treaties that help make copyright laws more consistent between nations. The WIPO treaties, negotiated in 1996 (by more than 100 countries), make it possible to fight piracy worldwide, regardless of the location of the copyright holder or the infringer. U.S. laws are in compliance with the treaties, for the most part, except for a provision in the Digital Millennium Copyright Act that makes it illegal to create or distribute software designed to defeat copy protection schemes. Once this provision is strengthened, U.S. laws will be in compliance with the intent of these treaties.

No Electronic Theft Act

The No Electronic Theft Act of 1997 amends the U.S. Copyright Act to define "financial gain" to include the receipt of anything of value, including the receipt of other copyrighted works.

Digital Millennium Copyright Act

The Digital Millennium Copyright Act of 1998 states that without permission from a song's owner, it is illegal to make copyrighted music available online for unlimited distribution. This law also puts specific limitations on the length of public broadcasts, the types of song and artist announcements and the frequency and sequence of songs played.

Digital Performance Rights in Sound Recording Act

The Digital Performance Rights in Sound Recording Act of 1995 provides copyright owners of sound recordings the exclusive right (with some limitations) to perform the recording publicly by means of a digital audio transmission. This is a departure from previous copyright laws, in which the owner of the musical work had exclusive public performance rights. This act also extends the provision for compulsory mechanical licenses to include downloadable music.

Doctrine of Fair Use

The Doctrine of Fair Use, embodied in section 107 of the Copyright Act, allows copies to be made without permission of the copyright holder under limited circumstances. Reproduction of copies for purposes such as criticism, news reporting, teaching and research is generally not considered infringement. Factors that must be considered in determining if a situation qualifies as fair use include the nature of the copyrighted work, the purpose and character of the use, the portion used in relation to the work as a whole, and the effect of the use on the market potential of the work.

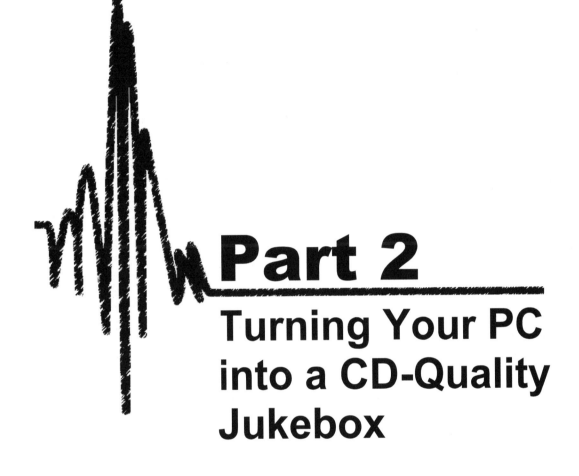

Part 2

Turning Your PC into a CD-Quality Jukebox

Chapter 6

Getting Started With MP3

This chapter provides an overview of what you need to get started with MP3. If you are already familiar with downloading and playing MP3 files, you can skip this chapter. Later chapters provide more detail on selecting, installing and using the individual products.

Check Your Configuration

To use MP3 you need at least a Pentium PC (133mHz or faster recommended) or a PowerPC Macintosh with a sound card and CD-ROM drive. If you are serious about audio or don't want to waste time waiting on the system, you should get a computer with a Pentium (II or III) or PowerPC (G3 or G4) processor.

You will need plenty of RAM, lots of free disk space, and a modem to download songs or listen to music streamed over the Internet. To convert your existing CDs into MP3 files, you'll need a CD-ROM drive that is capable of digital audio extraction (DAE)—commonly called ripping.

A more detailed list of system requirements is provided at the end of this chapter and in Chapter 8, *Choosing the Right Hardware*. Appendix B, *What and Where to Buy*, provides a list of recommended products and places where you can purchase them at reasonable prices.

Get Some Software

To play MP3 files, you need a player program or a portable player that supports MP3. The latest versions of Windows and Mac OS come with built-in players, but you'll be better off using a player like Winamp or MACAST because they have more features and are easier to use. To create your own MP3 files from prerecorded music, you'll need software for ripping the audio from CDs, or software that can record audio from external sources like records and tapes. You also need encoding software to convert the ripped or recorded files to MP3.

All-in-one programs like MusicMatch Jukebox, Real Jukebox and SoundJam MP include everything you need to create and play MP3 files. All of these programs are fairly easy to use, even for non-technical users. All support ripping from CDs, analog recording from records and tapes, and transferring MP3 files to portable players. Some all-in-one programs, such as Earjam and MusicMatch also support burning MP3 files directly to a CD recorder.

Advanced users may prefer a separate ripper/encoder, such as AudioCatalyst, because it provides them with more control over ripping and encoding, and a full-featured player like Winamp that supports advanced features like skins and plug-ins. Advanced users who do a lot of recording and want to edit sound files before they are converted to MP3 should get a good recording program like Cool Edit, Sound Forge or SoundEdit 16 (Mac).

New software is constantly being released, and existing software is constantly being updated, so check out the MP3Handbook.com Web site for information on the latest releases.

Get Some Music

To obtain songs in MP3 format you can download them from the Internet, create them from prerecorded music or purchase pre-made MP3 CDs. Web sites like MP3.com and EMusic.com offer thousands of downloadable songs in MP3 format. (See the tutorials in Chapter 19, *Basic Tasks,* for instructions on downloading MP3 files.) Many of these songs are free, and those that aren't usually cost only a dollar or so. A lot of other sites offer downloadable music, but you should be aware that many amateur sites continue to offer pirated music.

Since many of the MP3 files on the Web are from unknown artists or are pirated copies, you may want to start with your own record or CD collection. The RIAA maintains that it's illegal to make MP3 files from your own CDs[2], but nothing in copyright law explicitly prohibits this. In June, 1999 the U.S. Court of Appeals issued a ruling in the RIAA's suit against Diamond Multimedia that stated that the Doctrine of Fair Use (part of U.S. copyright law) protects consumers who make MP3 files from prerecorded music they own, as long as the files are for their own noncommercial use.

---

[2] Source: RIAA Web site (*www.riaa.com*)

Figure 5 - Obtaining Music in MP3 Format

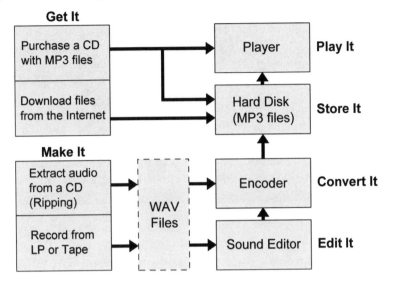

To create MP3 files from records or tapes you'll need to record them in real-time, using a sound card (see Chapter 14, *Hard Disk Recording*). You should use an all-in-one program like MusicMatch or RealJukebox or a good stand-alone recording program like Cool Edit or Sound Forge, since the sound recording applications that come with most computers are fairly limited.

If you want to create MP3 files from CDs, a better method is to bypass the sound card and rip the audio directly to your hard disk (see Chapter 15, *Digital Audio Extraction*). Ripping is better than recording through a sound card because it results in a perfect copy without added noise or distortion. Because it is a digital process, ripping is also much faster than recording. For example, a system with a fast CD-ROM drive can rip a four-minute song in less than 30 seconds. Recording the same song through a sound card will always take at least four minutes.

Audio CDs do not contain information such as artist names and album and song titles. To save you from having to enter this information manually, most rippers can automatically get this information from the CDDB (*www.cddb.com*) and use it to automatically name the files. (See Chapter 9, *Organizing and Playing Music*, for more information about the CDDB.)

> **CD-ROM Drive Compatibility**
>
> Not all CD-ROM drives support ripping, and many that do are slow or unreliable. If your drive won't rip, rips unreliably or rips slowly, the best solution is to purchase a newer drive that supports ripping (see Appendix B, *What and Where to Buy*).

Whether you rip or record, the song will end up either as an MP3 file or an uncompressed WAV (pronounced wave) file (see Chapter 12, *Digital Audio Formats*). The advantage of a WAV file is that you have the option of editing it to adjust the volume or trim off unwanted silence before it is converted to MP3. Some ripping programs can perform both of these functions automatically.

At this point, it's a good idea to play back the WAV file to check the sound quality. If you hear any popping, clicking or weird phasing noises, it means the audio data got scrambled and you need to tweak the settings and rip it again. You may have to try this a few times to find the settings that work best on your system.

If you ripped to a WAV file, it needs to be converted to MP3 format. This process is called encoding (see Chapter 16, *Making Your own MP3 Files*). Encoding compresses digital audio by removing sounds that most people can't hear. The size and sound quality of the MP3 file is a function of the bit-rate used—the higher the bit-rate, the larger the file and the better the sound quality.

Organize the Music

Now that you've created the MP3 files, you need a way to organize them. MP3 files can be organized in one big folder that contains all files, or they can be grouped in separate directories with similar music. It's up to you to decide which method to use, although if you have more than a few hundred songs you should organize them in separate directories. You may also need to delete leftover WAV files if your encoding software doesn't do this automatically.

Playlists are optional text files that contain the name and location of each audio file. Each playlist is like a tape with unlimited capacity, where songs can be added, deleted or moved around without the need to re-record the tape. Playlists can be created and read by text editors and most MP3 players.

If you have hundreds of songs, you may want to use software especially designed for creating and managing playlists. Programs, such as MP3 Explorer and Party DJ, can manage multiple playlists and can be used with player programs like Winamp.

A step up from a playlist is a database that holds information about each song, such as the type of music, the tempo and the situation it's most suited for (party, relaxation, romantic, etc.). Having this information in a database lets you easily sort and search for songs and use features like MusicMatch's Auto DJ to create playlists automatically based on the criteria you specify.

Kick Back and Let It Play

You can play songs from Windows Explorer or Mac Finder by double-clicking on them. If your system is set up properly, this should automatically launch the player software (if it's not already running). You can also play individual songs by launching the player and using its "File Open" function.

If you have created playlists, you can load one into your player, set the "repeat" mode on, and sit back and enjoy hours of continuous music. You can use the player controls to jump forward or backwards in the list, and you can click on individual songs to play them out of order. Good playlist managers allow you to add, delete and change the order of songs and save the playlist to a new file.

Table 3 lists the minimum configurations recommended for different types of users. The Basic configuration is for just playing audio files, but not creating or editing them. The Intermediate configuration is for creating and playing audio files, but not editing them. The Power User configuration is for creating, editing and playing audio files.

You may be able to get by with a processor slower than a Pentium 133, but you may end up sacrificing sound quality. You could also get by without the Plextor SCSI CD-ROM drive, but I highly recommend it for power users. Get double the amount (or more) of RAM listed if your system has room and you can afford it. You will be happier with the performance, especially when editing sound files or running multiple programs.

Table 3 - Recommended Minimum Configurations

INTEL PC			
HARDWARE	**BASIC** (Download and play audio files)	**INTERMEDIATE** (Create and play audio files)	**POWER USER** (Create, play and edit audio files)
Processor	Pentium 133	Pentium II or III	Pentium II or III
RAM	32MB	64MB	128MB
Sound Card	Basic sound card	Sound Blaster Live MP3	Sound Blaster Live MP3
CD-ROM	Basic CD-ROM	Must support DAE*	Plextor IDE or SCSI
SOFTWARE			
Ripper	N/A	MusicMatch Jukebox or RealJukebox	AudioGrabber
Encoder	N/A		Fraunhofer or Xing
Player	Sonique or Winamp		Winamp
Editor	N/A	N/A	Cool Edit
MACINTOSH			
HARDWARE			
Processor	PowerPC	PowerPC G3 or G4	PowerPC G3 or G4
RAM	32MB	64MB	128MB
Sound Card	Included	Included	Included
CD-ROM	N/A	Included	Included
SOFTWARE			
Ripper	N/A	SoundJam MP	MusicMatch Jukebox or SoundJam MP
Encoder	N/A		
Player	SoundJam MP		
Editor	N/A	N/A	SoundEdit 16

* DAE = Digital Audio Extraction, or "ripping."

Chapter 7

Choosing the Right Software

Dozens of programs that support MP3 are available and more are appearing every day. These programs fall primarily into the following categories: rippers, encoders, players, playlist managers, utilities and "all-in-one" programs. This chapter covers only the programs that can play digital audio (players, all-in-one, and DJ mixer programs). Other programs for recording, ripping, editing and encoding audio are covered in Part 4, *Recording Music on Your PC*.

Shareware and Freeware

Shareware is software that you can try before you buy. Shareware can be used for a limited time before you must either pay for it or stop using it. Freeware is software that you don't have to pay for, no matter how long you use it.

Shareware and freeware can be downloaded from the Internet and are sometimes included on CDs that are bundled with portable MP3 players and other MP3-related products. Some of this software is quite good, but much of it is not, and most has little or no documentation.

You can get all of the software you need for MP3 as shareware or freeware, but if you are a novice computer user and want technical support, you should get one of the commercial programs listed in this chapter.

If you are interested in exploring additional shareware and freeware software, see Appendix A, *Interesting Web Sites*. Many of these sites provide extensive listings of MP3-related software.

Players

I have divided the programs for playing digital audio into a few general categories to make it easier for new users to sort through all of the choices. With the proliferation of formats, most people will end up with multiple players installed on their computers. Some programs like FreeAmp and the Windows CD Player are limited to a single format, while others, such as RealPlayer and Winamp, can play multiple formats.

The Minimum You Need

At the minimum, you should install RealPlayer, Windows Media Player and a good full-featured player like Winamp. People who are into mixing music at parties should use a DJ mixer program or an all-in-one program like MusicMatch or RealJukebox. If you have a portable player, like the Rio, MusicMatch is a good choice because it can download songs from a playlist directly to the Rio's memory.

Single Format Players

Single format players usually play just one audio format and have fewer bells and whistles like equalizers, skins and visualization plug-ins. Most of the single format players are fairly limited compared to full-featured players like Winamp and Sonique. Use them if they are the only software that can play a particular format, but otherwise try to avoid them. Many proprietary players fall into this category. Often single format players will be included with a computer operating system or bundled with a secure music distribution system.

Windows CD Player

A good example of a single format player is the Windows CD Player program. It's designed to play standard audio CDs in your computer's CD-ROM drive, and nothing else. It comes in handy if you want to listen to tracks before deciding what to encode. Some ripping and encoding programs, such as AudioCatalyst, include a CD player function. Having this ability in a single interface is much more convenient than having to deal with a separate CD player program. Separate CD player programs can also conflict with ripping software over control of the CD-ROM drive.

MultiMedia Players

Multimedia players typically support multiple formats of downloadable music and streaming audio and video. Free versions are available for all of the Multimedia players listed in this section. The manufacturers of these programs usually make their money by licensing their technology and server software to other developers, Web hosting companies and corporate users.

QuickTime

QuickTime is a multimedia streaming audio and video system that can also play MP3 (version 4 and later). QuickTime is very good for streaming video. As with most streaming media players, the speed of your Internet connection directly affects the sound quality.

RealPlayer

The RealPlayer comes in two versions: a basic player, which is free, and a "plus" version, which costs $29.95. The free version is all you really need for a low bandwidth connection, but the RealPlayer Plus offers better audio quality and lets you record streaming audio (if the webcaster has enabled this feature), along with a few other bells and whistles.

Windows Media Player

Microsoft's Windows Media Player is a streamlined, easy-to-use multimedia player that is integrated with Microsoft Internet Explorer. The version of the Windows Media Player included with Windows is capable of playing WMA (Windows Media Audio), MP3 files and streaming video.

Full-featured Players

I consider an audio player to be full-featured only if it includes the following features: playlist support, equalizer presets, plug-ins and skins. A full-featured player should also support streaming audio. Based on this definition, only a handful of players qualify as full-featured. Winamp and Sonique are two of the best full-featured players for Windows PCs, and SoundJam MP is one of the best for the Mac.

Playlist support is essential for you to program your own music. Equalizers allow you to adjust the frequency response of your system. Plug-ins allow third-party developers to add useful features, such as automatic crossfading and support for remote controls, and other bells and whistles, such as visualization and sound effects. Skins allow you to customize the look of the player interface.

Winamp

With over 10 million copies downloaded, Winamp is currently the most popular full-featured MP3 player. Winamp is freeware and includes separate screens for a player, playlist manager, equalizer and a minibrowser. The equalizer can adjust the overall volume and boost or reduce the level in separate bands of frequencies. Equalization profiles can be created and saved for each song and automatically recalled each time the song is played.

Additional functionality can be added with third party plug-ins. The most useful is the crossfade plug-in, which automatically provides smooth transitions between songs like a professional DJ. Visualization plug-ins generate shifting patterns synchronized with the music. The more advanced visualization plug-ins generate complex 3D scenes with objects that move and morph to the music.

The appearance of Winamp can be customized by user designed "skins." Thousands of free Winamp skins are available via the Internet. These range from basic woodgrain and stone to futuristic steel and plastic. Skins can be created with any bitmap editor such as PC Paint or Corel Draw, and they can also be downloaded from Web sites like Winamp.com and MP3.com.

Sonique

Sonique is a Windows audio player capable of playing Microsoft's WMA files, MP3 files, audio CDs and more. Sonique can also play streaming MP3 audio from Icecast and SHOUTcast servers. It uses a unique windowless interface with a fully animated menu system.

Sonique has an extensive skins collection and includes a playlist editor and plug-in support, along with controls for adjusting pitch and a 20-band equalizer. It also includes a contextual help system and has a full-screen visual mode. Sonique is freeware, and well worth the time to check out.

MACAST

MACAST is a fully functional media player for the Macintosh and includes support for playlists, custom skins, plug-ins and equalizer presets. MACAST is designed for PowerPC Macs only. (See the description of MACAST Lite if you have an older Mac.)

The Open Source Initiative

To qualify as open source, software must include the source code and meet other criteria, including unrestrictive licensing. Modifications and additions by users are often incorporated into the main code for the benefit of all users. The Open Source Initiative is dedicated to promoting the Open Source trademark for the good of the programming community.

Other Players

Following are descriptions of several other digital audio players that don't fall into any of the categories above.

FreeAmp

FreeAmp is an open source effort to build a high quality digital audio player. Freeamp can play both downloadable and streaming MP3.

Hum

Utopiasoft's Hum is one of the first players to support the Windows CE platform. Hum enables a handheld PC with sound capability, such as the Cassiopeia or HP Jornada, to double as a portable digital audio player.

MACAST Lite

MACAST Lite is intended for older Macintosh systems with slower processors. It supports only basic features for playing audio, and not advanced features, such as plug-ins and skins, which are included in full-featured players like Sonique and Winamp.

DJ Mixers

DJ mixer software provides tools that allow you to mix music like a professional DJ. These programs allow you to queue up songs on multiple players, match tempos and crossfade between songs. Some software, like Party DJ, works in conjunction with a player like Winamp. Others, like Virtual Turntables, include their own player.

Party DJ

PartyDJ is for people who like to play DJ. It works with Winamp and provides a great interface for playing music at parties. PartyDJ allows you to toggle between a main and a support playlist and change the order of songs on the fly. It also keeps track of all songs that have been played during a session and warns you if you attempt to play the same song more than once.

PartyDJ's simple interface is especially useful at later hours when your motor skills may be impaired. Its Disco DJ feature allows you to control two instances of Winamp and mix songs like a professional.

Virtual Turntables

Virtual Turntables provides a way for anyone to mix music like a professional DJ. The software features real time mixing, pitch bends and visible cue markers. Settings for individual songs (cue positions, volume, notes, etc.) can be saved and reused.

Virtual Turntables also offers a built-in mixer with a crossfader and automatic pitch matching. It works with Winamp and has support for plug-ins. The buttons for scratching and backspin can be customized to make mixing with a keyboard easy.

PC-DJ

The PC-DJ family of software by VisioSonic was designed and built by professional DJs. The interface, which looks like a dual deck CD player, takes only a few minutes to learn. All of the PC-DJ programs include automatic crossfading and playlist support. PC-DJ Broadcaster supports streaming audio and allows you to easily create and stream your own Internet radio station.

PC-DJ is available in both freeware and professional versions. The professional version can instantly sort and start tracks and has 20 independent cue memories per track and automatic beat matching. Cue points can be graphically adjusted to a fraction of a millisecond.

All-in-one Programs

All-in-one programs include a ripper, encoder and player, along with advanced features for creating and managing playlists—usually with the help of a database. With a playlist, you have limited sorting and filtering capabilities, but with the information in a database you can quickly locate songs and easily sort them by artist, genre, tempo or other criteria. Most all-in-one programs can also copy MP3 files directly from a playlist to a portable player.

Earjam

Earjam is a user-friendly all-in-one media player. Earjam has EJ's, which are DJ's who access user preferences to create unique stations for individual users. The Earjam player can handle most audio formats, including MP3, Real Audio and WMA. Earjam can also burn MP3 files, directly to a CD.

MusicMatch Jukebox

MusicMatch Jukebox was the first all-in-one MP3 program on the market. It includes a ripper, an encoder, a player and a playlist manager. MusicMatch is a good choice for those who don't want to deal with a separate program for each function. It's also a good choice for the less technically inclined because it tests the CD-ROM drive and automatically configures itself for optimum performance.

MusicMatch has a straightforward interface designed to look like the front panel of a tape recorder. It also includes pull-down menus and dialog boxes for configuration settings. A unique feature is the AutoDJ, which automatically generates playlists based on user specified criteria. MusicMatch uses its own database, which includes fields like tempo, mood and situation for information that's not stored inside the ID3 tag of the MP3 file. (For an explanation of ID3 tags, see Chapter 13, *MPEG Audio*.) MusicMatch can also burn MP3 files directly from a playlist to a CD.

RealJukebox

RealNetwork's RealJukebox is a user-friendly program, which allows you to create and organize MP3s from audio CDs, records and tapes. RealJukebox has an easy to use Explorer-like interface. It automatically groups songs by ID3 tag information, so you can "drill down" through folders grouped by categories like artist, album and genre.

RealJukebox supports the CDDB, so it can automatically display the artist, album and title for each track. It also allows you to search for and download music from music Web sites. If you already have a large collection of MP3 files, you can import them and organize them with the RealJukebox playlist manager.

RealJukebox is available in both freeware and "Plus" versions. The freeware version doesn't have an equalizer or the ability to organize music by ID3 information, and limits the quality of encoded songs.

SoundJam MP

SoundJam MP is the first full-featured digital audio player for the Mac. It rips, records and encodes music into high quality MP3s. SoundJam allows you to view and sort your playlists by a variety of criteria, including album, artist, title, date and genre. SoundJam MP has a nice equalizer that can store presets for individual songs, and it can play streaming MP3 and QuickTime audio. It also can be customized with skins and third-party plug-ins.

Table 4 - Audio Player Software

Software	Developer	Web Site
PLAYERS		
FreeAmp	(open source)	www.freeamp.org
Hum (Windows CE)	Utopiasoft	www.utopiasoft.com
MACAST & MACAST Lite	@soft	www.macast.com
Sonique	Mediascience	www.sonique.com
Winamp	Nullsoft	www.winamp.com
Xmms (Linux/Unix)—formerly X11 Amp	Xmms Project	www.xmms.org
Xaudio MP3 Player (Unix)	Xaudio	www.xaudio.com
ALL-IN-ONE		
Earjam	Earjam.com	www.earjam.com
MusicMatch Jukebox (Mac and PC)	MusicMatch	www.musicmatch.com
RealJukebox	RealNetworks	www.real.com
SoundJam (Mac)	Cassidy & Greene	www.soundjam.com
DJ SOFTWARE		
Party DJ	DC Software	http://fon.fon.bg.ac.yu/~dcolak
Virtual Turntables	Carrot Systems	www.carrot.prohosting.com
PCDJ and PCDJ Pro Digital 1000 & 1200sl	VisioSonic	www.visiosonic.com

Chapter 8

Choosing the Right Hardware

Currently, to play MP3 and other downloadable music formats, you need a computer with a sound card or portable player like the Rio. You also need plenty of RAM, lots of free disk space and an Internet connection for downloading music and listening to Internet radio.

MP3-specific hardware, with the exception of portable players like the Rio, is still in the early stages of development. Many products under development do not require a computer and function much like standard home or car stereo system components. Until more of these products reach the market, most people will need a personal computer to work with any type of downloadable music.

Computers

Over the past few years, the price of computers and hard disks has dropped dramatically, making it possible to use a personal computer as a high-capacity digital jukebox and for high-end recording and mixing applications. A wide range of computers can be used to record and play digital music, but computers with the newer Pentium (II or III) and PowerPC (G3 or G4) processors work best. Many older systems will work to some degree but will be too slow for many applications. Slower systems are often suitable for downloading and playing music but not for ripping and encoding.

Processor

A Pentium 133 or a PowerPC (Mac) processor is the minimum for acceptable performance for playing MP3 files. Some players, such as Winamp, can be optimized for slower Pentium and 486 processors, but this will reduce the sound quality. Creating your own MP3 files is much more processor intensive than just playing them. Although you can create MP3 files on a slower system, a computer with at least a Pentium II or PowerPC G3 processor is recommended.

Processor Speed

Processor speed is more critical for playing MP3 files than creating them, even though creating MP3 files actually uses more processing power than playing them. This is due to the fact that a processor can crawl along at a snail's pace when creating an MP3 file with no ill effect, other than it taking a long time. But if you try to play an MP3 file on a system with a slow processor, it won't be able to keep up, because the file must be decoded in real-time. The sound will stop and stutter while the player waits for the processor to catch up.

Memory

The more RAM (Random Access Memory) you have, the better. Each program you run and each file that is opened uses up more of the computer's RAM. When the RAM is full, the computer uses the hard disk to handle the overflow. This "virtual" memory is many times slower than physical RAM. No matter how fast your processor is, the performance of your system will be severely limited if you don't have enough RAM.

Considering the fact that a four-minute WAV file takes up more than 40MB, 64MB of RAM would not be overkill for systems that are used for ripping and encoding. If you plan to edit WAV files before converting them to MP3, then 128MB or more of RAM would be better.

Hard Disks

Hard disk performance is not critical for playback, but it is more of a factor in encoding and editing sound files. Again, the larger and faster, the better. If you need more space to store digital audio files, you can find reasonably priced hard disks in the 20-40GB (gigabyte) range. Get the largest one you can afford, because it's easy to fill up a large drive, even with compressed audio files.

On most systems you can add a second hard disk and keep the original one. If for some reason you need to replace your existing hard disk, you can use a program like PowerQuest's Drive Image to copy a perfect image of the old disk to the new one. This eliminates the need to reinstall the operating system and application software. A good computer technician should be able install the new drive and transfer the data in less than two hours.

If you don't have room in your computer, or if you don't want to open it up, several companies make high-capacity external hard disks that connect to a parallel port or PC card slot. These drives are especially good for DJs and other users who have notebook computers, because replacement notebook drives tend to be much more expensive than external drives. Also, many notebook computers don't have room inside for additional hard drives.

Both IDE and SCSI drives work well, but SCSI generally performs better—although you will pay a premium for this performance. As of this writing, you can purchase a 30GB IDE drive for under $200 and a 30GB SCSI drive with controller for about twice as much. Either drive could hold over 7,000 high-quality songs in MP3 format.

CD Drives

The CD drives used in personal computers come in several different types: CD-ROM, CD-R and CD-RW. Most CD-R and CD-RW drives can also function as CD-ROM drives.

CD-ROM

CD-ROM stands for Compact Disc-Read Only Memory. CD-ROM drives found in computers can read data and multimedia CDs and play standard audio CDs. As the name implies, CD-ROM drives can only read information. They can't be used to record CDs.

CD-R

CD-R stands for CD-Recordable. Once you record something on a CD-R you can't erase or edit the information. CD-R drives can be used to record data CDs, which can only be read by CD-ROM drives, and to record Red Book audio CDs, which can be played by audio CD players and most CD-ROM drives.

CD-RW

CD-RW stands for CD-Rewritable. CD-RW drives allow you to write a CD and later erase or rewrite the information. Most CD-RW drives can also record CD-Rs. CD-RW discs reflect less light than CD-R discs and cannot be read by many older CD-ROM drives and audio CD players.

CLV and CAV Drives

Because audio CDs are designed to be played in real time, an audio CD player will spin faster as the disc plays at the inside and slower at the outside. This is called Constant Linear Velocity (CLV).

At the higher speeds used to read data CDs, imperfections in the CD cause vibration and noise to be a problem, so higher speed drives often spin at a Constant Angular Velocity (CAV). This means that the drive motor spins the CD at a constant RPM.

Drive Performance

CD-ROM drives are usually referred to as 12X, 16X, or some other "X" value. The X value refers to the data transfer rate relative to 150 KB/sec (1X). Early CD-ROM drives in the 4X-12X range typically read the data at a constant linear velocity, like an audio CD player.

A CD-ROM drive's speed rating usually refers to the fastest data transfer rate the drive will achieve on the outer-most tracks. The data transfer rate on the inner tracks can be substantially slower. Because CDs often don't use their full capacity and are recorded from inside to outside, CAV drives rarely read at their full rated speed.

Some newer CD drives such as the Plextor models use a combination of CAV on the inner tracks and CLV on the outer tracks to maximize the overall data transfer rate and reliability. This is called Partial CAV (P-CAV) and usually has two speed ratings (e.g., 12X-20X). The lower number is the speed for the inner tracks where the drive operates in CAV mode. As the drive approaches the outer tracks, it switches to CLV mode and operates at the higher speed for the remainder of the CD.

Many drive manufacturers only report the highest speed achieved on the outer tracks. The bottom line is that "X" speed ratings are not very useful for comparing the actual performance of 16X and higher speed drives. Only real-world tests with actual data are meaningful.

CD Technology

If you plan to do any ripping or burn your own CDs, it's useful to learn some of the basics of CD technology. This information can help you trouble-shoot ripping and recording problems, and maybe even avoid them in the first place.

A CD contains a single continuous 5.7km (about 3½ miles) long track of microscopic pits in a thin layer of metal. This track is only 1.6μm wide (1μm is one millionth of a meter). About 60 CD tracks would fit inside the groove of a vinyl record.

CDs are recorded at a constant linear density. This means that the same amount of data is recorded every cm (or inch) as the laser travels around the spiral track. This results in less data being recorded around the inner spirals and more around the outer spirals.

CDs are read from the inside to the outside. The diameter of the track at the inside is 50mm (about 2 inches), spiraling around over 22,000 times to the outside of the CD, where it is 117mm (about 4.5 inches) in diameter.

CD Capacity

A CD actually contains just over a gigabyte of data (1,073,741,824 bytes). Approximately 25% to 35% of the CD's capacity is used to store redundant information for error correction in case of scratches or manufacturing imperfections. The usable capacity of a CD depends on how it is formatted. The formatting is applied as the data is written to the CD.

Audio CDs

Audio data is recorded on CDs in chunks called frames (or sectors), each of which contains 588 16-bit stereo samples (1/75th of a second of music). A full 74-minute audio CD holds 333,000 frames, or about 765MB (783,216,000 bytes) of audio data. This is called the Red Book audio format and is named for the color of the book that describes the standard.

If a scratch causes more errors than can be corrected, an audio CD player will attempt to mask the error by interpolation. This fakes the value of a missing sample by taking a value that is in between two nearby samples, and the result is usually inaudible.

Data CDs

Because computer data is less tolerant of errors than our ears, CDs used for data storage use even more of the CD's gigabyte capacity to store data for error correction. This reduces the amount of computer data that can be stored on a CD to about 650MB—or about 65 minutes of uncompressed 44.1 kHz 16-bit stereo WAV files.

> **DVD**
>
> DVD stands for digital versatile disc. DVDs are similar to CDs and have capacities of up to 18.8GB. Most DVD drives currently on the market are read-only. Many, but not all, DVD drives can read prerecorded CDs and CD-Rs. Recordable DVD drives are currently available but the technology is still evolving and it may be a while before it is perfected.

Computer Interfaces

If you need to purchase a new drive, you should consider the pros and cons of the most common interfaces before making a decision.

IDE

IDE stands for Integrated Drive Electronics (also called ATA). This means that the controller circuitry is on the drive rather than on a separate card. ATAPI is the protocol that is used to communicate with non-hard drive IDE devices like CD-ROMs.

The IDE interface can support several types of devices, including hard disks, CD-ROM and CD-R drives. Most new PCs come with two IDE interfaces on the motherboard. Each channel can support two devices. If you have an IDE hard disk and CD-ROM or CD-R drive, they should be installed on separate channels. Otherwise, the slower CD drives can limit the performance of the hard disk.

SCSI

A SCSI (Small Computer Systems Interface)—pronounced "skuzzy"—interface can give you faster throughput and reduces the load on your computer's processor. Some SCSI drives, such as the newer Plextor models, will rip reliably at their maximum speed. Standard SCSI supports up to 7 devices (the controller counts as one) on the same channel; Wide SCSI supports up to 16 devices.

SCSI drives are optional on most personal computers, because they are more expensive and require a controller card. If you are purchasing a new system or replacing an existing drive, SCSI is well worth the additional cost. As a bonus, you can add additional SCSI devices (like a scanner or a CD-R drive) on the same controller.

Parallel

Some external drives can be connected to your system via the parallel port. Parallel is a good choice if your computer doesn't have room for more drives, and for drives that need to be used on more than one system. Although a key disadvantage of a parallel interface is that it puts more of a load on the computer's processor than IDE or SCSI interfaces. Parallel drives are also generally slower than IDE and SCSI drives.

Parallel drive interfaces are sometimes based on SCSI but are usually limited to just one device. Many drives and portable audio players with parallel interfaces include a pass-through connector so you can connect your printer and the drive to the same port. However, only one device can be active at a time. Multiple pass-through devices may be chained together on a single parallel port. This usually leads to trouble. It's better to add a second port or use another type of interface for the other devices.

USB

USB (Universal Serial Bus) is a relatively new, general purpose interface designed to overcome the limitations of serial and parallel interfaces. The USB offers much higher bandwidth than serial or parallel interfaces and supports multiple devices on a single port. Plug-and-play USB devices do not use interrupts or I/O addresses, which limit the number of serial and parallel ports that can be installed on a system.

Most new computers include at least one USB port, and low-cost hubs can be used to add additional ports. Since USB is relatively new, devices that support it are just starting to reach the market. USB products currently available include CD-R and CD-RW drives, printers, scanners, Zip drives and digital-to-analog converters. USB is supported by the current version of Mac OS, Windows 95 OSR-2, Windows 98, and Windows 2000. USB is not supported by Windows NT.

Sound Cards

Sound cards are one of the most overlooked links in computer audio. A sound card performs many functions. It handles analog to digital (A/D) and digital to analog (D/A) conversion, mixing, music synthesizing, sound effects and amplification.

The components inside a PC generate a tremendous amount of electrical noise. This noise can be introduced into the audio signal whenever it is in an analog format. Many inexpensive sound cards are poorly shielded and use low quality digital-to-analog converters. Therefore, you not only have noise introduced from the inside of the computer, but you also have distortion introduced by the sound card's electronics.

The problem with noise and distortion can be solved by purchasing a higher quality sound card. This will be adequate for most people, but a sound card with digital output is even better. However, this solution requires an external D/A converter or a preamplifier with digital inputs.

If you are purchasing a new sound card, get one of the PCI models if your computer supports this (most new PCs do). PCI cards place much less of a demand on the processor than ISA cards and conserve interrupts.

The Creative Labs Sound Blaster Live MP3+ and the Turtle Beach Montego II Quadzilla cards are good choices because they are well shielded and include digital outputs. The Sound Blaster Live Value and the standard Montego cards work well but don't include digital outputs. The Sound Blaster AWE64 Gold is a good choice if you need (or prefer) an ISA sound card.

External Audio Devices

During playback the digital signal from the MP3 or WAV file must be converted to analog. This conversion usually happens in the sound card. Since analog signals are much more susceptible to noise than digital signals, a good solution is to move the digital to analog conversion outside of the PC. You can accomplish this by using a sound card with a digital output and an external digital-to-analog converter, or by using a digital-to-analog converter with a USB interface.

Digital-to-Analog Converters

An external digital-to-analog converter sits between the digital output of your sound card and the analog input of your preamp. These devices vary widely in both cost and quality and are being eclipsed by low cost USB devices that bypass the sound card entirely. If you use an external digital-to-analog converter, make sure it uses connectors and signal levels that are compatible with your existing equipment.

USB Audio

A new generation of audio devices is taking advantage of the simplicity and flexibility of USB (Universal Serial Bus). These devices are basically outboard sound cards that connect to personal computers via the USB.

The Roland UA-30 (*www.edirol.com*) is, by far, the best USB audio device that I've tested. It supports both Macs and PCs and includes just about every type of input and output connector you might possibly need.

The UA-30 has optical and S/PDIF (coax) input and output jacks for digital signals, and stereo RCA jacks for analog connections. It also includes a switchable guitar/mic jack and a headphone jack. The UA-30 has separate level control sliders, with peak indicators, for the analog line-in and guitar/mic inputs. It also has a nice master output level control with level and peak indicators. The UA-30 even functions as decent 2-channel mixer.

Roland has another USB device, the UA-100 Audio Canvas, which combines the functions of a sound card, multi-channel mixer, digital signal processor and MIDI interface. DSP effects include reverb, chorus, and delay. The UA-100 allows you to mix recorded audio with vocal, guitar, and any other instrument or sound track with no loss of quality.

Speakers

Computer speakers are convenient because most have built-in amplification and use a minimal amount of desk space. However, even the best computer speakers are usually no match for a good set of stereo speakers.

If you want the best possible sound, you should hook your computer up to a good stereo system. (See Chapter 10, *Connecting Your PC to Your Stereo*.) If you plan to do this, make sure you have a good sound card. Otherwise, the high frequency response of your stereo system will make any noise and distortion more apparent. If you want to listen to high-quality audio while sitting at your computer, you'll need to spend at least $150 to obtain a high-fidelity computer speaker system.

Several new computer speaker systems use the Universal Serial Bus to bypass the sound card. These systems typically include a D/A converter, preamp and amplifier inside the speaker. Most of these speakers can also be connected to the analog outputs of a sound card if a computer doesn't have a USB port.

Digital speaker systems have much lower noise levels than speakers using analog inputs. But the noise from the computer, combined with the music, will often mask any noise, making it hard to notice any difference. I tried several of these and found that a good analog computer speaker system can sound just as good as a comparable USB system. The quality of the speakers and the D/A converter has much more impact on sound quality than whether you use a digital or analog connection.

Roland's MA-150U system includes a pair of two-way bass reflex speakers, each with its own amplifier. The MA-150U has a USB port and two sets of analog line inputs, along with a dynamic enhancer control that can improve the sound at lower volume levels.

The MicroWorks from Cambridge SoundWorks is an excellent speaker system that includes a subwoofer and two satellite speakers. Cambridge SoundWorks also offers the FPS2000™ digital surround sound speaker system. It's designed for serious gamers and includes a powered subwoofer and four satellite speakers. Altec Lansing and Bose also make very good computer speaker systems.

The MicroWorks speakers have a very smooth response and sound better than many home stereo system speakers that cost twice as much. The MA-150 does not have quite as smooth a response as the MicroWorks, but it's more efficient and well-suited for use as a portable PA system.

It's important to listen to any speakers before you purchase them, because sound quality is very subjective and the quality of different models can vary widely, even within the same brand.

Dual-Mode MP3/Audio CD Players

The current generation of audio CD players will only play standard audio CDs, which are limited to 74 minutes of music. With MP3 at 128 kbps, you can fit more than 12 hours of high-quality music on a single data format CD.

Figure 6 - Dual-Mode MP3/Audio CD Player

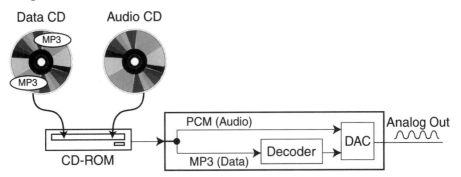

A new type of dual-mode CD player is now available that operates independently of a computer and gives you the flexibility to play both standard audio CDs, and data CDs with MP3 files. Prerecorded CDs with music in MP3 format are already available from MP3.com and other online sources. Following are just a few examples of newer CD players that support MP3.

AudioReQuest

AudioReQuest by ReQuest (*www.audiorequest.com*) is a combination MP3/CD recorder and player. It includes a CD-ROM drive and hard disk and has the capability to record directly from CDs and external sources to MP3 and other formats. The AudioReQuest supports playlists and can use either a USB or parallel interface to share files with PCs and portable players. It operates with a remote control and connects to a TV or computer monitor to provide a graphical interface for playlist editing and navigation, and to display visualization effects.

Brujo

The Brujo by netDrives (*www.netdrives.com*) is a basic MP3/CD player that supports CDs, CD-Rs and CD-RWs. It features 63 memory locations, repeat and shuffle play and a 31-key infrared remote control.

D'Music

The D'Music SM-200C by Pine (*www.pineusa.com*) is one of the first portable CD players to support the MP3 format. The SM-200C includes support for ID3 tags, which allow it to display the song title and artist name. The unit uses 2 AA batteries and includes a 5 band equalizer and an anti-shock mechanism for skip free playback of audio CDs.

Portable Players

Portable MP3 players began to reach the market in late 1998. As with the first generation of any new product, prices were fairly high, and glitches were common. None of these players have built-in speakers. You must use them with the included headphones or with amplified speakers like the ones sold for use with computers.

First Generation Players

Two of the first portable MP3 players to reach the market were Diamond Multimedia's Rio and Saehan Information Systems' MPMan. Several other portable MP3 players have since been announced by other manufacturers. By the time you read this there will be a much wider range of players to choose from, and prices should begin to drop due to the increased competition. Most of the first generation players use solid-state memory, which makes them mostly immune to shock and vibration but also limits their capacity.

Rio 300

The Rio PMP 300 (*www.rioport.com*) is about the size of a cigarette pack and includes 32MB of on-board memory and accepts SmartMedia cards to expand its capacity up to 64MB. It uses a single AA battery and connects to your computer with a parallel cable. The Rio has well-designed controls and several preset equalization settings. The newer SE (Special Edition) version of the PMP 300 comes with 64MB of onboard memory.

MPMan F20

The MPMan (*www.mpman.com*) is sold in the U.S. by Eiger Labs (*www.eigerlabs.com*). It includes 32MB of onboard memory and accepts SmartMedia cards to expand its capacity up to 64MB. The F20 uses a single AA battery and connects to your computer with a parallel cable. The MPMan includes higher quality earphones than most other portable players and has a nice bass boost feature.

Second Generation Players

Second generation portable audio players have already begun to reach the market. These players typically include larger LCDs that can display song titles, built-in FM radio tuners, and microphones that allow them to be used as portable recorders. One player, the MPIO (*www.digitalway.co.kr*), even has a digital camera attachment that uses the same memory as the player.

I-Jam

The I-Jam MP3 player (*www.ijamworld.com*) from I-Jam MultiMedia is one of the smallest MP3 players available. It uses removable MultiMedia cards that can be interchanged like cassette tapes. The I-Jam operates on two AAA batteries and is available with either a USB or parallel interface. It also includes an FM tuner and is available in multiple colors.

Lyra

The Lyra (*www.lyrazone.com*) by Thompson Consumer Electronics (sold in the U.S. by RCA) is the one of the first portable players to use CompactFlash cards. The Lyra doesn't have any onboard memory but it is available with either a 32MB or 64MB CompactFlash card and supports both Type I and II cards.

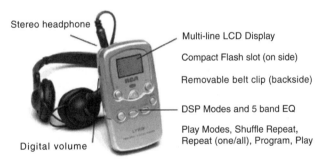

Stereo headphone

Multi-line LCD Display

Compact Flash slot (on side)

Removable belt clip (backside)

DSP Modes and 5 band EQ

Play Modes, Shuffle Repeat, Repeat (one/all), Program, Play

Digital volume

NOMAD II

The NOMAD II portable MP3 player by Creative Labs (*www.nomadworld.com*) has a built-in FM tuner and a built-in microphone so it can also be used as a portable radio and digital recorder. The Nomad II has no onboard memory and uses a single removable SmartMedia card.

rave:mp 2200 & 2300

The rave:mp (*www.ravemp*.com) *by* Sensory Science, is a portable MP3 player that can also be used as an audio recorder and personal digital assistant (PDA). The rave:mp 2200 has a USB interface and comes with 64MB of memory, which can be expanded to 128MB with a SmartMedia card. The rave:mp 2300 uses 40MB removable Clik disks to store music. Both units have built-in microphones, and the 2200 also has an FM tuner.

Rio 500 & 600

The Rio 500 (*www.rioport.com*) uses a USB interface and is designed to work with both Macs and PCs. The 500 includes 64MB of onboard memory and accepts SmartMedia cards to expand its capacity to up to 128MB. The 600 only has 32MB of onboard memory but can be expanded to up to 372MB with snap-on backpacks. Both units have backlit LCDs for displaying song titles, but do not include an FM tuner or microphone. A nice feature of the Rio 500/600 player is the ability to organize music in multiple folders.

Handheld PCs

Handheld computers that use Windows CE and have sound capability can play MP3 and WMA files using programs like the Hum player from Utopiasoft. These are the ultimate portable players because they can be used for so many other purposes, such as e-mail, address books and Web access.

Cassiopeia

The Cassiopeia is a Windows CE handheld computer that includes the ability to play stereo audio (MP3 and WMA format) and movies. The Cassiopeia includes a backlit color TFT display, up to 32MB RAM and a Compact Flash slot for expansion. It also has a built-in microphone and speaker, and options for a 56k modem and serial port.

Getting Music on the Player

To play music on a portable player, you first must get the files on a computer and then download them to the player. Eventually, you'll be able to download files from the Internet directly to these players and purchase prerecorded digital music on flashcards or small disks that can be used just like cassette tapes or CDs.

Personal Jukeboxes

Several manufacturers have developed hard-disk based portable players that function as high-capacity personal Jukeboxes. The HanGo PJB-100 was the first to reach the market and has been followed by the Nomad Jukebox by Creative Labs. These devices hold over 1,000 songs and connect to a PC via a USB port. The Nomad Jukebox is the size and shape of a typical portable CD player. The PJB-100 is about the size of a brick but only about 1" thick. The Nomad Jukebox also includes the ability to record audio from external sources via its line-in jack.

Computer Interfaces

First generation portable players use a parallel interface to connect to the computer. Many of the second generation players use USB, which is better because it eliminates conflicts with other devices.

Memory Capacity

First generation portable players include between 16MB and 64MB of onboard memory and are limited to about 96MB total. The amount of music they can hold is a function of the amount of memory installed and the bit-rate of the MP3 files. (See Table 25 on page 187 to see the relationship between bit-rates and the amount of music that can be stored in player memory.)

A portable player with 64MB of storage and will hold about 68 minutes of MP3 music encoded at 128 kbps (close to CD quality). If the music were encoded at 96 kbps, it would hold about 106 minutes. Many people find the 96 kbps rate acceptable because the sound quality is comparable to a portable cassette player.

The capacity of portable players will continue to increase as the price of memory drops and manufacturers take advantage of more efficient storage media. Portable players that use small hard disks offer much more capacity, but most of these are still in the early stages of development.

Memory Cards

Memory cards provide compact, convenient, removable storage for portable MP3 players, digital cameras and hand-held computers. Groups of songs can be copied to different memory cards and they can be interchanged and used just like cassette tapes and CDs. With today's technology, you could carry the equivalent of a dozen or more CDs in your wallet using memory cards.

As costs continue to drop and capacities increase, you might some day be able to carry your entire music collection in your pocket using memory cards.

Two main types of memory cards are used in portable MP3 players: SmartMedia and CompactFlash. Both types were originally developed for use in digital cameras and are sometimes referred to as digital film. Although they are both about the size of a matchbook, each is incompatible with the other and each has unique advantages and disadvantages. Most memory cards available today use Flash RAM technology, which is non-volatile memory that can retain data, even when the power is turned off.

SmartMedia

SmartMedia is the most common type of memory card used by first generation portable MP3 players. It is also called SSFDC (Solid State Floppy Disk Card). At present, SmartMedia cards are currently available in sizes up to 64MB, with higher capacities expected. At 45mm x 37mm x 0.76mm thick (about 1-3/4" x 1-1/2" x 1/32"), it's the thinnest type of memory card currently available.

The main advantage of SmartMedia is simplicity. It's just a flash RAM chip on a card, with no controller or supporting circuits (it might be more accurate to call it "dumb media"). The disadvantage is that the required controller circuits must be included in the player or camera. This means that compatibility with newer, larger cards is not guaranteed. Many of the first digital cameras (developed when the largest card was 8MB) had to be returned to their manufacturers to be upgraded when 16MB and 32MB cards became available.

If you have a digital camera that uses SmartMedia cards, don't try to use your camera card in a Rio player. Camera SmartMedia cards contain format information in their memory that will be erased when used in the Rio. The card will then no longer be usable in the camera. Because of copyright issues, the Rio uses a proprietary format on its memory cards to prevent files from being copied from the player. A program called *Dreaming of Brazil (www.parkverbot.org/harald/download)* can be used to reformat SmartMedia cards for camera use after they have been used in Rio players.

CompactFlash

CompactFlash (also known as CF) cards were first introduced in 1994. Most new digital cameras use Compact-
Flash cards, and they are starting to appear in some MP3
players, such as the Lyra. CompactFlash cards can hold
up to 320MB, but they are very expensive.

CompactFlash cards come in two varieties, Type I and Type II. Both types
are 43mm x 36mm (about 1.7" x 1.4"). Type I cards are 3.3mm (about 1/8")
thick, and Type II cards are 5mm (about 3/16") thick. Type I cards are currently available in capacities up to 192MB. Type II cards are available in capacities up to 320MB.

CompactFlash cards conform to the PCMCIA-ATA standard and act like a
hard disk drive when inserted in a PC. This allows MP3 files to be copied on
and off a CompactFlash card, without special software. The controller circuitry is included on the card, so any device that is designed to use a CompactFlash card can use any brand of card (as long as it meets the Compact-
Flash Association standards).

Unlike SmartMedia cards, as larger capacity and faster CompactFlash cards
become available, they can be used without requiring upgrades or changes to
players and cameras. The built-in controller handles defect management and
error correction independent of the player or camera. CompactFlash cards are
serialized, and future implementations of secure music systems may attempt
to tie songs to specific cards.

CompactFlash cards are electrically the same as the larger PC (formerly
known as PCMCIA cards). They use a 50-pin connector (vs. the PC card's 68
pins) and can be plugged directly into a laptop computer's PC card slot with
a simple adapter. (PC card slots can also be added to desktop computers.)
The best solutions for desktop computers provide both PC card and CompactFlash card slots and connect to the PC's parallel port.

The IBM microdrive

The additional thickness of a CompactFlash Type II card
allowed IBM to develop a miniature hard disk called the
microdrive. The microdrive fits in a CF Type II slot and
performs like a standard IDE hard drive.

Other Memory Cards

The **Memory Stick** (50mm x 22mm x 2.8mm) was introduced by Sony in 1998 for use in their digital still and video cameras and other products. It uses an on-board controller like CompactFlash cards but uses a proprietary interface and is not compatible with CompactFlash or SmartMedia cards. Because of its proprietary nature, it has not caught on for use in MP3 players, except for those manufactured by Sony.

The **Miniature Card** (38mm x 33mm x 3.5mm) was introduced by Intel in 1996. Like SmartMedia cards, it has no on-board controller. In 1998, Intel conceded the market for portable consumer devices to SmartMedia and CompactFlash cards, and it is rarely seen today.

MultiMedia Cards (32mm x 24mm x 1.4mm) are similar to Compact-Flash cards but they have smaller form factor. They are used primarily in cellular phones, pagers and a few of the smaller portable MP3 players.

The **Iomega Clik!** drive fits in a PC card Type II slot and uses removable 40MB disks that cost $10-15, depending on quantity.

ATA Flash PC cards are the same as CompactFlash cards, but larger and are designed to fit into a notebook computer's Type II PC card slot.

PC Card Hard Drives are even larger and require a Type III slot (twice as thick as a Type II slot).

With capacities of up to 1GB, the microdrive could revolutionize the portable MP3 player market. Imagine 18 hours of music in a device the size of a matchbook that weighs only 16 grams (about 1/2 ounce). Many hand-held computers, such as the Cassiopeia and HP Jornada, can take advantage of the microdrive and function as high-capacity portable audio players.

MP3 for Your Car

Most of the early MP3 car stereos are small PCs with CD-ROM or hard drives, LCD screens and remote controls. Full-featured, consumer quality MP3 car stereos are just beginning to reach the market. Most of these cost several hundred to a thousand dollars. Prices should drop quite a bit over the next few years as more players reach the market.

Commercial Car Stereos

Following are descriptions of some of the more capable MP3 car stereos.

Aiwa CDC-MP3

The Aiwa CDC-MP3 in-dash AM/FM stereo (*www.aiwa.com*) is just the beginning of the new generation of digital media players that will soon be available. The CDC-MP3 plays both audio CDs, and MP3 format CD-Rs and CD-RWs. It comes with a detachable face plate and a remote control. The CDC-MP3 supports ID3 tags, long file names and up to 8 levels of sub-directories. It supports multiple bit-rates from 32kbps to 320 kbps. The player includes a 45W amplifier, which is sufficient for most vehicles.

Clarion AutoPC

The Clarion AutoPC (*www.autopc.com*) combines a full-featured in-dash computer with an FM radio and CD player. Clarion has not yet incorporated MP3 player technology into the AutoPC but plans to do so in the near future. The AutoPC includes a GPS (Global Positioning System) with the NavTech Map Database, making it possible to always know where you are and how to get where you are going. The CUE auto FM receiver lets you receive E-mail, pager alerts and traffic reports. The AutoPC supports Compact Flash Cards, which can be used to transfer data from your PC to the AutoPC.

empeg-car

The empeg-car (*www.empeg.com*) is a Linux-based digital music player that can store over 7,000 high-quality songs, instantly accessible through the player interface in your dashboard. The main unit can have up to 28GB of disk storage. A quick-release mount is included for security reasons and to make it easier to load new tunes into the system. Other features include an FM Stereo tuner with RadioText display and a credit card size IR remote control. Software for organizing and downloading music from your PC is provided. The empeg-car requires a separate amplifier; however, it does come with four line-output connectors (front and rear pairs) for connecting to external amplifiers. Future versions of the empeg will include an Ethernet interface for faster file transfers.

Kenwood eXcelon Z919

The eXcelon Z919 (*www.kenwood.com*) is an in-dash AM/FM car stereo that also plays audio and MP3 format CDs. It comes with a remote control, but the face plate is not detachable. The Z919 currently does not support ID3 tags, but it does support long file names. The Z919 includes a 45W amplifier.

> **Cassette Player Audio Adapters**
>
> A way to play MP3s through your existing car stereo without spending a lot of money is to use a portable player like the Rio, along with an adapter that plugs into a cassette player. You can purchase these adapters at Best Buy, Circuit City or Radio Shack for about $20. These adapters also can be used with any boom box or stereo system that has a cassette player.

MP-ROM

The MP-ROM (*www.carplayer.com*) is one of the most versatile MP3 car players on the market. Not only can it play MP3 files, it also can play CDs, CD-Rs, DVDs, DVD-Rs and CD-RWs. It comes complete (no extra equipment is required to use it) with a fully enclosed case and all cables. The MP-ROM can run on AC or DC. It features track seeking, shuffle play, programmable memory and a 31-button remote control to make it easier to use while driving.

Do It Yourself

A notebook PC with a 12-volt adapter and cassette player adapter works well for do-it-yourselfers who already have a decent car stereo. Currently, you can purchase a new Pentium 133 notebook PC with a 2GB hard disk and CD-ROM drive for under $800. This is a couple of hundred dollars cheaper than a high-end MP3 car stereo, and you end up with a fully functional PC.

To connect your notebook PC to your car stereo, insert the mini phone plug of the adapter's cable into the line-out or headphone jack of the notebook. Insert the adapter into your cassette player and press Play. If you use a headphone jack with an external volume control, avoid turning it up more than one fifth of the way to avoid overdriving the head of the cassette player.

Additional Resources

Web Site	Address
CompactFlash Association	www.compactflash.org
MP3Car.com	www.mp3car.com
Personal Computer Memory Computer International Association (PCMCIA)	www.pc-card.com

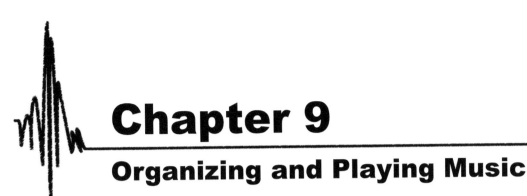

Chapter 9

Organizing and Playing Music

Once you have your music collection in MP3 format, you gain an enormous amount of flexibility and control. You have instant access to any song, and you can organize your music in ways that were not previously possible. With playlists, you can easily program dozens of hours of continuous music. Instead of swapping tapes or CDs, you can click on a playlist and let the computer do the rest. With DJ mixer software, you can use your PC to mix songs on the fly and play requests, just like a professional DJ.

Your CD player or tape deck and all of the equipment that a DJ uses for mixing and playing music are replaced by software on your computer. With software, it's much easier to mix music because so much can be automated. You can even configure some programs to choose which songs to play and automatically crossfade between songs.

If someone has a request, or you want to change the music to match the mood, you can do it in seconds (by remote control, if necessary). A side benefit is that if someone doesn't like a particular song, you can tell them (while trying to keep a straight face) that the computer controls the music, and that you have absolutely no control over what songs it chooses.

To get started (assuming you have the right type of computer and a decent music collection), you'll need to convert your music to a compressed format like MP3. You'll also need a good full-featured player like Sonique or Winamp and lots of disk space (see Chapter 7, *Choosing the Right Software* and Chapter 8, *Choosing the Right Hardware*).

Storing Music

Many types of drives and media can be used to store digital music on a PC. However, hard disks and CD-Rs are the best choices for most people.

Hard disks offer a great combination of good performance, reasonable cost, ease of use, and reliability. CD-Rs offer much lower cost and very good reliability at the expense of performance and ease of use. CD-RWs are also a good choice if you want to work with reusable media. If you have a newer computer with a large hard disk and plenty of free space, you're in good shape. Otherwise, you'll need to upgrade to a larger hard disk or store your music on CD-R or CD-RW media.

Some people may prefer to use removable disks (Zip, Jazz, etc.), but removable drive media is significantly more expensive than CD-R and CD-RW media. Data tapes are used primarily for backups and are not suitable for playing MP3 files. This is because tapes are a linear media and are slow for accessing individual files.

Disk Space

Even with compressed audio formats like MP3, digital audio requires lots of disk space. The actual disk space required depends on the lengths of the songs and the bit-rates used to encode them. Figure on getting about 275 to 350 songs per GB of disk space for good quality sound (128 kbps) and 175 to 250 songs per GB for high quality sound. (See Table 25 on page 187 to see the relationship between bit-rates, sound quality and the amount of music that can be stored on various types of media.)

If you plan to edit sound files, you'll need plenty of disk space for the uncompressed WAV files and the temporary files of the sound editing software. Each minute of uncompressed audio in WAV format requires about 10MB of disk space, and it doesn't take long to fill up even a large hard disk with a few dozen four-minute songs. Even if you don't plan on editing sound files, you'll still need to create WAV files (at least temporarily) if you want to record your own audio CDs from prerecorded music.

Hard Disks

Hard disks are a great way to store digital audio files, but many people, especially those with older computers, don't have enough hard disk capacity to store a large music collection. Fortunately, the price of hard disks has dropped dramatically, while the capacity has continued to increase. As of this writing, you can purchase a 30GB hard disk for less than $200. That's not a bad price for the capacity to store more than 7,000 high-quality songs.

CD-Rs and CD-RWs

Recordable and Rewritable CDs are a good option for storing your music (and for backing up your system). Currently, you can fit about 150 four-minute MP3 songs on a single CD (at 128 kbps). To create these you need a CD-R or CD-RW drive, both of which can be found for under $200. It's a good idea to put playlists on each CD so you can insert the CD and double-click on a playlist file instead of having to select individual songs. (For more information creating custom CDs, see Chapter 18, *Recording Your Own CDs*.)

Storage Cost

Hard disk storage currently costs less than $10 per GB, while CD-R storage costs anywhere from 50 cents to $2 per GB, and CD-RW storage costs about $2 to $5 per GB. Recordable DVDs will eventually offer much higher capacity and lower costs per GB than CDs, but the technology is still evolving. I recommend waiting until the technology stabilizes and the prices are lower before purchasing a DVD recorder.

Playing Music

Digital audio files can be played by selecting individual files or groups of files using Windows Explorer (or Mac Finder). You can also select files from within your audio player program, and you can use playlists to program continuous music. A few concepts that will make it easier to understand these options are covered below.

Files

Most songs in digital formats like MP3 exist as individual files. The player software needs to "open" a file to play it. You can use the File Open feature of a player to play a song, similar to the way you would open a document from within a word processor. You can also double-click on the file itself. If the player is not already running, the system will launch the player associated with the file type and then open and play the file. Another way to play a file is to right-click on it and select **Play** from the pop-up menu.

File Type Associations

Any time you double-click on a file, the operating system checks to see which program is associated with the default action (play, edit, etc.) for the file type. The operating system then launches the program and automatically loads the file. The links between file types, actions and programs are referred to as "file type associations."

In Windows, file type associations control which choices appear on the popup menu that displays when you right-click on a file. Each choice launches the associated program and executes a specific action, like **Open**, **Edit** or **Play**. The choices on the right-click menu will be different depending on the file type, but most file types will have at least an **Open** choice.

File type associations are controlled by file extensions. Multiple actions can be associated with a single file type and each action can have a different program associated with it. Each combination of action and program will show up as a choice when you right-click on a file.

File type associations are normally established when you install software, but it is possible to change them later. (See Chapter 19, *Basic Tasks*, for instructions on changing file type associations.) Below are descriptions of common actions associated with digital audio files.

Open, as the name implies, means that the file will be opened in the associated program when you double-click on it. It may also start playing, depending on how the action is defined. If the file name shows up in the player or playlist window and doesn't play, click on the **Play** button of the software. The **Play** action should always open and play the file.

Enqueue means the file will be added to a list of files waiting to be played in the active playlist of the player program. To add multiple files to a playlist, you can highlight them (shift-click or control-click), then right-click and select **Enqueue** to add the files to the current playlist.

Edit is used to load a file into an application with the intention of editing it. Functionally, it's the same as **Open**, but it may be associated with a different application. A good example is a WAV file. The default (double-click) action would likely be **Play,** associated with a player program like Winamp. The **Edit** action could be associated with a program like Sound Forge or Cool Edit. The **Open** action may not be defined, or it could be associated with another player or editor.

If you plan to install more than one player on your system, you'll need to decide which program will be associated with each type of digital audio file. For example, if you have more than one MP3 player, you will need to specify one to be the default—i.e., the player that will be launched when you double-click on an MP3 file.

Some players provide an installation option to be associated with certain audio file types. A few players have the nasty habit of automatically associating themselves with audio file types, even if the file types have already been associated with other programs. Winamp and Sonique can be configured to automatically restore file type associations whenever they are run. You can also manually change file type associations through Windows Explorer (see the tutorial on modifying file type associations in Chapter 19, *Basic Tasks*).

Adjusting the Volume

When you play music on a PC, there are several places where you can adjust the volume. Setting the right level for each volume control will help minimize distortion and noise. A general rule to follow is to keep input levels relatively high and power amplifier levels relatively low. High input levels help minimize noise, and lower power amplifier levels provide headroom that helps minimize distortion and clipping.

The Windows Volume Control program controls the input and output levels of the sound card and has separate screens for setting recording and playback levels. The Playback Control screen has a control labeled Wave (or Wave/Direct Sound) that sets the input levels of audio files played through the sound card. A Master level control (sometimes labeled Play Control, Speaker Control or Volume Control) sets the output level of the sound card.

Most player programs have their own volume control, which may be linked with the Wave playback control. Some players like Sonique and Winamp also have preamps that can be used with equalizer presets to adjust the levels of individual songs. Avoid setting preamp levels too high because this will cause distortion.

Generally, the level of the Wave playback control should be set close to the maximum and the volume should be regulated through the volume control of the player software. When playing music through a stereo system, the volume control on the receiver (or amplifier) should be set at about the level you would normally use when listening to a tape or CD. If you are using amplified speakers, you should begin with their volume control about one third of the way up. The master volume control should be set low enough so there is no distortion when the input level is at 100%.

To access the Volume Control, double-click the speaker icon in the system tray, or launch it via the Start Menu, by selecting **Programs**, **Accessories**,

Figure 7 - Playback Volume Controls

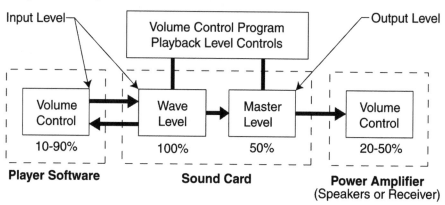

Multimedia (or Entertainment), then **Volume Control**. Figure 7 shows typical volume control settings, with the player software's volume control used to regulate the overall level. (See Chapter 14, *Hard Disk Recording*, for more information on using the Volume Control program.)

Working with Playlists

A playlist is a file (or database) that contains a list of songs. A simple text playlist contains the names and locations of each audio file and nothing else. The standard extensions for playlist files are .M3U and .PLS.

Playlists can be used like tapes and CD changers but without the limitations of physical recording media. You can create a playlist with hundreds songs in a few minutes with a wordprocessor or playlist editor. It would take a couple of hours to program the same number of songs on a CD changer, and several days to record them on tape.

You can have as many playlists as you want. The same song may appear in multiple lists and even multiple times on the same list. A playlist could contain just one song or it could have thousands of songs. Playlists can contain a mix of audio file types as long as the player software supports these.

You might want to create a playlist that includes every song in your collection, and you might want other playlists for specific occasions or moods. You can create playlists of dance music, romantic music, or whatever else you want. Of course, don't forget that you need the audio files to go with the list.

MusicMatch's Auto DJ

If you're having a party and someone suggests that you play some killer dance music, you can use MusicMatch's Auto DJ to automatically create a playlist. You could specify criteria that include all songs released later than 1990, but only those that are coded as suitable for dancing. You could also specify that the tempo must be fast, and that the genre be either rock or techno, but not funk or disco. Songs that meet these criteria will be selected and added to the playlist. You can then play individual songs or all songs on the list, and you can save it for future occasions.

Creating and Editing Playlists

Once you have a playlist, it's very easy to add and delete songs or change the order. Most playlist editors allow you to drag songs up or down the list to change the order. Some even allow you to add a file by dragging and dropping it into the playlist editor.

Individual files, groups of files and entire directories can be added to a playlist by the **Open** and **Add** functions of the playlist editor. Files can also be added to playlists by highlighting them in Windows Explorer and then right-clicking and selecting **Enqueue** from the pop-up menu.

Using Playlists

Since standard playlists are files, they can also be associated with programs and actions, just like audio files. Double-clicking on a playlist file or right-clicking on it and selecting **Play** will load the playlist and start playing the first song. Right-clicking on a playlist file and selecting **Enqueue** will add the songs to the player's current playlist, but will not start playing them.

Once a playlist is loaded, you can play individual songs by double-clicking on them in the playlist window or by highlighting them and clicking the **Play** button. Most players also have **Loop** (repeat) and **Shuffle** (random play) features. These two features are useful in combination with playlists for long stretches of continuous music. If you have 100 songs in a playlist and you set the player on both **Loop** and **Shuffle**, you are less likely to get bored with the music because the order of the songs will be different each time.

Playlists files can be printed for easy reference. If someone compliments you on your music selection, you could give them a copy of the playlist, and they could use it as a shopping list. Just don't give them copies of the audio files on the list, because that would be copyright infringement.

Databases

Some all-in-one programs, like MusicMatch and RealJukebox, use a database to organize music. The songs still exist in separate files, but the database can store much more information about a song than a text-based playlist. This information can then be used to sort and filter the songs and to automatically generate playlists.

MusicMatch uses its database for its Music Library and its Auto DJ feature. With information for each song entered in the database, you can program the Auto DJ to automatically create playlists based on criteria like genre, tempo, year and mood. RealJukebox uses a database to organize songs and playlists into Explorer-like folders. You can easily sort music and drag and drop files between folders to create playlists.

The CDDB

The CDDB (*www.cddb.com*) is a comprehensive Web-based database with information on thousands of audio CDs. Before the CDDB, when you played a CD on your computer there was no way for the player software to display the album and artist name and song titles unless you manually entered the information.

Many player and ripping programs can access the CDDB to obtain this information. To locate the proper record in the CDDB, the program uses an algorithm to calculate a unique identifier from the CD's table of contents. The program then finds the CDDB record with a matching "key."

The information about the songs can be displayed by the player or used for other purposes, such as generating file names or filling in the ID3 tag of an MP3 file. Many players and rippers write the information to the CDPlayer.ini file and can retrieve it from there without accessing the CDDB each time the CD is played. The size of the CDPlayer.ini file is limited to 64K and entries will be overwritten once that limit is reached.

Table 5 - File Names Generated Automatically from the CDDB

Default File Names	File Names Generated from CDDB Info
Track 1.wav	White Wedding.wav
5b9a97_Trk01a.wav	Billy Idol – White Wedding.wav

Organizing Your Files

A good system for organizing your MP3 files and playlists will make it easier for you to find songs. If you have only a few dozen files, a single folder will work fine. But if you are like most MP3 aficionados, sooner or later you'll end up with hundreds of MP3 files, and a single folder will not be practical.

Folders

Most people will be better off dividing their MP3 files into logical groups and storing them in separate folders (subdirectories). It's a good idea to have no more than two or three levels of folders, because each additional level will make it more difficult to manage your files. Most programs let you specify a default folder for storing files. If you have a lot of levels and folders and do a lot of ripping and editing, you'll spend a lot of time browsing for files, moving files between folders or changing the default folder location.

File Names

It's important to have a good system for naming and organizing your files. Otherwise, you may end up with hundreds of files and no easy way to quickly locate the ones you want. Currently, there are no standards for naming MP3 files, although efforts are underway to develop these. The key is to choose a system that works for you and stick with it.

I prefer a simple system using just the artist name and song title, separated by a dash. Some people will prefer different systems, but the advantage of using both the artist name and song title is that you can easily sort songs by the name of the artist, then by the song title. Another advantage of this method is that many players display the file name when a song is played, and a simple name is easier to identify. Other information, such as the album title and genre, can be stored in the ID3 tag. (See Chapter 13, *MPEG Audio*, for more information on ID3 tags.)

File Names

Whichever system you choose to organize your music, you'll have to deal with file names at some point. If you are downloading MP3 files, chances are they'll already have names that make sense, but if you are creating your own MP3 files, you should use a logical naming system.

Many ripping and encoding programs can use information from the CDDB to automatically name files in a way that makes sense to the user. For example: **Billy Idol-White Wedding.MP3** is easier to recognize than **5b9a97_Trk01a.MP3**. The information from the CDDB can also be stored in the ID3 tag of the MP3 file.

Most rippers let you control how the information from the CDDB is used to create file names. Some programs provide you with full control over file names, although a few only let you specify the directory where files will be stored. Unless you specify otherwise, or if the information can't be obtained from the CDDB, ripping programs will create file names based on the CD identifier and/or track number.

Encoders usually keep the same name and add the .MP3 extension. When the song is encoded, the information from the CDDB can also be written to the ID3 tag of the MP3 file. Many players can display the information from the ID3 tag to identify the song that's playing.

Figure 8 shows several examples of filing systems. The first example is a simple system with separate folders for MP3 files, WAV files and playlists. The second example has one folder for all playlists and separate folders for each category of music. The third example has one folder for playlists and separate folders for each artist.

Figure 8 - Organizing Files

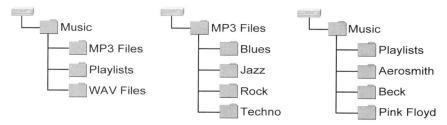

> **Don't Want to Deal With Files and Folders?**
>
> If all this talk about naming files and working with folders sounds like too much work, you can use an all-in-one program like MusicMatch Jukebox or RealJukebox to handle this for you. These programs make it easier for you to manage your files, although you still should have at least a basic understanding of how to work with files and folders.

Music Library Managers

Whichever filing system you use, several products exist to help you search and organize the audio files on your computer. All-in-one programs like MusicMatch Jukebox and RealJukebox are good at helping you keep things organized. Other programs like MP3 Explorer are useful for advanced users who may not like using an all-in-one program.

The MusicMatch Music Library provides a nice interface for sorting and locating songs. Its playlist manager is a nice tool for managing multiple playlists. RealJukebox has a very easy to use Windows Explorer-like interface that groups files in "virtual folders," based on the ID3 tag fields. You can also drag and drop files to create playlists that can be organized by folder.

MP3 Explorer

MP3 Explorer is a good tool for managing MP3 files. It uses a Windows Explorer-like interface and can sort through files on your hard disk to locate all playlists and MP3 files. Once it locates these files, you easily sort them, and drag and drop them to create custom playlists. You can also use MP3 Explorer as a front-end for a player like Winamp to manage playlists and quickly locate any MP3 file in your collection.

MP3 Explorer can display properties for MP3 files, as well as copy, rename and delete them. It can also extract information from the names of MP3 files and enter it in the ID3 tag. This comes in handy if you named your files logically and need to add the information contained in the names to the ID3 tag.

Bells and Whistles

Once you have organized your music and are comfortable playing MP3 files and working with playlists, you may want to experiment with some of the customization options of the full-featured players like Sonique and Winamp. Both of these programs can be customized with skins and plug-ins.

Skins

Skins are files that change the look of the player's interface. The default skin that comes with Winamp is pretty dull, but there are thousands of skins that can liven it up. Most of these are created by Winamp users and are freely distributed. Following are screen shots of some of my favorite skins. Links for downloading these skins are posted on the *MP3Handbook.com* Web site. Hundreds of other skins can be found at *www.1001winampskins.com* and *www.customize.org*.

Plug-ins

A plug-in is a small program used to add features to other programs. Plug-ins may be created by the developer of the main program or by other developers. For example, Winamp uses its own plug-ins for many of its features. Hundreds of third-party plug-ins for everything from visualization to sound effects are available from other developers. The following plug-ins can be downloaded from *www.winamp.com*.

Crossfade

The SqrSoft® Advanced Crossfading plug-in automatically eliminates silence and fades smoothly between songs. This plug-in allows anyone to play a seamless mix of music like a professional DJ. Once you install the plug-in it loads automatically every time you run Winamp.

Sonique Default and Battle Angel Skins

Winamp Skins

AudioStocker

AudioStocker and RockSteady are DSP (digital signal processing) plug-ins for Winamp that automatically adjust the volume of individual songs so they all play at about the same loudness. Both programs can also apply dynamic range compression to prevent clipping.

Visualization

Many plug-ins are for visualization. "Vis" plug-ins generate geometric forms and objects that change colors and move and morph to the music. These are great for parties, and many of the visual effects are very spectacular. My favorites are the Dancing Can, Geiss, Triplex and WhiteCap.

Geiss produces a constantly changing stream of colored waves and various geometric forms. Triplex is similar, but the forms are 3D objects. The Dancing Can is a 3D soda can that morphs to the music on a dance floor with special lighting effects. There is also a plug-in for the Dancing Baby that you may have seen on the Web or on the Ally McBeal TV show.

Many of the best 3D plug-ins require that your graphics card support graphic languages like DirectX or OpenGL. A few even require a special 3D graphics card. So, unless you are a hardcore visualization fanatic, you may want to stick to good 2D visualization plug-ins.

Remote Controls

One last thing required to make your system as convenient as your TV is a remote control (You don't want to have to get up and go to the computer every time you want to skip a song or adjust the volume, do you?)

Fortunately, technology that lets you control your audio player with a standard remote control is relatively inexpensive and easy to use. A simple infrared receiver connects to the serial port of your computer and transmits the commands from your remote control to your player.

The simplest remote control software functions as a plug-in for players like Winamp. More sophisticated remote control software can be used to control any type of program. The plug-in type is the easiest to set up and use. Basically, you "train" the plug-in to recognize commands from the remote and map them to functions of the player.

Irman

The Irman remote control from Evation (*www.evation.com*) costs around $35 and lets you control Winamp, Wplay and X11Amp with most standard infrared remote controls. Just install the plug-in, connect the receiver to a serial port with a short cable, and then configure the plug-in to learn the codes from your existing remote. The Irman can control most player functions and even load predefined playlists.

MP3 Anywhere

MP3 Anywhere by X10 (*www.X10.com*) allows you to control your computer remotely and send digital audio to your stereo through a wireless transmitter. MP3 Anywhere sells for under $100 and includes X10's BOOM software and Mouse REMOTE, which allow you to control most popular audio player programs, including MusicMatch, RealJukebox and Winamp.

Chapter 10

Connecting Your PC to Your Stereo

If you've taken the time to put your music collection on your computer, you'll probably want to listen to it through a good stereo system. Even if your stereo isn't in the same room as your computer, there are several low-cost options for connecting the two. (If you already know how to hook up audio equipment, feel free to skip this chapter.)

There are two main types of PC-to-stereo connections: direct cabling and wireless connections. Each has distinct advantages and disadvantages. A direct cable connection is the least expensive, but the high frequency response can suffer if the cable is too long. Wireless connections eliminate the need to run cables, but they are prone to noise and interference from other devices. There are solutions for both methods that can work well over distances up to several hundred feet.

Connection Fundamentals

Connect Inputs to Outputs. The most basic concept of connecting audio equipment is that inputs must always be connected to outputs. Sometimes you will still get sound if you mistakenly connect a sound card output to an output of a stereo receiver. The sound may be distorted or very low volume, and the input selector may not work as expected. When in doubt, connect the sound card output to the CD jack on your stereo—it's always an input.

A common mistake is to confuse the input and output functions of the tape record and the tape play jacks. The tape play jacks on a receiver are always inputs, and the record jacks are always outputs. On tape recorders these functions are reversed: The play jacks are outputs and the record jacks are inputs. See Tables 5 and 6 for more information on the functions of the input and output jacks typically found on sound cards and stereo receivers.

Match Signal Levels. Connect high-level (also called line-level) outputs to high-level inputs, and connect low-level outputs (such as a microphone) to low-level (Mic) inputs. Do not use the receiver's phono input jack because this is designed for a very low-level signal and has a special equalization circuit. Avoid using the sound card's headphone or speaker out jack to connect to other equipment unless you have no other choice. This jack is driven by an extra amplifier to provide power for driving headphones or small non-powered speakers. The higher level may overload other inputs, and the extra amplifier adds distortion to the signal.

Some notebook computers and low-cost sound cards omit the line-out jack. On notebook computers, headphone jacks may have a volume control knob or slider nearby. If you must use the headphone jack to connect to an external stereo, start with the volume control at about one fifth of the way up to minimize distortion. A better solution for notebooks is to use an external digital-to-analog converter, such as the SONICport, that connects to the USB. With any type of connection, always start with the volume control of your stereo receiver or preamp turned all the way down and adjust it only after your computer is turned on and all cables are connected.

Use Good Quality Shielded Cables. The quality of the cables you use will have a noticeable effect on the quality of the sound. This is true for both interconnect cables and speaker cables. Audio interconnect cables have an insulated wire in the center surrounded by a braided or foil shield. Monster Cable (*www.monstercable.com*) is one of the most popular brands of high-quality audio cables and can be found in most stores that sell stereo equipment. MusicMatch also sells good quality shielded cables with the right type of connectors for connecting a sound card to a stereo system.

Make sure that any cables you use with stereo 1/8" mini-phone jacks have stereo plugs, because mono plugs look similar. Stereo plugs have two thin rings of plastic insulation, while mono plugs only have one. Some 1/8" mini-phone cables are made as headphone extension cords, and some cables with RCA connectors are used for connecting speakers. These cables are unshielded and will pick up lots of noise and hum.

Use Low-Capacitance Cables for Long Runs. Capacitance is the load that cables place on a signal. The load is greater for higher frequencies and increases with the length of the cable. The effect is to reduce the high frequencies delivered to your stereo. Low-capacitance cables are usually thicker than standard cables and can be found where high-end stereo equipment is sold.

Pro Sound Equipment

The outputs of professional sound equipment generally have a much higher level than those used on consumer equipment, and problems can occur if you mix the two types. Generally, pro amplifiers, tape and CD decks will work fine with consumer equipment, but mixers, preamps and signal-processing devices are likely to cause problems.

Sound Card Inputs and Outputs

Sound cards have several types of input and output jacks. Lower-priced sound cards generally will have 1/8" mini phone jacks. A mono jack is used for the microphone input, and stereo jacks are used for the line-in, line-out and headphone. Stereo jacks carry both the left and right signals and are used to save space.

Better sound cards may have separate RCA jacks for the left and right channels. These are the same kind of jacks found on home stereo systems. High-end sound cards may also have connectors for digital inputs and outputs. These can be used to connect to digital devices such as MiniDisc recorders or external digital-to-analog (D/A) converters.

Figure 9 – Typical Sound Card Input and Output Jacks

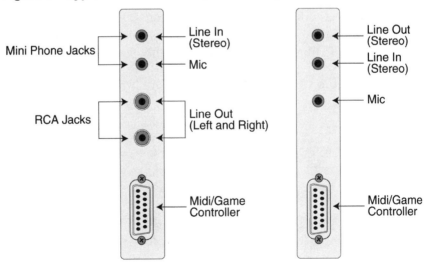

Table 6 - Sound Card Inputs and Outputs

Type	Input	Output	Level	Connectors
Mic	X		Low	Mono mini-phone
Line In	X		Line	Stereo mini-phone or two RCA jacks
Line-Out		X	Line	Stereo mini-phone or two RCA jacks
Headpho nes		X	High	Stereo mini-phone
Digital In	X		S/PDIF	Single RCA, DIN or special connector
Digital Out		X	S/PDIF	Single RCA, DIN or special connector

The most common type of digital interface is coaxial S/PDIF (Sony-Phillips Digital Interface), which usually uses a single RCA connector for both input and output and carries left and right channels in a single digital signal. Some sound cards like the Sound Blaster Live Value can be upgraded to S/PDIF with the addition of a small daughter card. A cable is provided to run the S/PDIF signals to jacks that mount in an unused slot of your PC.

Stereo Receiver Inputs and Outputs

Most home stereo equipment uses RCA jacks for all analog inputs and outputs. Digital connections found on some CD players, DAT recorders and MiniDisc recorders use an optical S/PDIF connector (also called Toslink), which requires special fiber optic cables. If you need to connect equipment that has different types of S/PDIF connectors, you will need a converter. Midiman (*www.midiman.com*) makes a decent bi-directional optical-to-digital S/PDIF converter that is reasonably priced.

Figure 10 - Typical Stereo Receiver Input and Output Jacks

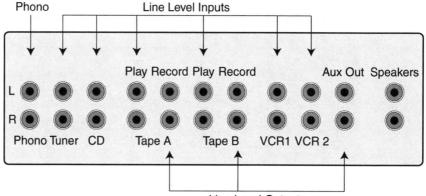

Table 7 - Stereo Receiver Inputs and Outputs

Type	Input	Output	Level	Connectors
Headphones		X	High	Stereo phone or mini-phone
Phono	X		Phono	Two RCA
CD	X		Line	Two RCA
Tuner	X		Line	Two RCA
Tape - Record		X	Line	Two RCA
Tape - Play	X		Line	Two RCA
VCR - Record		X	Line	Two RCA
VCR - Play	X		Line	Two RCA
Aux. In	X		Line	Two RCA
Aux. Out		X	Line	Two RCA
Preamp Out		X	Line	Two RCA
Digital In	X		S/PDIF	Single RCA or Toslink (optical)
Digital Out		X	S/PDIF	Single RCA or Toslink (optical)

Analog Connections

The simplest connection between a computer and a stereo system is to run a cable directly from the sound card line output to a line input of the stereo (see Figure 11).

If your sound card's line output is an 1/8" stereo mini-phone jack, you'll need an adapter or splitter to separate the left and right signals to two RCA connectors. An adapter may be either a solid one-piece type or a short length of cable with different connectors on each end.

Figure 11 - Analog Connection to Stereo

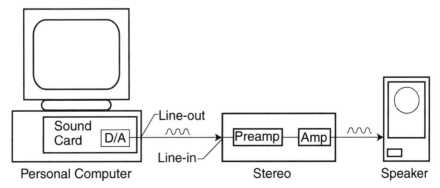

Avoid the solid adapters because they put a strain on the jack. A splitter cable (male 1/8" stereo mini-phone plug to two female RCA jacks) will allow you to use a standard male-to-male RCA cable of any length to connect to your stereo.

MusicMatch sells a 100' cable with a male 1/8" stereo mini-phone plug on one end and two male RCA plugs on the other end that works well for connecting sound cards to stereo receivers and does not require an adapter.

To record from your stereo system to your computer, connect a cable (and adapter, if necessary) from a line-out (or record) jack on your receiver to the line-in jack on your sound card.

Digital Connections

The best quality sound can be obtained by running a digital signal all the way from your PC to your stereo. This is ideal because there will be no high frequency loss or noise picked up along the way. Some newer stereos have digital inputs and can be connected directly to sound cards with digital outputs.

Figure 12 - Digital Connection to Stereo

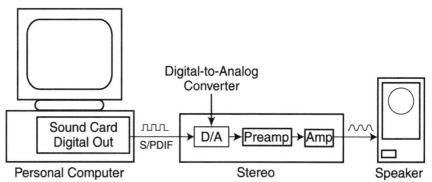

External Digital-to-Analog Converters

If you have a sound card with digital output, you can connect it to a stereo via an external digital-to-analog converter. A good external digital-to-analog converter can give you better quality than the D/A converters in most consumer sound cards. Many MiniDisc and DAT recorders have digital inputs and can also function as external D/A converters.

Digital Cabling

For short cable runs (less than 10'), you can use a standard RCA stereo cable. For longer runs, use 75-ohm coax cable (the same as used for cable TV). You will need adapters to connect pre-made TV-type (RG-58) cable to RCA S/PDIF jacks, or you can get the parts you need to make your own cable at your local Radio Shack store.

Figure 13 - External Digital to Analog Converter

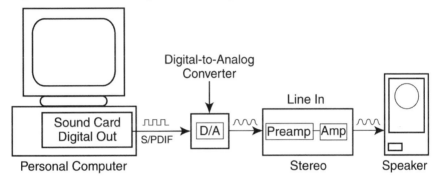

USB Devices

USB audio devices can be used to perform the basic functions of a sound card. These devices provide various combinations of analog and digital inputs and outputs and can be used for both recording and playback. The USB audio driver sends a digital signal through the USB port directly to the external digital to analog converter. This is a good solution for notebook computer users who want higher quality sound.

USB is still in its infancy and has a few drawbacks. Running other programs and CPU intensive tasks can interrupt the smooth flow of audio data and cause clicks and pops. USB audio is supported by the current version of Mac OS, Windows 95 OSR-2, Windows 98, and Windows 2000. USB is not supported by Windows NT.

The Roland UA-30 is a USB audio device that works very well. It supports both Macs and PCs and includes just about every type of input and output connector you might possibly need. If you use any USB audio device, make sure you install the latest USB service packs for your operating system.

Figure 14 - USB Audio Connection to Stereo

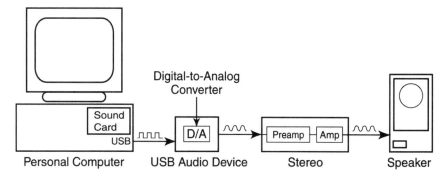

Personal Computer   USB Audio Device   Stereo   Speaker

Wireless Connections

Several manufacturers offer wireless devices that can transmit a stereo audio signal up to 300 feet. Some of these are designed strictly to work with the manufacturer's own amplified speakers or headphones. Others include receivers with standard RCA line output jacks and can be used to transmit a signal from a computer to a remote stereo system. Many wireless audio devices use the same 900 mHz technology used by cordless phones. Some of these devices are capable of delivering good sound quality, but interference and noise can be a problem in many locations.

The MP3 Anywhere Digital Audio Sender by X10 (*www.X10.com*) is the ultimate wireless audio device for MP3 users. It sells for under $100 and uses the 2.4 gHz spectrum to reduce interference and provide a high quality digital connection. The MP3 Anywhere also includes a remote control and software, which allow you to control most popular player programs.

Other 2.4 gHz wireless systems are the LeapFrog WaveMaster from Terk (*www.terk.com*) and the WAVECOM Sr. from RF-Link Technology (*www.rflinktech.com*). They each sell for under $100 and can transmit both audio and video, along with signals from infrared remote controls.

Power System Transmitters

Several products use the electrical wiring of a building to transmit audio signals. These devices tend to pick up 60-cycle hum from the electrical system. This may not be noticeable with "noisy" rock music, but I don't recommend these products because you can get much better results from a good wireless unit. Power system audio transmitters definitely aren't suitable for any type of critical listening.

Part 3

Understanding Digital Audio

Chapter 11

A Digital Audio Primer

Many people don't care about the technology behind their stereo system. As long as it sounds good and they can press a button and listen to music, everything is fine. However, when you start working with audio on computers and the Internet, it's important to understand a few key principles to achieve good results.

What is Sound?

Sound reaches our ears as waves of rapidly varying air pressure caused by a vibrating object, such as a guitar string. As the string moves in one direction, it pushes on nearby air molecules, causing them to move closer together. This creates a small region of high pressure on one side of the string and low pressure on the opposite side. As the string moves in the opposite direction, the areas of high and low pressure reverse.

Sound waves occur as these repeating cycles of higher and lower pressure move out and away from the vibrating object. The frequency (pitch) of a sound is the number of times per second that these cycles occur. The amplitude (intensity) of sound is the size of the variations.

Figure 15 - Conversion of Sound Wave to Analog Signal

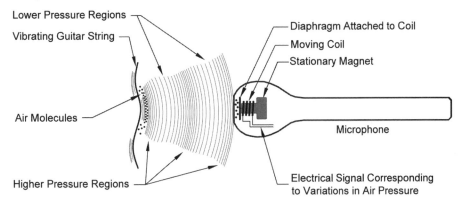

Measuring Sound

Our ears respond to sound logarithmically. As a sound gets louder, increasingly larger changes in sound intensity must occur for us to perceive the same amount of change in loudness.

Decibels

The term decibel (dB) means one-tenth of a Bel—named after Alexander Graham Bell. (This is why the B in dB is capitalized). A Bel is the base 10 logarithm of the ratio between the power level of two sounds or signals.

Figure 16 - Relationship of Sound Pressure Level to Sound Intensity

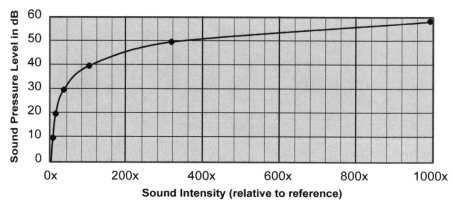

Sound Pressure Level

The intensity of sound is called the sound pressure level (SPL) and is measured in decibels (dB SPL). Decibels are a logarithmic scale that represents how much a sound level or audio signal varies from another signal, or reference level. You might refer to a sound as being 10dB louder than another sound or 3dB softer. A 3dB change is about the minimum change in sound level that most of us can perceive. A 10dB change sounds about twice as loud.

Decibels are always relative. To use decibels to represent a specific quantity, you need to know the reference, or 0 dB level. In the case of sound intensity, 0 dB SPL represents the threshold of hearing of a young undamaged ear (a pressure of about 3 billionths of a pound per square inch). In this case, all sound pressure levels are positive numbers that show how much louder a sound is than the threshold of hearing.

Figure 17 - Relative Loudness of Common Sounds

Relative Level	SPL	Sound
10,000,000x	140	Colt 45 Pistol (25 ft)
	130	Fire Engine Siren (100 ft)
1,000,000x	120	Jet Takeoff (200 ft) ←—Threshold of Pain
	110	Rock Concert (10 ft)
100,000x	100	
	90	Loud Classical Music
		Heavy Street Traffic (5 ft)
10,000x	80	Cabin of Cruising Jet Aircraft
	70	
		Average Conversation (3 ft)
1,000x	60	
	50	Average Suburban Home (night)
100x	40	Quiet Auditorium
	30	
		Quiet Whisper (5 ft)
10x	20	Rustling Leaves
	10	
Reference Level	0 Decibels	←—Threshold of Hearing

Loudness

Loudness is subjectively how we perceive different sound intensities. The sound intensity of a jet taking off 200 feet away is about 120dB SPL, or a million times more intense than the threshold of hearing. The sound intensity of rustling leaves is about 20dB SPL, or 10 times higher than the threshold of hearing. The sound of the jet is 100,000 times more intense than the rustling leaves (100dB). We actually perceive the jet to be about 1000 times louder than rustling leaves rather than 100,000 times louder.

Frequency

The frequency of a sound is measured in Hertz (Hz), which means cycles per second. A kilohertz (kHz) is a thousand cycles per second. We perceive pitch exponentially. A unit of pitch all musicians are familiar with is the octave. An octave is the interval between any note and the next higher note with the same name. Notes that are one octave apart sound similar, but one is twice the frequency of the other. For example, the note A below middle C is at a frequency of 220Hz, the note A above middle C is at 440Hz, and the next higher A is at 880Hz.

Figure 18 - Octave Intervals and Frequencies for Musical Notes

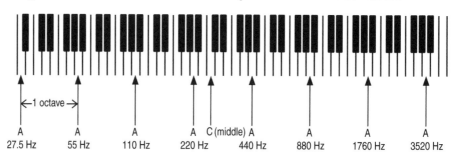

Analog Audio

The term analog means something that is similar in function or position. The varying voltage produced by a microphone is analogous to the pressure variations of a sound wave. On a cassette tape, variations in magnetic flux in a metal coating on the tape represent pressure variations in the sound wave. On vinyl records, variations in the width of the groove correspond to the pressure variations. The position along the groove or tape corresponds to time.

In an analog audio system, voltages represent sound pressures. These signals are amplified from the millivolt level (1000th of a volt) produced by microphones, playback heads and phono cartridges by about 1000 times (60dB) to the levels found inside stereo preamps. A power amp boosts the voltage level from the preamp to a loudspeaker, which creates sound waves in the air by vibrating rapidly in response to the audio signal.

Digital Audio

In digital audio, the representation of the audio signal is no longer directly analogous to the sound wave. Instead, the value of the signal is sampled at regular intervals by an analog-to-digital (A/D) converter (or ADC), which produces numbers (digits) that represent the value of each sample. This stream of numbers represents a digital audio signal, which can be stored as a computer file and transmitted across a network.

In order to listen to a digital audio signal, it must be converted to analog by a digital-to-analog (D/A) converter (or DAC). In most home stereo systems, the D/A conversion takes place inside the CD player. Computer sound cards, MiniDisc recorders and DATs have both A/D converters (for recording) and D/A converters (for playback). Many home systems have a combination of digital and analog components, but all audio systems end with analog signals at the speakers or headphones.

Sampling

To convert an analog signal to a digital format, the voltage is sampled at regular intervals, thousands of times per second. The value of each sample is rounded to the nearest integer on a scale that varies according to the resolution of the signal. The integers are then converted to binary numbers.

The sampling rate is how many times per second the voltage of the analog signal is measured. CD audio is sampled at a rate of 44,100 times per second (44.1 kHz). DAT (Digital Audio Tape) supports sampling rates of 32, 44.1 and 48 kHz. Other commonly used sampling rates are 22.05 kHz and 11.025 kHz.

Figure 19 - Sampling and Converting a Waveform to PCM

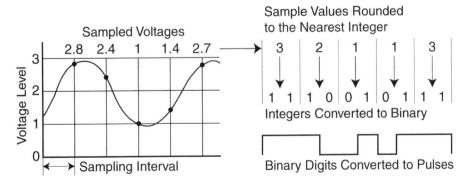

The sampling rate must be at least twice as high as the highest frequency to be reproduced[3]. The range of human hearing is roughly from 20 to 20,000 Hz, so a sampling rate of at least 40 kHz is needed to reproduce the full range.

Higher sampling rates allow the use of filters with a more gradual roll-off. This reduces phase shift, which can affect the stereo image at higher frequencies.

The 44.1 kHz sampling rate for CDs was chosen to allow headroom for filters and other types of signal processing. MPEG AAC and DVD Audio support sampling rates of up to 96 kHz.

Figure 20 - Effect of Increased Resolution and Sampling Rates

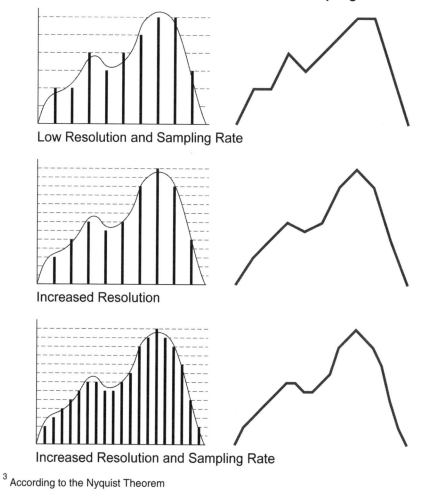

Low Resolution and Sampling Rate

Increased Resolution

Increased Resolution and Sampling Rate

[3] According to the Nyquist Theorem

Resolution

The resolution of a digital signal is the number of values that can be assigned to each sample. CD audio uses 16 bits per sample, which provide 65,536 (2^{16}) possible values. Higher resolution increases the dynamic range and reduces quantization distortion and background noise.

Quantization

Quantization is the process of selecting whole numbers to represent the voltage level of each sample. The A/D converter must select a whole number that is closest to the signal level at the instant it's sampled. This produces small rounding errors that cause distortion.

Quantization distortion increases at lower levels because the signal is using a smaller portion of the available range, so any errors are a greater percentage of the signal. A key advantage of audio encoding schemes, such as MP3, is that more bits can be allocated to low-level signals to reduce quantization errors.

Dithering

A process called dithering introduces random noise into the signal to spread out the effects of quantization distortion and make it less noticeable. Some audiophiles don't like the notion of noise that is deliberately added to a signal, but the advantages of digital audio are so great that the end result is still better than most analog systems.

Figure 21 - Quantization Errors

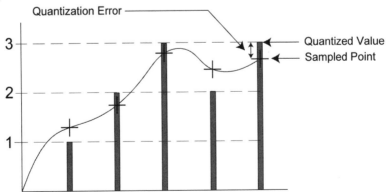

Clipping

Levels in a digital audio signal are usually expressed in dB, measured by their relationship to 0 dB, the highest possible level. One of the rules of digital audio is that a signal can never exceed 0 dB. If the level of a signal is raised too much, the peaks will be clipped at the 0 dB level. Clipping causes extreme distortion and should be avoided at all costs.

Figure 22 - Clipping

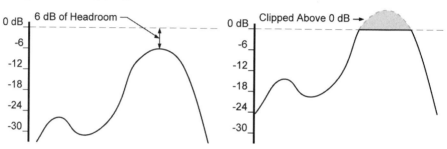

Bit-rates

The term "bit-rate" refers to how many bits (1s and 0s) are used each second to represent the signal. The bit-rate for digital audio is expressed in thousands of bits per second (kbps) and correlates directly to the file size and sound quality. Lower bit-rates result in smaller file sizes but poorer sound quality, and higher bit-rates result in better quality but larger files.

The bit-rate of uncompressed audio can be calculated by multiplying the sampling rate by the resolution (8-bit, 16-bit, etc.) and the number of channels. For example, CD Audio (or a WAV file extracted from a CD) has a sampling rate of 44,100 times per second, a resolution of 16 bits and two channels. The bit-rate would be approximately 1.4 million bits per second (1,411 kbps).

Table 8 - Calculating Bit-rates

Sampling Rate	x	Resolution	x	# of Channels	=	Bit-rate
44,100	x	16	x	2	=	1,411,200

Dynamic Range

Dynamic range is the range of the lowest to the highest level that can be reproduced by a system. Red Book audio CDs have a dynamic range of 96 dB. The dynamic range of vinyl records and cassette tapes is much lower than audio CDs and varies depending on the quality of the recording and playback equipment. The dynamic range of cassette tapes also varies depending on the type of tape.

Signal-to-noise Ratio

The signal-to-noise ratio is the ratio of the background noise (hiss, hum and static) level to the highest level that can be reproduced. Each additional bit of resolution corresponds to an increase of 6 dB in signal-to-noise ratio. Audio CDs achieve about a 90 dB signal-to-noise ratio.

Figure 23 shows the relationship between dynamic range and signal-to-noise ratio.

Figure 23 - Dynamic Range and Signal-to-noise Ratio

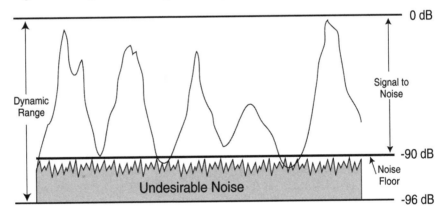

Encoding

Encoding is the process of converting uncompressed digital audio to a compressed format such as MP3. The algorithm used in the encoding (and decoding) software is referred to as a codec—as in *cod*ing/*dec*oding. There is often more than one codec for a particular format, and different codecs can vary widely in quality and speed, even for the same format.

Advantages of Digital Audio

For years, audiophiles and engineers have debated the merits of digital audio versus high-end analog systems, and to this day, there are audiophiles who swear by their analog systems. Digital audio has emerged as the winner by most accounts, but it's still useful to understand the advantages of digital versus analog audio, because many audio systems contain a mix of digital and analog components.

The advantages of digital audio can be summed up as follows: wider dynamic range, increased resistance to noise, better copyability and the ability to use error correction to compensate for wear and tear. Many types of digital media, such as CDs and MiniDiscs, are also more durable than common analog media, such as vinyl records and cassette tapes.

Wider Dynamic Range

Digital audio at 16 bits theoretically can achieve a dynamic range of 96 dB, compared to less than 80 dB for the best analog systems. This is especially important for classical music where levels within the same composition can range from the relative quiet of a flute solo to the loudness of dozens of instruments playing simultaneously.

Increased Resistance to Noise

In analog systems, crackling noise and hum from electromagnetic frequency (EMF) interference is picked up along the way as the signal passes through analog circuits. Background hiss is also generated by thermal noise from analog components. Digital signals are virtually immune to picking up these types of noise, although any noise that enters the signal before it's converted to digital will be reproduced along with the rest of the signal.

Better Copyability

Digital audio can be copied from one digital device to another without any loss of information, unlike analog recording, where information is lost and noise introduced with every copy. Even the best analog systems lose about 3dB of signal-to-noise ratio when a copy is recorded. After several generations of analog copies, the sound quality will deteriorate noticeably. With digital audio, unlimited generations of perfect copies can be made.

This ability to make perfect copies is one reason why the RIAA has gone to so much trouble to introduce the Serial Copy Management System (SCMS) for consumer audio equipment, and why they are so concerned about the proliferation of MP3 files. SCMS prevents multiple generations of copies (copies of copies) from an original and is required by the Audio Home Recording Act of 1992 to be used on all consumer digital audio recording devices sold in the United States. Currently, there is no way to prevent multiple generations of perfect copies from a single MP3 file.

Digital copies can also be made much faster than analog copies, which usually must be made in real time. For example, with an analog device like a cassette deck, it always takes at least 60 minutes to record 60 minutes of music from a CD. With digital audio, the same 60 minutes of music can be copied to a hard disk in as little as 5 minutes on a system with a fast CD-ROM drive.

Of course, if you are making an original recording with digital equipment, it will take the same amount of time as with analog equipment. (Uncle Jack playing the kazoo for half an hour still takes half an hour to record). But once a digital recording is on your PC, you can make a digital copy in a fraction of the time it would take to record a copy with analog equipment.

Error Correction

Most digital audio media, such as CDs and DATs, have built-in error correction. On an audio CD, approximately 25% of the disc is used for error correction data. If a bad scratch causes an error that can't be corrected, the player will attempt to reconstruct the missing data by interpolation.

Durability

Digital media such as CDs and MiniDiscs are much more durable than any analog media. This improved durability is one of the main reasons people were so eager to migrate from vinyl records to CDs.

Each time you play a record or tape, microscopic bits of vinyl or oxide are scraped away, adding to the cumulative wear. Vinyl records are particularly prone to warping and scratching, and tapes gradually become demagnetized. A CD or MiniDisc can be played hundreds of times, with no loss of quality, as long as there is not excessive physical damage.

Both analog and digital tapes can suffer degradation from magnetic fields, but some popular digital formats like DAT are much more durable than analog tapes (especially cassettes) because the tape is stronger and the oxide coating is thicker.

File Size and Bandwidth

Digital audio can create large files that quickly use up hard disk capacity and require a tremendous amount of bandwidth to transmit over a network. Network bandwidth is like a pipe that carries a stream of bits. The size of the pipe imposes a limit on how many bits can be moved in a given time period. Multiple users competing for the same bandwidth limit the amount of bandwidth available to any one user.

File sizes and bandwidth requirements for uncompressed audio can be calculated by multiplying the sampling rate by the resolution, the number of channels and the time in seconds. The bit-rate has a direct relation to the file size—if you do something that changes the bit-rate, the file size will change proportionally. The bandwidth requirement of a digital audio signal is the same as the bit-rate. This is true whether the signal is compressed or not. Table 9 shows the formula for calculating file sizes for uncompressed audio.

Table 9 - Calculating File Sizes

Sampling Rate	x	Resolution	x	Number of Channels	x	Time in Seconds	/	Bits / Byte	=	File Size (in Bytes)
44,100	x	16	x	2	x	60	/	8	=	10,584,000

You can do several things to control the size of digital audio files, but there will always be a trade-off between file size and sound quality. Lowering the sampling rate will produce a smaller file, but will also lower the frequency response. Lowering the resolution also produces a smaller file but reduces the accuracy and allows more noise and distortion to be introduced due to increased quantization errors. A mono signal, used in place of stereo, will cut the size in half (uncompressed audio only).

Table 10 shows how different combinations of sampling rates, resolution and numbers of channels can be used to control file sizes for uncompressed audio. These parameters will also affect the file size after the audio is encoded in a format like MP3, but the effect will not be as predictable as with an uncompressed file because the encoding software will do its own optimizing.

Table 10 - File Sizes for a One-minute Audio Clip

Sampling Rate	Resolution	Number of Channels	Bit-rate	File Size (in Bytes)
44,100	16	2	1,411,200	10,584,000
44,100	16	1	705,600	5,292,000
22,050	16	1	352,800	2,646,000
11,025	16	1	176,400	1,323,000
11,025	8	1	88,200	616,000

Compression

Limited network bandwidth and hard disk capacity have been major driving factors behind the development of compressed audio formats. Until recently, only a small number of people used their computers to store CD-quality music. A few people would copy their favorite songs from a music CD and use a CD-Recordable drive to create a compilation CD, similar to the way many people make cassette tapes from prerecorded music.

Audio and electronics engineers have been working to solve the bandwidth bottleneck ever since networks were invented. They work on both sides of the problems by increasing bandwidth (larger pipe) and compressing data (higher pressure). High speed Internet connections such as cable modems and ASDL have been developed to increase the size of the pipe, and compression schemes such as JPEG and MPEG have been developed to squeeze more data through it.

MP3 provides relief by compressing files up to approximately 10=1 without significant loss of quality. Four minutes of CD audio (44.1, kHz 16-bit stereo) requires about 40MB of disk space and would take more than 3 ½ hours to download with a 28.8 kbps modem. At this rate, a 2GB hard disk would hold about 50 four-minute songs.

With MP3 encoded at 128 kbps, each four-minute song would take up less than 4MB of space and could be downloaded in less than 20 minutes with a 28.8 kbps modem. A 2GB hard disk could now hold more than 500 songs. This much compression, coupled with the larger and cheaper hard disks that are now available, makes it possible to use a PC as a high-capacity, CD-quality jukebox in place of tape decks, turntables and CD players.

Table 11 - Typical Download Times* for Four-minute Songs

Format	28.8 k Modem	56 k Modem	Dual ISDN 128 kbps	Cable 1.5 Mbps	T1 Line 1.5 Mbps	ADSL 500 kbps+
CD Audio	3.6 hrs	2 hrs	44 min	4 min	4 min	7 min
MP3 at 128 kbps	19.7 min	9 min	4 min	20 sec	20 sec	39 sec

* Actual speed will usually be less.

Newer generations of MPEG Audio, such as AAC (Advanced Audio Coding), offer even higher levels of compression and better sound quality but have not yet reached the consumer market because of high licensing costs.

Lossy vs. Lossless Compression

There are two basic categories of compression: lossless and lossy. Lossless compression works by encoding repetitive pieces of information with symbols and equations that take up less space but provide all the information needed to reconstruct an exact copy of the original. Lossy compression works by discarding unnecessary and redundant information (sounds that most people can't hear) and then applying lossless compression techniques for further size reduction.

Figure 24 - Typical MP3 Compression

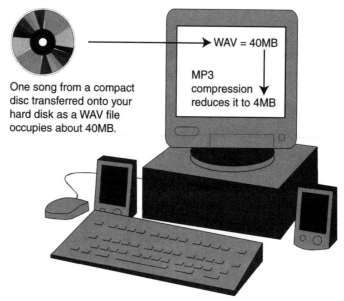

One song from a compact disc transferred onto your hard disk as a WAV file occupies about 40MB.

WAV = 40MB

MP3 compression reduces it to 4MB

Dynamic Range Compression

Dynamic range compression reduces the range in dB between the lowest and highest levels of a signal, but does not affect the file size or bandwidth requirement. Dynamic range compression is often used by recording engineers to make songs sound louder without clipping.

There is an ongoing debate among audiophiles about the merits of lossless versus lossy compression. With lossless compression, there is never a loss of fidelity (unless an error gets introduced during the process)—there is no debate about that. With lossy compression (such as MPEG Audio), there is always some loss of fidelity that becomes more noticeable as the compression ratio is increased. The goal then becomes producing sound where the losses are not noticeable; or where the losses are noticeable but not annoying.

The highest compression ration for lossless audio is about 2 to 1, but the quality will always be indistinguishable from the original. With lossy compression, the quality will vary according to factors such as the bit-rate, the complexity of the music and the quality of the encoding software. Some forms of lossy compression, such as MPEG AAC, can achieve compression ratios of up to 11 to 1, with quality indistinguishable from the original. Numerous controlled tests with trained listeners have verified this.

Even with the best lossy formats, a few people with very sensitive ears may be able to tell the difference between the original and encoded file when listening to critical material (complex music) on expensive hi-fi systems. Most people will not be able to detect any differences at the higher bit-rates, but a few people will feel like they are being cheated when they know something has been taken away. And even if they can't hear the difference, they may imagine one anyway.

Chapter 12
Digital Audio Formats

Digital audio comes in many different formats, and multiple formats will be a fact of life for the foreseeable future. Groups like MPEG have created open standards, but even formats based on the same MPEG standard may not be compatible with each other because of proprietary components.

Fortunately for consumers, many hardware and software players are able to support multiple formats—so if you purchase digital music in any of the major formats (AAC, MP3, WMA, etc.) you will be in a good shape. If a format does become obsolete, plenty of tools are available for converting digital audio to different formats.

Digital Audio Files

An audio file has two main parts: a header and the audio data. The header is used to store information about the file, including the resolution, sampling rate and type of compression. Often a "wrapper" is used to add features, such as license management information or streaming capability.

The format of a digital audio file refers to the type of audio data within the file. The file type refers to the structure of the data within the file. It is common for the same format to be used by more than one file type. For example, the PCM format is found in both WAV and AIFF files.

Figure 25 - Digital Audio File Structure

Table 12 - Common Digital Audio Formats

Type	Extensions	Codec
AIFF (Mac)	.aif, .aiff	*PCM
AU (Sun/Next)	.au	*u-law
CD audio (CDDA)	N/A	PCM
MP3	.mp3	MPEG Audio Layer-III
Windows Media Audio	.wma	Proprietary (Microsoft)
QuickTime	.qt	Proprietary (Apple Computer)
RealAudio	.ra, ram	Proprietary (Real Networks)
WAV	.wav	*PCM

* Can be used with other codecs.

WAV

WAV is the default format for digital audio on Windows PCs. WAV files are usually coded in PCM format, which means they are uncompressed and take up a lot of space. WAV files can also be coded in other formats, including MP3.

AIFF and AU

AIFF is the default audio format for the Macintosh, and AU is the default format for SUN systems. Both of these formats are supported on most other platforms and by most audio applications. Each of these formats can be compressed, but compression sometimes creates compatibility problems between platforms.

Streaming Audio

Streaming audio avoids many of the problems of large audio files. Instead of having to wait for the entire file to download, you can listen to the sound as the data arrives at your computer.

Streaming audio players store several seconds worth of data in a buffer before beginning playback. The buffer absorbs the bursts of data as they are delivered by the Internet and releases it at a constant rate for smooth playback.

Many digital audio formats can be streamed by wrapping them in a streaming format, such as Microsoft's ASF (Active Streaming Format), which can be used to stream WMA, MP3 and other formats.

Table 13 - Streaming Audio Systems

Type	Primary Format	Developer
Windows Media Technologies	Windows Media Audio / Active Streaming Format (ASF)	Microsoft
Icecast (open source)	MP3	The Icecast Team
QuickTime	QuickTime	Apple Computer
RealSystem	RealAudio	RealNetworks
SHOUTcast	MP3	Nullsoft

Standard Formats

Standard formats make it easier for software developers and equipment manufacturers to produce products that are less costly and more compatible with each other. The compatibility provided by standard formats helps assure consumers that their music and equipment won't become obsolete. Cassette tapes, compact discs and PCM are examples of standard audio formats that have benefited both consumers and manufacturers.

PCM

PCM (Pulse Code Modulation) is a common method of storing and transmitting uncompressed digital audio. Since it is a generic format, it can be read by most audio applications—similar to the way a plain text file can be read by any word-processing program. PCM is used by Audio CDs and digital audio tapes (DATs). PCM is also a very common format for AIFF and WAV files.

PCM is a straight representation of the binary digits (1s and 0s) of sample values. When PCM audio is transmitted, each "1" is represented by a positive voltage pulse and each "0" is represented by the absence of a pulse. Figure 26 shows how binary data is converted to a PCM signal.

Figure 26 - Pulse Code Modulation

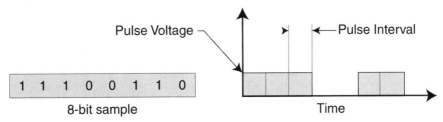

DPCM

DPCM (Differential Pulse Code Modulation) is a simple form of lossy compression that stores only the difference between consecutive samples. DPCM uses 4 bits to store the difference, regardless of the resolution of the original file. With DPCM, an 8-bit file would be compressed 2=1, and a 16-bit file would be compressed 4=1.

ADPCM

ADPCM (Adaptive Differential Pulse Code Modulation) is similar to DPCM except that the number of bits used to store the difference between samples is varied depending on the complexity of the signal. ADPCM works by analyzing a succession of samples and predicting the value of the next sample. It then stores the difference between the calculated value and the actual value.

u-LAW and a-LAW

u-LAW (pronounced "mew-law") and a-LAW are compression schemes commonly used in telecommunications networks. u-LAW is used in North America and Japan. a-LAW is used in Europe and the rest of the world.

MPEG Audio

MPEG Audio is a family of open standards for compressed audio that includes MP2, MP3 and AAC. (See Chapter 13 for more detailed information on MPEG Audio.)

MPEG-Based Proprietary Formats

Several proprietary formats are based on MPEG audio. Some of these are used in special applications, such as voice mail systems, high definition TV and satellite radio. Others compete directly with MP3 and are based on AAC or MP3, with proprietary wrappers. The sound quality of some of these is very good, but their proprietary nature makes them incompatible with many programs and portable players.

a2b

AT&T's a2b music is a sophisticated music distribution system with many features, such as watermarking and encryption, to support copyright protection and royalty tracking. It is based on the MPEG-2 AAC Low Complexity Profile. The Policy Maker feature of a2b is a flexible electronic licensing system, which can control how music is used and distributed. Music encoded with a2b can include artwork, credits, lyrics and links to the artist's Web site.

> **Proprietary Formats**
>
> Even though MPEG Audio is based on open standards and widely used, many companies continue to develop proprietary formats. This may be due to the fact that companies involved in the development of MPEG Audio hold patents on many of the algorithms used in the standard and charge royalties to software developers and hardware manufacturers who use them. The marketplace, which tends to favor open standards with reasonable licensing costs, will ultimately decide which formats will prevail.

MP4

Global Music Outlet uses the term MP4 to describe its proprietary music delivery system. It's based on an enhanced version of MPEG AAC and includes an embedded player (each song is an .EXE file). Album graphics and links to the artist's Web site can be embedded in the file.

Liquid Audio

Liquid Audio is a sophisticated music distribution system based on Dolby Digital and MPEG AAC. It supports both downloadable and streaming audio and uses watermarking and encryption for copyright protection. Music encoded with Liquid Audio can include artwork, lyrics, notes and pricing, along with links to a Web site where the song or album can be purchased. Liquid Audio has a playlist feature and allows you to burn songs to a CD if you have a supported CD-R drive.

QuickTime

QuickTime is a widely used multimedia format from Apple Computer that supports both streaming audio and streaming video. Much of the MPEG-4 standard is based on QuickTime, and it is widely used for streaming video on the Web.

Non-MPEG Proprietary Formats

Several digital audio formats exist that are entirely proprietary. Many of these are quite good and are widely used.

Dolby Digital (Formerly AC-3)

Dolby Digital is a very high quality audio encoding and noise reduction system that is the audio component of High Definition Television (HDTV) and digital broadcast TV (DTV). It is also used in DVDs, laser discs, digital cable and direct broadcast satellite (DBS) systems.

> **Ogg Vorbis**
>
> Ogg Vorbis (*www.vorbis.com*) is a high-quality, non-proprietary, patent-free, open source, compressed audio format and streaming technology. Ogg Vorbis supports fixed and variable bitrates from 16 to 128 kbps/channel and is reported to be similar in quality to MPEG AAC.

EPAC

EPAC is a perceptual audio encoding scheme based on PAC—developed by Bell Labs, the research and development arm of Lucent Technologies. EPAC is reported to produce quality indistinguishable from the original CD at 128 kbps. However, I participated in one listening test where the audience was able to consistently tell the difference between original CD tracks and the same tracks encoded in EPAC at 160 kbps.

Windows Media Audio

Microsoft's Windows Media Audio (WMA) format is a relatively late entry into the field of proprietary audio formats. WMA performs well at lower bit-rates and is reported to produce quality indistinguishable from the original CD at 128 kbps. WMA is supported by most full-featured player programs and by many portable players. WMA is royalty-free when incorporated into software that runs on the Windows platform.

RealAudio

RealAudio was the first widely used system for streaming audio and video over the Internet. It is a proprietary format, but it is used by many online music stores for sample clips of songs.

TwinVQ (VQF)

TwinVQ (Transform-domain Weighted Interleave Vector Quantization) is an encoding scheme developed by the NTT Human Interface Lab in Japan. TwinVQ is reported to provide higher quality than MP3, but encoding times are reported to be much longer, and CPU utilization is reported to be higher during playback.

Additional Resources

Organization	Web Site
Audio Engineering Society	*www.aes.org*
Internet Sound Institute	*www.soundinstitute.com*
MIT Media Lab – Machine Listening Group	*http://sound.media.mit.edu*

Chapter 13

MPEG Audio

MPEG stands for Moving Picture Experts Group. The MPEG committee was established in 1988 and works under the direction of the International Standards Organization (ISO). MPEG's purpose is proposing standards for encoding audio, video and interactive graphics. Thanks to MPEG, we now have technologies such as DVD, DirecTV and MP3.

MPEG Standards

Organizations from all over the world are involved in developing MPEG standards. Fraunhofer-Gesellschaft of Germany and Thomson Multimedia of the United States provided key technology related to MPEG Audio Layer-III (MP3). Dolby Labs was heavily involved in the development of MPEG AAC. Each of these organizations holds patents related to the technologies they contributed.

The MPEG committee works in phases and meets several times a year. To date, MPEG has released three families of standards: MPEG-1, MPEG-2 and MPEG-4. (If you are wondering about MPEG-3, it was merged into MPEG-2). All MPEG phases include standards for both audio and video. This chapter is concerned only with MPEG Audio.

It typically takes several years from when a standard is released to when consumer products that support it reach the market. MPEG-1, which includes MP3, was released in 1992. However, it took more than four years for software players, such as Winamp, to appear, and almost six years for the first portable MP3 players to become available.

MPEG standards for digital audio cover encoding of audio, either by itself or as the audio component of a multimedia file or stream. MPEG Audio is based on perceptual encoding techniques, which take advantage of the characteristics of human hearing and remove sounds that most people can't hear.

MPEG-1

MPEG-1 (which includes MP3) was approved in November 1992. It works with bit-rates up to 1.5 mbps (million bits per second) and supports both mono and stereo audio, but not multi-channel surround sound. MPEG-1 supports sampling rates of 32, 44.1 and 48 kHz.

MPEG-2

MPEG-2 adds support for surround sound, lower sampling rates of 16, 22.05 and 24 kHz and bit-rates as low as 8 kbps. MPEG-2 can have up to five channels for surround sound and one low frequency enhancement channel for subwoofers. A multilingual extension adds support for up to seven more channels.

MPEG-4

MPEG-4 is intended to be an all-purpose encoding standard for multimedia systems of the future. It's designed to handle applications ranging from simple voice systems that require very low bandwidth to high quality "audiophile" and professional sound systems. MPEG-4 can integrate synthetic and natural audio, including MIDI and text-to-speech systems. A large part of MPEG-4 is based on Apple's QuickTime multimedia format.

MPEG-4 is made extensible by a language called MSDL (MPEG Syntax Description Language). The support for interactivity allows manipulation of the presentation of audio and visual data. MPEG-4 supports a wide range of storage and transmission media and will work over networks and wireless mobile connections.

MPEG-7

MPEG-7 is also referred to as Multimedia Content Description Interface. It defines a structure that supports searching, filtering and management of multimedia data. MPEG-7 is expected to be released in 2001.

Table 14 - MPEG Phases

MPEG-1 (approved Nov. 1992)
Single (mono) and dual (stereo) channel encoding of audio at 32, 44.1 and 48 kHz sampling rates and bit-rates from 32 to 448 kbps.

MPEG-2 (approved Nov. 1994)
A backwards compatible extension to MPEG1 with up to five channels, plus one low frequency enhancement channel. Adds support for 16, 22.05 and 24 kHz sampling rates for bit-rates between 32 to 256 kbps for Layer-I, up to 384 kbps for Layer-II, and from 8 to 320 kbps for Layer-III.

MPEG-2 AAC
Supports a wider range of sampling rates (from 8 kHz to 96 kHz) and up to 48 audio channels, plus up to 15 auxiliary low-frequency enhancement channels and up to 15 embedded data streams. AAC works at bit-rates from 8 kbps for mono speech and in excess of 320 kbps for very-high-quality audio.

MPEG-4 Version 1 (approved Oct. 1998)
All-purpose encoding standard for multimedia systems of the future. Supports coding and composition of both natural and synthetic audio at a wide range of bit-rates.

MPEG-4 Version 2 (scheduled to be approved Dec. 1999)
Builds on previous standards for digital television, interactive graphics applications and interactive multimedia.

MPEG-7 (scheduled to be approved July 2001)
Also called Multimedia Content Description Interface. Provides information search, filtering and management for multimedia data.

Licensing

Once a standard is released, it is up to private industry to develop products and technologies to take advantage of it. Often, these companies are required to pay licensing fees to companies that hold patents on technologies related to the standard. The only requirement from MPEG is that any licensing fees be fair and equitable.

Many people are surprised to learn that licensing fees are required to develop products based on an open standard. These licensing fees help compensate companies that contribute technology and other resources towards developing MPEG standards. If these companies had no way to recoup their investment, there would be little incentive for them to spend money developing technologies that their competitors could then use free of charge.

> ## MPEG 2.5
>
> A non-ISO extension called "MPEG 2.5" was created by the Fraunhofer Institute to improve the performance of MPEG Audio at lower bit-rates. At lower bit-rates, this extension allows sampling rates of 8, 11.025 and 12 kHz. Higher sampling rates at very low bit-rates would require a trade-off in reduced resolution. Lowering the sampling rate reduces the frequency response but allows the resolution to be increased. The result is much better quality audio, even though the frequency response is reduced.

MPEG Layers

Several related audio encoding schemes fall under the MPEG umbrella. These are referred to as Layers I, II and III, which exist under both MPEG-1 and MPEG-2. (Another audio encoding scheme that's part of MPEG-2 is MPEG AAC, which is not compatible with Layers I - III.)

Each layer uses the same basic structure and includes the features of the layers below it. Higher layers offer progressively better sound quality at comparable bit-rates and require increasingly complex encoding software. This, in turn, requires more processing power for encoding and decoding the audio.

Layer-I

Layer-I was originally designed for the Digital Compact Cassette (DCC) and is not widely used.

Layer-II

Layer-II (also referred to as MP2) is widely used within the broadcasting industry. It was designed as a trade-off between complexity and performance and offers very high quality sound at higher bit-rates. It also has lower encoding delays than MP3, which is important for live broadcasting.

Layer-III

Layer-III (MP3) was designed for better quality at lower bit-rates. The high level of compression achieved by MP3 is very important because of the limited bandwidth of the Internet and the limited space of hard disks. This compression also makes MP3 well suited for portable players that use expensive solid-state memory cards.

AAC

AAC (Advanced Audio Coding) is not an MPEG layer, although it is based on a psycho-acoustic model. Sometimes referred to as MP4, AAC provides significantly better quality at lower bit-rates than MP3. AAC was developed under MPEG-2 and also exists under MPEG-4.

AAC supports a wider range of sampling rates (from 8 kHz to 96 kHz) and up to 48 audio channels, plus up to 15 auxiliary low frequency enhancement channels and up to 15 embedded data streams. AAC works at bit rates from 8 kbps for mono speech and up to in excess of 320 kbps for high-quality audio. Three profiles of AAC provide varying levels of complexity and scalability.

AAC software is much more expensive to license than MP3 because the companies that hold related patents decided to keep a tighter reign on it. Most AAC software is geared towards professional applications and secure music distribution systems, and it may be a while before you see AAC support in consumer-oriented products.

AT&T's a2b music, Global Music's MP4 and Liquid Audio are systems for music delivery that are based on AAC. They both include schemes for copyright identification, encryption and royalty tracking. It's important to remember that these systems are proprietary, even though they are based on an open standard.

Even though AAC is a better format for digital audio, it's not clear whether or not it will eclipse MP3 in consumer products. MP3 can sound just as good as AAC at the expense of using more disk space or memory, and disk space and memory are getting cheaper all the time.

Compatibility

The various flavors of MPEG Audio are compatible with each other to some degree. Layers I, II and III are backwards compatible. For example, a Layer-III decoder should also be able to decode a Layer-I or II stream, and a Layer-II decoder should be able to decode a Layer-I stream. AAC is not backwards compatible with any of the MPEG layers and is sometimes referred to as "NBC," or "not backwards compatible."

MPEG-1 layers, and the same layers under MPEG-2, are compatible with each other to a limited degree. MPEG-2 decoders must be able to decode

MPEG-1 files, and MPEG-1 decoders should be able to play the left and right channels of an MPEG-2 signal.

Most MP3 players are compatible with both MPEG-1 and MPEG-2 files, and most mainstream MP3 encoders and players are compatible with each other (though there have been compatibility issues reported with a few of the freeware encoders and some players).

Compatibility between proprietary formats based on MPEG is another story. Most of the proprietary formats based on MPEG Audio, such as AT&T's a2b music and Liquid Audio, are not compatible with each other or with software that supports only pure MPEG formats.

Some features added to MPEG Audio (such as watermarking) should not affect compatibility, but many proprietary formats use encryption. And any form of encryption is likely to make these formats incompatible with each other and with products that support only pure MPEG Audio.

MPEG Encoding

MPEG Audio uses what's referred to as perceptual encoding (a type of "lossy" compression. To compress audio, MPEG encoders first apply a psycho-acoustic model to identify parts of the signal that most people can't hear. The encoder removes these sounds from the signal and then applies standard lossless data compression techniques.

This technique does not work perfectly because the sensitivity of each person's hearing is different. But the sensitivity of human hearing does fall within a finite range, and researchers can determine a range that applies to the vast majority of people.

Sub-bands

The encoder first divides the signal into multiple sub-bands, so the encoded signal can be better optimized to the response of the human ear. For example, most of stereo information below 100 Hz can be discarded because the ear cannot determine the direction of very low frequency sounds; but at higher frequencies the ear is more sensitive to direction of sounds, so more stereo information needs to be retained.

Figure 27 - MPEG Audio Encoding

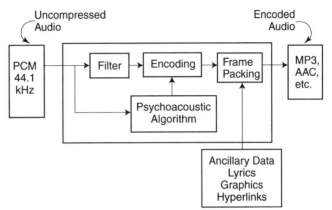

Minimum Audible Threshold

The level below which all sounds are inaudible to the human ear is called the threshold of hearing, or minimum audible threshold. This threshold varies according to frequency because the human ear does not have a linear response.

Sounds below this threshold can be removed by the encoder, and most listeners will not detect any difference between the encoded signal and the original. The ear is most sensitive to frequencies between 2 kHz and 4 kHz, so less information can be removed from this range without affecting the quality of the sound.

Figure 28 shows the Fletcher-Munsen curve, which illustrates how the threshold of human hearing varies according to frequency.

Masking Effect

Quiet sounds are "masked" by louder sounds that are close to them in frequency and time. Since you can't hear these sounds, they can be removed from the signal without affecting the perceived quality. An example is the hiss and other background noise you hear when a song is paused or blank tape is playing. When the music plays above a certain level, you can no longer hear the background noise, but it is still there in the signal. If you remove it, you shouldn't notice any difference in the sound.

Figure 28 - Fletcher-Munsen Curve

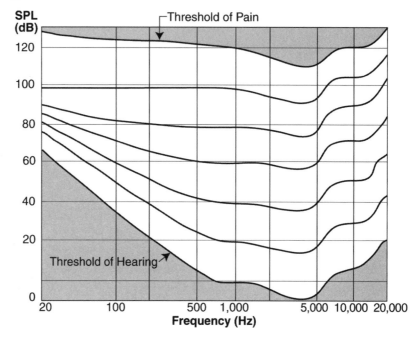

Reservoir of Bits

Certain musical passages need to be encoded at higher bit-rates to maintain fidelity, so MP3 creates a reservoir by setting aside bits from less complex passages. These extra bits can then be applied to more complex passages, where they are needed more. This is different from variable bit-rate encoding, because a fixed number of bits are allocated—they just are shifted to where they are needed most.

Stereo Modes

Stereo audio normally requires twice the bandwidth of mono because it uses two separate channels. Much of the information is identical on both channels. For example, any sounds positioned at the center of the stereo image will be carried by both channels. This wastes a lot of space because the information is identical. MPEG Audio has several ways of handling stereo information. Each method varies in the amount of compression and the fidelity to the stereo image.

Simple Stereo (mode 0) is the closest to a normal stereo signal. It uses independent channels; therefore, any duplicate information will be retained, and some bandwidth will be wasted. The MPEG encoder can vary the allocation of bits between channels according to the complexity of the signal. The overall bit-rate remains constant, but the split between the channels varies according to the dynamic range of each channel.

Joint Stereo (mode 1) uses MS (middle/side) Stereo, where one channel carries the information that is identical on both channels and the other carries the difference. Joint Stereo retains all the original stereo information and uses bandwidth very efficiently.

Intensity Stereo encodes only the stereo information that is perceived as important to the stereo image. Intensity Stereo provides the highest level of compression, but the stereo image will suffer at lower bit-rates.

Although Simple Stereo is the closest to a normal stereo signal, it is not the best option to use with MPEG Audio. In most cases, Joint Stereo will produce higher quality sound because the bits can be allocated more efficiently.

Huffman Encoding

In any musical composition, certain sound patterns are repeated—some more often than others. These patterns can be coded with symbols to save space, and then decoded into the original pattern when played. Huffman encoding increases compression by using shorter codes for more common sound patterns. It's similar to replacing every word in a document with a number and using the smaller numbers for the most common words.

Bit-rates

MPEG Audio supports constant and variable bit-rates ranging from 8 kbps to 1.5 mbps. Just as with uncompressed audio, the bit-rate of MPEG Audio has a direct relationship to sound quality and file size.

Constant bit-rate (CBR) encoding is not very efficient because it uses the same number of bits, regardless of how complex or simple the passage is. Variable bit-rate (VBR) encoding varies the number of bits depending on the complexity of the music and is more efficient than CBR. For example, a simple passage with just a vocalist and acoustic guitar needs fewer bits than a passage with a full symphony.

Resolution and MPEG Audio

MPEG encoders rely on the resolution used in the uncompressed audio file to set the range of resolution that will be used for the encoded file. The resolution of the encoded file is varied according to the complexity of the signal to achieve compression. Many encoders are optimized to work with 16-bit resolution input, and some will only accept 44.1 kHz, 16-bit WAV files as input.

Table 15 shows the file sizes and relative amounts of compression for different bit-rates. As the bit-rate increases, so does the sound quality, along with the file size. This table also shows how many hours of audio or four-minute songs, a 1GB hard disk will hold at each rate.

Table 15 - File Size vs. Bit-rate

Bit-rate	File Size (4-min. song)	MB per Minute	Compression Ratio	Hours per GB	4-min. Songs per GB
1,411 kbps (CD Audio)	41.3MB	10.3	None	1.7	25
320 kbps	9.4MB	2.3	4.4 = 1	7.3	109
256 kbps	7.5MB	1.9	5.5 = 1	9.1	137
192 kbps	5.6MB	1.4	7.3 = 1	12.1	182
160 kbps	4.7MB	1.2	8.8 = 1	14.6	218
128 kbps	3.8MB	0.9	11.0 = 1	18.2	273
80 kbps	2.3MB	0.6	7.6 = 1	29.1	437

Signal Delays

The process of encoding and decoding audio introduces a slight delay into the signal. This is not a problem for home use, but it is a factor for applications where a short delay is critical, such as two-way voice conversations, where a delay of more than 10 ms (milliseconds) can be disturbing. Delays for MPEG Audio typically range from 19 ms for Layer-I to more than 60 ms for Layer-III and AAC. The actual delay depends on the hardware and software used.

Embedded Data (ID3 Tags)

MPEG Audio is frame-based, which allows it to support the insertion of additional program information in the form of text, graphics and other types of data. The standard is flexible enough that software developers can include almost any type of data, such as copyright information, lyrics, album artwork and even links to artist's Web sites.

ID3 Tags

An informal standard called ID3 tagging has emerged that specifies a format for storing non-audio data inside MP3 files. The ID3 information can be displayed and edited by MP3 players such as Winamp. The ID3 tag is placed at the very end of the MP3 file, which makes it unsuitable for streaming audio.

ID3 Version 1 is limited to 128 bytes of data and 30 characters per field and contains fixed length fields for title, artist, album, year, comments, track number and genre. Most audio CDs do not contain this information, so it needs to be entered manually or obtained from a database, such as the CDDB (see Chapter 9, *Organizing and Playing Music*). The identification field must contain the characters "TAG" to indicate ID3 version 1 compliance.

ID3 Version 1.1 takes the last two characters of the comments field and uses them for the number of the CD track that the song originated from.

Table 16 - ID3 Tag Version 1.1 Fields

Position	Length (Bytes)	Field
0-2	3	Identification
3-32	30	Title
33-62	30	Artist
63-92	30	Album
93-96	4	Year
97-125	28	Comments
124	1	0 (zero)
125	1	Track Number
126	1	Genre

ID3v2

ID3 Version 2 is designed to be more flexible and expandable than version 1.1. Each tag contains smaller chunks of data, called frames. Each frame can contain any type of data, such as lyrics, album cover graphics and links to a band's Web site. The ID3v2 tag is placed at the beginning of the file, which

---

Key Features of ID3v2

- Uses a container format.
- Tag data is at beginning of the file, which makes it suitable for streaming.
- Has an "unsynchronization" feature to prevent ID3v2 incompatible players from attempting to play the tag.
- Maximum tag size is 256MB; maximum frame size is 16MB.
- Supports Unicode and the capability to compress data.
- Has several new text fields, including composer, conductor, media type, beats per minute (BPM) and copyright message.
- Able to contain both plain and synchronized lyrics (for karaoke).
- Can contain volume, balance and equalizer settings.
- Supports encrypted information, images and hyperlinks.

---

makes it useful for streaming applications. A unique feature called the Popularimeter can be used to keep track of how often you listen to each song, and this information could be used by future programs to automatically construct playlists based on your personal tastes.

Measuring Sound Quality

Sound quality is subjective, so traditional measures like total harmonic distortion (THD) and signal-to-noise ratio are not useful for rating perceptual encoding schemes. The perceived quality of the sound is more important than any characteristic that can be measured with test equipment. Controlled tests with trained listeners are the best way of measuring the performance of perceptual encoding schemes.

During the MPEG-1 development process, three international listening tests were performed using the CCIR (Centre for Communication Interface Research) impairment scale shown in Table 17. At 128 kbps, MP3 scored between 3.6 and 3.8. This indicates that listeners detected a difference between the MP3 and the original but the difference was not annoying. At 240 kbps and above, MP3 scored at the high end of the scale, and most listeners found it difficult to distinguish between the MP3 and the original version.

Table 17 - CCIR Impairment Scale

5.0 - Imperceptible (indistinguishable from the original)

4.0 - Perceptible (perceptible difference, but not annoying)

3.0 - Slightly annoying

2.0 - Annoying

1.0 - Very annoying

Variables That Affect Sound Quality

The major variables that affect the sound quality of encoded audio are the type of encoder, the bit-rate, the type of music and the sensitivity of the listener's hearing. The quality of commercially available encoders is generally very good, and most people would find it difficult to tell the difference between two MP3 files encoded from the same song by different encoders. Assuming you've already decided on using MP3, the bit-rate is the biggest factor that you can control.

In general, music that is more complex will require higher bit-rates. A good example is classical (or symphonic) music. Classical music is generally more complex, because there are more instruments and a wider dynamic range compared to most other types of music, such as blues and rock. Variable bit-rate encoding is a good choice for all types of music because it provides significantly better quality than constant bit-rate encoding at a similar rate. This is because the bits are allocated where they are needed most, which also helps maintain a more constant signal-to-noise ratio.

Table 18 shows the bit-rates for various digital audio formats that will produce high quality sound for most types of music.

Table 18 - Bit-rates for High Quality Sound

Format	Bit-rate	Compression
Red Book (CD)	1.4Mbps	None
MPEG Layer-I	384 kbps	3.6=1
MPEG Layer-II	256 kbps	5.5=1
MPEG Layer-III (MP3)	192 kbps	7.3=1
	VBR Normal/High	7=1 to 10=1
MPEG AAC	128 kbps	11=1

Table 19 - ID3 Tag Genre Codes

0 Blues	20 Alternative	40 Alternative Rock	60 Top 40
1 Classic Rock	21 Ska	41 Bass	61 Christian Rap
2 Country	22 Death Metal	42 Soul	62 Pop/Funk
3 Dance	23 Pranks	43 Punk	63 Jungle
4 Disco	24 Soundtrack	44 Space	64 Native American
5 Funk	25 Euro-Techno	45 Meditative	65 Cabaret
6 Grunge	26 Ambient	46 Instrumental Pop	66 New Wave
7 Hip-Hop	27 Trip-Hop	47 Instrumental Rock	67 Psychedelic
8 Jazz	28 Vocal	48 Ethnic	68 Rave
9 Metal	29 Jazz+Funk	49 Gothic	69 Showtunes
10 New Age	30 Fusion	50 Darkwave	70 Trailer
11 Oldies	31 Trance	51 Techno-Industrial	71 Lo-Fi
12 Other	32 Classical	52 Electronic	72 Tribal
13 Pop	33 Instrumental	53 Pop-Folk	73 Acid Punk
14 R&B	34 Acid	54 Eurodance	74 Acid Jazz
15 Rap	35 House	55 Dream	75 Polka
16 Reggae	36 Game	56 Southern Rock	76 Retro
17 Rock	37 Sound Clip	57 Comedy	77 Musical
18 Techno	38 Gospel	58 Cult	78 Rock & Roll
19 Industrial	39 Noise	59 Gangsta	79 Hard Rock

Source: *www.dv.co.yu/mpgscript/mpeghdr.htm*

Additional Resources

Organization	Web Site
American National Standards Institute (ANSI)	*www.ansi.org*
Centre for Communication Interface Research (CCIR)	*www.ccir.org*
Fraunhofer Gesellschaft	*www.iis.fhg.de/amm/techinf*
ID3 Tag Specification	*www.id3.org*
International Standards Organization (ISO)	*www.iso.ch*
Moving Picture Experts Group (MPEG)	*http://drogo.cselt.stet.it/mpeg*

Part 4

Recording Music on Your PC

Chapter 14

Hard Disk Recording

The Internet and CDs aren't the only sources for digital music. You may have old records that have never been released on CD that you would like to convert to a digital format. You may have deteriorating tapes you would like to preserve. Or maybe you want to record live music, create audio books or record sound effects for a multimedia presentation.

Any type of analog audio can be preserved (and sometimes improved) by recording it in a digital format. Once the audio is in digital format, it's easy to clean it up or add special effects. Digital audio also takes up less physical space than analog audio, even without compression.

The process of recording and storing the audio on a computer is called hard disk recording. Dedicated hard disk recorders costing thousands of dollars have been available to professional recording engineers for years. Now, with the right hardware and software, you can produce professional quality digital recordings on your computer for much less money.

Hard disk recording works much the same as tape recording. Audio is recorded in real-time from analog sources, such as records or cassette tapes, or from digital sources, such as MiniDiscs or DATs. One hour of audio still takes 60 minutes to digitally record. But once audio is in a digital format, you are no longer limited to working in real-time. You can then use playlists to program continuous music in a fraction of the time it would take using a tape recorder and you can also easily edit the sound with a program like CoolEdit.

You can record directly from a microphone or any other source fed into your sound card's inputs. With the right sound card and software, anything you hear on your computer can also be recorded (for example, sounds from other programs or streaming audio from the Internet). Audio from your computer can also be recorded to a tape or MiniDisc recorder through the line output of your sound card. This is useful for recording programs from Internet radio stations to cassette tapes for portable listening. The same process can also be used to record music from MP3 files to cassette tapes.

Figure 29 - Hard Disk Recording

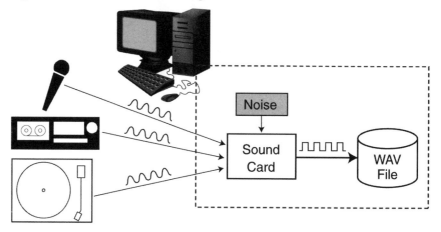

The recording capacity of your computer is limited only by the amount of free space on your hard disk. The total time will vary, depending on the sampling rate, resolution and number of channels. (See Chapter 11, *A Digital Audio Primer*, for more information on calculating file sizes.)

Recording from Analog Sources

Even though ripping and direct digital recording produce better quality sound, there are many cases where you have no choice but to use analog recording. You may have a record or tape you want to preserve, or you may want to record acoustical instruments or vocals, using a microphone.

Recording with a sound card in this manner starts out with an analog signal, so the signal will degrade slightly during the A/D conversion process. The result, however, will be a digital signal stored in a file that will not degrade, unlike records and analog tapes that will degrade a little bit each time they are played.

To record an analog source, it must be connected to your sound card's line input with the right type of cable. (See Chapter 10, *Connecting Your PC to Your Stereo*.)

MiniDiscs and DATs

MiniDiscs use a lossy encoding scheme similar to MPEG Audio. The player must first decode the audio before outputting a digital signal, which results in some loss of quality. Recording digitally from a DAT requires no decoding.

Direct Digital Recording

If you have a piece of audio equipment with digital output (such as a DAT or MiniDisc player) and your sound card has a digital input, you can make a direct digital recording. This bypasses the A/D converter and analog circuits in the sound card and results in a better quality recording. Direct digital recording is still a real-time process, like analog recording.

Recording Software

Most operating systems include a basic recording program such as the Windows Sound Recorder, which is limited in functionality. If you plan on doing a lot of recording, you should purchase a specialized program like Cool Edit, Sound Forge or SoundEdit 16 (see Appendix B, *What and Where to Buy*). Specialized recording programs generally work better, have more features and can handle large files better.

Some sound cards come bundled with stripped-down versions of full-featured recording and editing software. These "lite" programs usually are adequate for basic recording and editing functions, such as removing silence or normalizing a file. The Sound Blaster Live comes bundled with Sound Forge XP (a good deal considering the software alone sells for about $50). Most bundled programs offer a reasonable cost upgrade to the full version.

Cool Edit

Cool Edit (*www.cooledit.com*) is a great sound recording and editing program, well liked by many users. You can use CoolEdit to remove the blank spaces at the beginning or end of a song, normalize audio files, remove noise from recordings and more. Cool Edit 2000 is a "lite" version and offers the basic recording and editing features needed by most users. Cool Edit Pro adds more extensive capabilities, including multi-track recording.

Recording Directly to MP3

Most sound editing programs do not have the capability to record directly to MP3, so the audio is normally first stored in a WAV file and then converted to MP3 in a separate step. A few of the all-in-one programs such as MusicMatch Jukebox, RealJukebox and the Macintosh version of AudioCatalyst can record directly to MP3.

Even though these programs can record directly to MP3, it's often better to record to a WAV file first. This gives you the chance to clean up the file before it's encoded. Also, more things can go wrong when you encode while recording because the computer has to work harder. Any interruptions can ruin an otherwise good recording.

Sound Forge

Sound Forge (*www.soundforge.com*) is a high-end professional sound recording and editing program. It reads and writes to almost any format and can process studio-quality audio files and optimize files headed for the Internet. Sound Forge XP is a "lite" version of Sound Forge and offers the basic recording and editing features needed by most users.

Total Recorder

Total Recorder (*www.highcriteria.com*) is a universal sound recording tool that allows you to record digital and analog audio from multiple sources. TotalRecorder can also record sound that is being played by other media programs, including live Internet broadcasts. You can use its scheduler to record a streaming audio program, even if you can't be there when it is happening. It's almost like having a VCR for the Internet.

Sound Card Mixing Functions

In addition to performing digital to analog conversion, sound cards work with software to perform the functions of a mixing console. On Windows systems, the Volume Control program provides the interface to the sound card's mixer functions. Some recording programs provide their own mixer interface in place of the Volume Control program.

Volume Control

The Volume Control program provides controls for adjusting the volume and balance for each channel supported by the sound card. Separate screens are used for recording (input) and playback (output) controls.

Figure 30 - Sound Card Mixing Functions

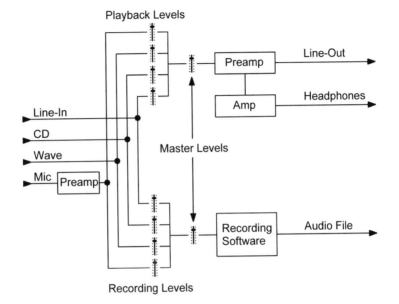

Most sound editing and player programs have their own volume control that usually links to the Volume Control program. Changing the volume in these programs will cause one of the sliders in the Volume Control program to move (and vice versa).

Many sound card drivers replace the built-in Volume Control program and add or modify channels. Depending on which sound card is installed, the playback and recording controls may be labeled differently. The playback level screen is usually labeled "Volume Control," but the sound card software may change it to "Play Control" or "Speaker Control." The recording level screen is usually labeled "Recording Control" or "Record Control." Regardless of the labels, the basic functions are the same.

Playback Control

The Playback Control screen provides level and balance controls for each input supported by the sound card. The inputs most people will use are CD Audio, Line-in, Mic and Wave. The Wave control is used to adjust the playback level of digital audio files (MP3, WAV, etc.). The **Advanced** button on some channels provides access to tone controls and special effects like 3D sound and reverberation.

Playback Control

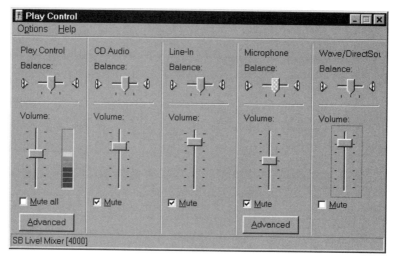

Levels can be adjusted individually for each channel and the master volume control sets the overall level sent to the line-out and headphone jacks. Check the **Mute** checkbox on any unused channels to reduce noise.

Channels can be displayed or hidden by clicking on the **Options** menu, then **Properties,** and checking the box next to each channel you want displayed. This makes the screen less cluttered by displaying only the channels you need. For example, if you are playing a CD and want use a microphone to make a voice-over announcement, you might want to display only the CD and microphone sliders.

Recording Control

The Recording Control provides separate level and balance controls for each input supported by the sound card. These sliders are independent of the playback control sliders and are used to set the levels of signals sent to the recording program. The playback levels only affect how loud the music is played and have no effect on the level of the signal recorded. It is possible to have a source playing very loud, yet a recording level that is much too low.

When you launch the Volume Control, it defaults to the Playback Control screen. To adjust recording levels, select **Options** from the pull-down menu, then **Properties**, and then **Recording**. The screen with the recording controls will appear.

Recording Control Properties

Below each slider is a checkbox (labeled "Select") that activates that source. In the example below, Line-In is the only source selected, so only the signal from the sound card's line input jack will be recorded.

Some sound card software adds a master volume control and recording level meter to the Recording Control screen. If your Recording Control screen doesn't have a master recording level meter, you can use the meter in your recording program—which is usually more accurate.

Recording Control With Line-In Selected

> **Sound Blaster Live**
>
> The Recording Control of the SoundBlaster Live only allows you to select one device at a time, unlike most other sound cards, which allow you to select multiple devices. To record a mix of sound from multiple sources, select the "What U Hear" control. Then go to the Playback Control and select the sources you want to record.

Recording Levels

It's important to set input levels as high as possible to obtain a good signal-to-noise ratio and maximum dynamic range. However, they should not be set so high that the meter stays constantly in the yellow level, except for occasional peaks. If the meter reaches the red level, the recording level is approaching the maximum, or clipping level. You should avoid clipping at all costs because it causes extreme distortion.

Programs like Cool Edit and Sound Forge have their own level meters that are more precise than the simple meter in the Recording Control. These meters are usually labeled in dB, with 0dB equal to the maximum level. Levels below the maximum are shown in negative dB and the lowest possible level is referred to as infinity.

When using this type of meter to set recording levels, make sure the peaks average around -6 dB and don't exceed -3 dB. This will normally give you enough headroom to avoid clipping, while maintaining a good signal to noise ratio. These meters usually have a peak reading marker to show the highest level measured during a recording session.

The Recording Process

Although hard disk recording is similar to tape recording, there are several additional steps. Below is an outline of the basic process. (See Chapter 20, *Software Tutorials*, for instructions on recording with Cool Edit.)

Setting Audio Parameters

Before you start recording, you must specify the sampling rate, resolution and number of channels. For CD-quality audio, you would choose 16-bit stereo at 44.1 kHz. For voice or background music, you could choose mono to save space. You could also choose 8-bits or a lower sampling rate for voice or for music that does not need to be high quality.

> **Tip**
>
> If you need to switch back and forth between playback and recording controls, instead of going back and forth through the pull-down menus, you can launch two instances of the Volume Control program and set one to display the playback controls and the other to display the recording controls.
>
> To do this, click on the Volume Control icon to launch one instance of it, then click on the icon again to launch a second instance. Both instances will default to playback controls, so switch one of them to display the recording controls. You can now switch between them by clicking on their icons in the Windows Task Bar.

Selecting the Source

The source, whether internal or external, needs to be selected from the Recording Control screen of the Volume Control program. For an external source, select **Line In**, **Mic** or **S/PDIF-In**. For an internal source, you would normally select **Wave** (or **Wav/Direct Sound**). If you have a Sound Blaster Live, you can select **What U Hear** to record everything that passes through the sound card.

Make sure to only select the channel for the source you want to record, otherwise noise on other selected channels may get mixed in with the recording. It's also a good idea to zero the sliders on unused channels to prevent noise leakage.

Setting the Recording Level

Just like when recording a tape, you should set the level as high as possible without the signal being clipped. If the level is too low, the signal will not take advantage of the full dynamic range and will be noisy. If the level is too high the signal will be clipped and distorted.

To set the level, start the source playing, and watch the level meters. Adjust the level control sliders so the peaks stay below the red area (about -3 dB).

Skip forward to the loudest part of the song to make sure those peaks are not too high. Once you are satisfied with the level, rewind or reset the source and pause it at the beginning of the track.

> **Dynamic Range Compression**
>
> If you can't achieve a high enough average level without clipping, some programs allow you to apply dynamic range compression to raise the apparent loudness of a signal. This type of compression is usually not necessary when recording prerecorded music. Dynamic compression can be applied in a WAV file with a sound editor, or when the song is played with a plug-in like AudioStocker.

Recording

Now you are ready to record. In quick succession, click on the Record button in the recording program, then press or click (if the source is another program) the Play button on the source. If the level meters start moving and you don't hear anything, the playback level control is probably muted. To monitor the sound while recording, go to the Playback control and uncheck the mute buttons for Wave or Direct Sound and adjust the volume sliders.

When the playback is complete, stop the source and also click the stop button in the recording program. Zoom out and view the whole recording. This will show you quickly whether or not there are any gaps or clipping. You may notice a section of silence at the beginning and end of the recording. This can be removed using the trim feature of the recording software (see Chapter 17, *Editing Sound Files*). You may want to keep a half second of silence at either end. This is a matter of preference, and the appropriate amount of silence will vary depending on the song.

File Formats

Before you save the file, you must specify the format (e.g., WAV, AU, AIFF, etc.). Some recording programs require that you select the format before recording. Choose PCM WAV with a sampling rate of 44.1 kHz and 16-bit resolution if you plan to convert the file to MP3 format.

Reducing Background Noise

Noise can be introduced into an audio signal in many places and can ruin an otherwise good recording. A good test, before recording on a system for the first time, is to record a few seconds of silence from the gaps between tracks on a record or tape and then play it back.

> **Tip**
> Place your sound card in the slot farthest away from the computer's power supply and processor and place your video card as far away from the sound card as possible. This can help reduce the introduction of electrical noise from other components inside the computer.

Listen for hum, hiss and pops. Hum may indicate a faulty cable or improperly grounded equipment. Hiss is unavoidable on tapes, but hiss when the source is paused indicates electrical noise from inside the computer or the tape player or turntable. Pops indicate scratches or dust on a record.

When recording from vinyl records, clean the record and make sure your turntable's stylus and cartridge are in good shape. When recording from tape, make sure the heads are clean and demagnetized. In either case, use good quality shielded cables to reduce noise from electrical interference. Set the highest possible recording level, without clipping, to help mask noise and maximize the dynamic range.

The quality of your sound card will have a big effect on the quality of your recordings. When you record through a sound card, the A/D conversion process adds distortion from quantization errors and electrical noise can be picked up from other components in the computer.

Many lower priced sound cards are poorly shielded, which makes them more susceptible to noise. Some lower priced sound cards also have low resolution A/D converters, which will introduce more distortion from quantization errors.

If you plan to make analog recordings, consider using a better sound card such as the Creative Sound Blaster Live MP3 or the Turtle Beach Montego II, or use an external A/D converter, such as the Roland UA-30. (See Appendix B, *What and Where to Buy*, for more information.)

Record and Tape Preservation

Many people have collections of vinyl records or tapes they would like to preserve. Often these recordings are not available in digital format (or they may not be replaceable in any format). Digitizing a recording (recording it in a digital format) is an excellent way to preserve the music and avoid wear and tear each time the record or tape is played.

Many recording programs can also be used to remove clicks, pops and background noise. Most sound editing programs have special filters for removing unwanted noise. A few programs, such as Adaptec's Spin Doctor, are specifically geared towards recording and cleaning up audio from vinyl records and tapes. You can also use Cool Edit and Sound Forge to remove noise, although Spin Doctor is somewhat easier to use.

Spin Doctor allows you to set separate levels for noise filtering and pop removal. Cool Edit lets you select a section of silence so it can develop a noise profile to apply to the rest of the file. Cool Edit allows you to save noise profiles and use them to remove noise from similar files. Sound Forge is slightly more difficult to use but works well.

Whichever program you use, you must be careful to avoid removing audible parts of the music along with the noise. It's a good idea to try several settings and listen to the result before you remove any noise permanently.

Table 20 - Sound Recording and Editing Software

Program	Manufacturer	Comments
Cool Edit 2000	Syntrillium	Great, low-cost sound recorder and editor
Audio Clean-Up Plug-In	Syntrillium	Plug-in for removing hiss, clicks, pops and crackle
Cool Edit Pro	Syntrillium	Professional version of Cool Edit
GoldWave	Chris Craig	Nice low-cost sound recorder and editor
MPEG Tape Deck	Marcus Kuenzel	Records and encodes audio from external sources to MPEG format
Peak LE (Mac)	Bias, Inc.	Good low-cost sound recorder and editor
SoundEdit 16 (Mac)	Macromedia	High-end, professional-quality sound recorder and editor
Sound Forge	Sonic Foundry	High-end, professional sound recording and editing
Sound Forge XP	Sonic Foundry	Lite version of Sound Forge (bundled with Sound Blaster Live)
Total Recorder	High Criteria	Records audio from any source, including other programs

Additional Resources

Site	Address
Audio Cafe	www.audiocafe.com
Home Recording	www.homerecording.com
Mix Online	www.mixonline.com

Chapter 15

Digital Audio Extraction

Digital audio extraction (DAE), commonly referred to as ripping, is the process of copying audio data directly from a CD. Because it bypasses the sound card, ripping normally results in a perfect copy with no introduction of noise or loss of fidelity.

Ripping is the fastest way to get songs from a CD onto your computer. Since it is a digital copying process, the speed of ripping is limited only by the performance of your hardware and software, unlike recording, which is always a real-time process.

When you record a CD through a sound card, the digital audio data is converted to analog, then resampled and converted back to digital. While the signal is in analog form, it can pick up noise from the interior of the computer. When the signal is converted back to digital, quantization distortion will be introduced by the A/D converter in the sound card.

When you record a four-minute song from a CD, it will always take at least four minutes to record, whether you use a tape recorder, sound card, or any other recording method. However, with a fast CD-ROM drive, the same song can be ripped in less than 30 seconds.

Figure 31 - Recording Audio From a CD

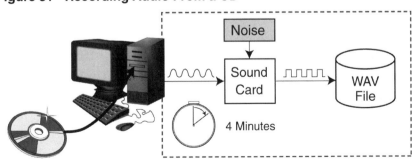

Figure 32 - Ripping Audio From a CD

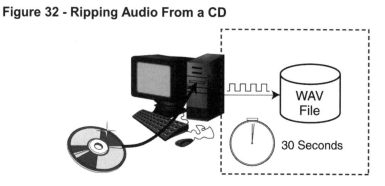

Ripping Software

Specialized software is required for ripping. All-in-one programs, such as MusicMatch Jukebox and RealJukebox, include rippers, encoders, players and playlist managers in one program. A few manufacturers, like Plextor, include ripping software with their CD-ROM drives. Audiograbber (also used in AudioCatalyst) is one of the best ripping programs available. MusicMatch also has a very capable ripper.

Will Your Drive Rip?

The performance of your CD-ROM drive is the single biggest factor in the success of ripping. Not all drives support digital audio extraction, and most manufacturers do not include digital audio extraction performance in their specifications. This may be because manufacturers worry that advertising this capability would make them subject to the royalty requirements for digital recording devices marketed for consumer use.

Table 21 lists resources for understanding CD-ROM technology and CD formats. The CD Digital Audio Extraction Page includes a list of drives that support digital audio extraction. This lists is by no means complete, but if your drive is listed, the information may be useful for troubleshooting.

Table 21 - CD-ROM Resource Sites

Organization	Web Site
CDDB	www.cddb.com
CD Digital Audio Extraction Page	www.tardis.ed.ac.uk/~psyche/cdda/
CD Page	www.cdpage.com

To determine the model number of your CD-ROM drive (in Windows 95 or later), click the **Start** button, and select **Settings**, then **Control Panel.** Double-click on the **System** icon, then select the **Device Manager** tab. Click on the plus (**+**) symbol to the left of the CD-ROM icon. This will display a second CD-ROM icon labeled with the manufacturer and model number of your drive.

Windows Device Manager

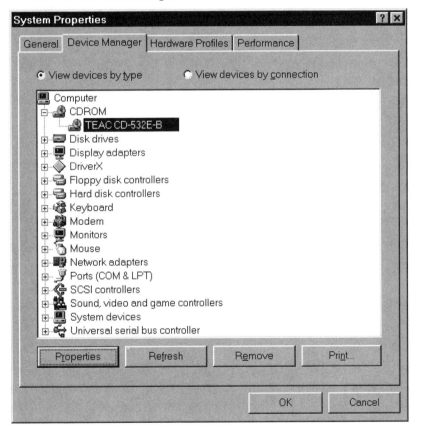

Keep in mind that even if a CD-ROM drive supports ripping, it doesn't mean the drive will work well on your system. Many variables affect ripping performance, including processor speed, hard disk fragmentation, the type of ripping software, and the CD-ROM access method used (e.g., ASPI vs. MSCDEX). Other factors, such as bad cables, software incompatibility and incorrect configuration settings, can prevent even a good CD-ROM drive from ripping.

If your drive is listed as being able to rip but doesn't work properly, your software or system configuration may be at fault. If your drive is listed as not being able to rip, it doesn't necessarily mean it can't. It just means that someone else with the same model drive tried ripping with it and was unsuccessful. If you can't get your drive to rip after trying a few different settings, you are probably better off replacing it rather than struggling to get it to work.

If your CD-ROM rips but frequently has problems, it's well worth the cost of a new drive that works more reliably. When I started ripping my CD collection, I probably wasted 20 to 30 hours messing with a marginal CD-ROM drive. Once I installed a new drive, 95% of my ripping problems went away.

Jitter

Pops or breaks in the sound of a ripped audio track are often caused by jitter. Jitter is caused by the inability of many CD-ROM drives to accurately seek a specific sector (also called a frame) on an audio CD.

CDs were originally designed for audio and then adapted to computer data. In an audio CD player, once the laser read head is in position, the data is read in a continuous stream. The head does not have to jump to a new position while playing, it simply follows the spiral track. Computers read information from CDs in blocks, rather than in a continuous stream.

Programs that extract CD audio must first read a block of sectors, then write this data to the hard disk. The drive must then seek the beginning of the next block of sectors. The Red Book CD audio specification states that a CD player only needs to be accurate to within 1/75th of a second. Because of this

Figure 33 - Jitter

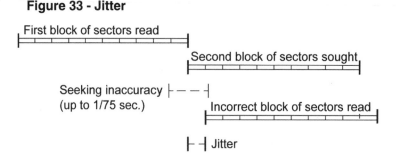

Figure 34 - Jitter Correction

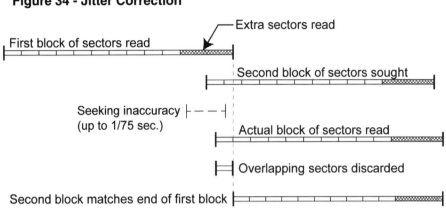

$1/75^{th}$ of a second tolerance, when a program is extracting CD audio, it can't be sure that the sector returned by the drive is the exact one it requested.

Most ripping software has settings for jitter correction (sometimes referred to as synchronization or error correction) that can correct this problem. With jitter correction enabled, the ripping software reads sectors in blocks, and overlaps the reads by a specified number of sectors. It can then compare the blocks and discard the sectors that overlap.

Jitter correction slows down ripping because it takes more time to read the overlapping data. Older drives tend to have more jitter problems than newer models. Drives with poor seeking accuracy may rip unreliably or not at all, even with jitter correction. Some newer drives, such as the Plextor models, perform jitter correction internally.

Seek Errors

Not all CD-ROM drives can produce identical files extracting the same track at different times. This doesn't necessarily mean that the track was ripped inaccurately. Because of the $1/75^{th}$ second positioning inaccuracy, the CD-ROM drive can't tell exactly where the recording started on a track. Jitter correction can't help since there is no previous block to synchronize with.

If you extract the same track twice, there's a chance it will start at a slightly different position. The extracted track may contain slightly more or less silence at the beginning. This changes the binary data slightly but doesn't affect how a track sounds. This type of inconsistency is more common with lower-cost CD-ROM drives. Many of the better drives can rip the same tracks multiple times and consistently produce identical files, even when different ripping software is used.

Jitter Correction Settings

The settings of your ripping software, especially those for jitter correction, play a big part in ripping performance. It pays to experiment with several settings and compare the files to see which one works best. If you have one of the Plextor drives, always rip with jitter correction disabled, since the drive handles this internally. Otherwise, the ripping will take longer than necessary because of the extra time required for the overlapping reads of the software jitter correction.

MusicMatch

MusicMatch is very good at optimizing itself for jitter correction (MusicMatch uses the term "error correction") because it tests the CD-ROM drive and automatically configures itself. You can toggle jitter correction on and off but you shouldn't have to tweak any of the advanced settings. If your drive will not rip, you can try changing a few of MusicMatch's advanced settings, but there's a good chance the problem lies elsewhere.

AudioCatalyst

AudioCatalyst (and Audiograbber) use the term synchronization in place of jitter correction. AudioCatalyst provides more control over the ripping process than MusicMatch, but you must manually configure it. Buffered and unbuffered burst settings provide no jitter correction. Dynamic sync varies the amount of correction depending on the data. Fixed width sync provides progressive levels of jitter correction from 1 to 10.

If you need to use a higher level than 4 or 5 you should consider replacing your CD-ROM drive. AudioCatalyst supports both ASPI and MSCEDX ripping, but ASPI is much better. MSCDEX should only be used if there is no other choice. For step-by-step instructions for ripping with AudioCatalyst, see Chapter 20, *Software Tutorials*.

Successful Ripping

Once you have determined optimum settings for ripping on your system and have successfully ripped at least one CD, you generally should not have to change them. Although, in some cases, changes in your computer's configuration may affect ripping performance and require reconfiguration of the ripping program.

Tips for Successful Ripping

- Use a CD-ROM drive that supports digital audio extraction and has good seeking accuracy.

- Make sure your system is not running unnecessary programs or processes when it's ripping

- Keep your hard drive defragmented.

- Make sure your CD-ROM drivers are up-to-date.

- Use the ASPI method of accessing the CD-ROM.

- Use jitter correction (sometimes called error correction or synchronization) unless your drive handles this directly.

- Disable auto insert notification for your CD-ROM drive.

- Don't waste your time with a marginal CD-ROM drive or one that does not rip at 4X or better speed.

- Test with a few tracks from different CDs and listen to the WAV files to verify the quality before ripping your entire CD collection.

One of the first things to do if you have trouble either ripping or encoding is to exit all other programs. On Windows systems you can press the Ctrl, Alt and Del keys simultaneously to display the Windows Task Manager and see a list of all programs that are in memory. See Chapter 18, *Recording Your Own CDs,* for tips on optimizing your system.

Programs running in the background may cause problems because they put more of a load on the system's processor and tie up memory that otherwise would be available. Idle programs, like a wordprocessor or a spreadsheet, normally will not cause problems, but they still use memory. Any program that puts a load on the processor or writes frequently to the hard disk can also cause problems.

Ripping Speed

A good CD-ROM drive should rip reliably at 4X or better. This means that a four-minute song should take less than one minute to rip. Only a handful of drives, such as those made by Plextor, can rip reliably at their full rated speed. If you plan to do a lot of ripping, the Plextor drives are certainly worth the $200 or so you will spend for the drive plus a SCSI controller.

> **Tip**
>
> If you have enough disk space, keep the WAV files until you are satisfied with the sound quality of the MP3 file. You may listen to a few seconds of a WAV file and think that it is good, but later on, when you listen to the MP3, you may find problems further into the file.

You may notice that some tracks rip faster or slower than others. This is normal for CAV drives (see Chapter 8, *Choosing the Right Hardware*) because CDs are read from the inside out and CAV drives spin at a constant RPM. CAV drives will rip slower on the inner (lower number) tracks and faster on the outer (higher numbered) tracks. CLV drives should rip at similar rates on all tracks, but sometimes they have problems on the inner tracks. This is because they must increase the RPM to maintain the linear velocity, and vibration at the higher speeds can cause seek errors.

If you have a slow CD-ROM drive, you may be tempted to work on other tasks while it's ripping, but you risk ruining the ripped file. This is another reason why it's worthwhile it to get a fast SCSI CD-ROM like the Plextor 12/20 Plex, which can rip a full CD in under five minutes. And, if you do run other programs while it's ripping, it will have fewer problems than an IDE CD-ROM drive because the SCSI interface puts less of a load on the system's processor.

On a fast system, you might be able to get away with working in a spreadsheet or wordprocessor program while you are ripping, but you should still be careful, because a track can appear to rip successfully, but the WAV file will be full of errors and sound horrible.

Disabling Auto Insert Notification

The auto insert notification feature of Windows senses whenever a CD is inserted into the CD-ROM drive and automatically executes the instructions in the autorun.inf file or starts playing it if it is an audio CD. Auto insert notification can interfere with ripping and recording CDs, so it should be disabled.

To disable auto insert notification, click the **Start** button, select **Settings**, then **Control Panel.** Double-click on the **System** icon, then select the **Device Manager** tab. Click on the plus (**+**) symbol to the left of the CD-ROM icon. This will display a second CD-ROM icon. Highlight the second CD-ROM icon and click **Properties**. Select the **Setting**s tab and uncheck the **Auto insert notification** box.

Rip Offset

Some CD-ROM drives have problems recording the first or last tracks of CDs because the drive inaccurately reads the start and end times by a few frames (sectors). AudioCatalyst and MusicMatch allow you to enter an offset value to compensate for this. Generally a value of 10 to 30 will work. Higher numbers may cut in to the audio data.

Ripping Under Windows NT

To rip under Windows NT you must have an ASPI driver installed. If you have a SCSI controller, ASPI is probably installed on your system. ASPI was originally developed for SCSI devices but also works with some IDE CD-ROMs.

ASPI versions 4.01 through 4.53 will not work with most IDE drives. To see which version of ASPI is installed on your system, find the file **wnaspi32.dll** in the **\Windows(or \WinNT)\system32** directory and right-click on it. Select **Properties**, then select the **Version** tab and click on **Product Version**.

Ripping to WAV Files or Direct to MP3?

Ripping usually produces a WAV file, although some software can rip and create an MP3 file in one operation. The advantage of ripping to a WAV file is that it can be edited to adjust the volume or to trim off silence. A WAV file can also be used to encode several MP3 files at different bit-rates without the need for the original CD. Ripping directly to an MP3 file is a bit riskier than ripping to a WAV file because it is more taxing on your system and there are more things that can go wrong.

File Names

Many rippers can use information from the CDDB to automatically name files in a way that makes sense. For example, Billy Idol-White Wedding.WAV is easier to remember than Trk01.WAV. Encoders usually keep the same name and just add the .MP3 extension.

Some rippers provide you with full control over file names and folders, although a few only allow you to specify the folder where the files will be stored. Unless you specify otherwise, or if the information can't be obtained from the CDDB, most rippers will create file names based on the CD identifier and/or track number (e.g., 5b9a97_Trk01a.WAV).

See Chapter 9, *Organizing and Playing Music*, for more information on file names and the CDDB.

Verifying the Quality

Before ripping your entire music collection, you should rip a few tracks to WAV files and listen to them to verify that the results are satisfactory. Most problems with WAV files that weren't ripped properly are fairly obvious, even when played through computer speakers. Clicks and pops or phasing noises are signs that the audio data got scrambled during the ripping process.

Once you have successfully ripped a few WAV files and are satisfied that your configuration is optimal, you may want to try ripping a few test tracks directly to MP3 (if your software supports this). If the tracks ripped directly to MP3 sound OK, then you can probably rip your whole collection this way.

Error Indicators

A good ripping program will warn you of any errors during ripping and include tools for determining if the rip was successful or not.

MusicMatch uses a color-coded indicator to tell you whether or not the track was ripped successfully. A green indicator means the track was ripped with no errors, yellow means there were some errors (but the entire track was ripped), and red means the process was aborted.

AudioCatalyst warns of "possible speed problems" and outright failures but does not verify if the rip was successful. It does calculate a checksum for each ripped track, but this does not necessarily mean the rip was successful. Unless you have a checksum from the same track that was ripped successfully to compare, there's no way to tell if the checksum is valid. Even then, the checksum could be different because of a seek error at the beginning of the track, which would not affect the quality.

With a good CD-ROM drive, if you rip the same track more than once, the checksums and the WAV files should always be identical. Ripping the same track twice and comparing the files or checksums is a good way to test the accuracy of a CD drive and the effects of different ripping settings.

AudioCatalyst has a file comparison feature for this purpose. If the WAV files or checksums for the same track do not match exactly, then at least one of them has errors. Sometimes the WAV files may be different, but still usable if the differences are just in the first few or last few bytes. The only way to be sure is to listen to the files.

Analog Ripping

Many CD-ROM drives are simply incapable of ripping. Some CDs may be scratched or otherwise damaged to the point where they cannot be ripped. If your CD-ROM doesn't support ripping, or you have CDs that are so badly scratched they won't rip, you may have no other choice than to record them via analog (see Chapter 14, *Hard Disk Recording*).

Some programs refer to this as "analog ripping," but that term is really a misnomer. Analog ripping is the same as any other analog recording process except that the source starts out as digital and is converted to analog, and then converted back to digital in the sound card.

Figure 35 - Analog "Ripping" a Four-Minute Song

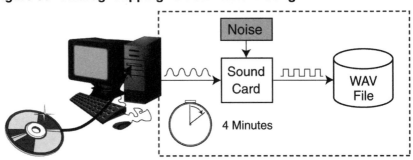

MusicMatch will automatically switch to analog recording if it detects too many errors during ripping. AudioCatalyst and RealJukebox will also let you record CDs via analog. You can accomplish the same thing by playing the CD and using a program like CoolEdit or Sound Forge to record it, but it's easier to use an all-in-one program.

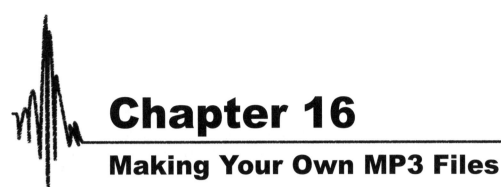

Chapter 16

Making Your Own MP3 Files

Since most music by major artists is not yet available in MP3 or other downloadable formats, you may want to create MP3 files from music you already own. Keep in mind that while it's legal to create MP3 files from music you have purchased, it's not legal to give these to your friends or post them on a Web site without permission (see Chapter 5, *Digital Music and Copyright Law*).

To create an MP3 file from a record, tape or other external source, you first record it and save it as a PCM WAV file. Then you convert it to MP3 with an encoding program. To create an MP3 file from an audio CD, you digitally extract (rip) the audio data to a WAV file and then convert (encode) it to MP3. Some programs like MusicMatch and RealJukebox can rip or record and encode in parallel. Figure 36 shows several options for creating your own MP3 files.

Figure 36 - Options for Creating MP3 Files

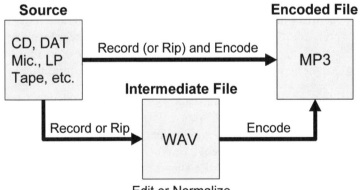

Encoding

Encoding is the process of converting uncompressed digital audio into a compressed format such as MP3. Ripping (see previous chapter) just copies the audio from a CD to a WAV file (or AIFF file on a Mac). The underlying format remains PCM. Encoding actually converts the file to a new format. When you play the encoded file, it must first be decoded before being processed by the D/A converter in your sound card or portable player.

Compared to ripping, there are fewer things that can go wrong with encoding. However, there are more parameters that affect the file size and sound quality. The goal of ripping is to create a perfect copy every time. The goal of encoding is to create files with the best possible sound quality, given the constraints of file size or available bandwidth.

Encoding is a game of trade-offs between speed, file size and sound quality. MPEG provides programmers with a lot of flexibility as to how they implement a particular standard. The result is that there can be substantial differences in sound quality between different encoders, even for files encoded at the same bit-rate. The differences between encoders are usually more apparent in the sound quality they achieve at lower bit-rates. At higher bit-rates (above 256 kbps), it's difficult to tell the difference between encoders.

Encoding audio is much more time consuming and processor-intensive than decoding it. A fast 486 computer might be adequate for playing encoded audio but would be unbearably slow for encoding it. A fast Pentium class system is needed to encode MP3 files in real-time. On a Pentium II 266Mhz system, a four-minute song can be encoded in about a minute. On a 486 system, this could take 15 minutes or more. Some newer formats, such as MPEG AAC, take even longer to encode because the algorithms used to achieve higher compression are more complex and require more processing time.

Xing Technologies makes a very fast encoder that is used by both MusicMatch and AudioCatalyst. The Xing encoder used with the VBR option produces files with a good balance of sound quality and file size. The Fraunhofer Institute was heavily involved in developing the standard for MP3 and makes an excellent MP3 encoder that many people believe produces superior sound quality at lower bit-rates. Unfortunately, it's very expensive to license, so it's found primarily in higher priced ($100+) products. It's also much slower than the Xing encoder.

> **Recording or Ripping Directly to MP3**
> Some programs, such as AudioCatalyst, MusicMatch and RealJukebox, allow you to rip and encode (or record and encode) in a single process.

Bit-rates

As mentioned in Chapter 11, *A Digital Audio Primer*, the term bit-rate refers to how many bits (1s and 0s) are used each second to represent a digital signal, and the bit-rate correlates directly to the size and sound quality of an MP3 file. MP3 files can be encoded at anywhere from 8 kbps to 320 kbps. Lower bit-rates result in smaller files, with reduced sound quality, and higher bit-rates result in better sound quality, but larger files. Table 22 shows the formula for calculating the file size for four minutes (240 seconds) of audio encoded at 128 kbps.

Table 22 - Calculating File Sizes for Encoded Audio

(Bit-rate x Length) /	(Bits/Byte x 1KB) /	1024	=	File Size
(128,000 x 240) /	(8 x 1024)	/ 1024	=	3.8MB

Sound Quality

Because sound quality is subjective and varies depending on the encoding program, the bit-rate required to obtain a certain quality level will vary. At higher bit-rates (192 kbps+) on typical home stereo systems, many people will not be able to tell the difference between the encoded file and the original (although audiophiles with good ears and expensive systems often can).

Table 23 - Comparable Sound Quality for MP3 at Different Bit-rates

Bit-rate	Mode	Quality
8 kbps	Mono	Telephone
16 kbps	Mono	Short-wave Radio
32 kbps	Mono	AM Radio
64 kbps	Stereo	FM Radio
128 kbps	Stereo	Near CD
256 kbps	Stereo	Equal to CD

Other Encoders

Many freeware MP3 encoders are available that are quite capable. Blade and Lame are two that are fairly popular. BladeEnc is a freeware and supports multiple platforms, including Linux and Solaris. Lame is an open source encoder that is available only as source code.

MP3 at 128 kbps is sometimes referred to as CD-quality. But anyone who refers to 128 kbps as CD-quality either has poor hearing or has never done a side-by-side comparison. There are so many other factors, such as the type of music and the encoding algorithm, that affect sound quality, it's best not to infer that a specific bit-rate is equal to a certain quality level. Fortunately, mainstream MP3 encoders like Xing continue to improve, and if MPEG AAC encoders become available for a reasonable price, CD-quality sound at 128 kbps will become a reality for the average user.

Hard disk capacity is so cheap these days that it doesn't make sense to use lower encoding rates just to save disk space. Today you can purchase a 30GB hard disk for under $200. With variable bit-rate encoding at the normal/high setting, this disk would hold over 7,000 songs. That's more songs than in many people's CD collections (especially if you count only the songs they actually listen to).

Lower bit-rates may produce files that sound fine with your present stereo system, but someday you may own a higher-end system where you can tell the difference. It's less work to use higher rates now than to have to recreate the files at a later date. Lower rates do make sense for music intended for a portable player like the Rio (where storage space is at a premium) or for voice recordings (where high frequency response is less critical).

Constant Bit-rate Encoding

Constant bit-rate (CBR) encoding uses the same number of bits each second to record a section of silence as it does to record a complex passage of music. This is like taking out the trash every day regardless of how full it is.

An advantage of constant bit-rate encoding is that it will always produce a predictable file size. The file size can be determined by multiplying the bit-rate by the length of the song in seconds (see Table 22 on page 183). A disadvantage of CBR is that bits will be wasted on simple or quiet passages, when they would have been better used for more complex passages.

Variable Bit-rate Encoding

Variable bit-rate (VBR) encoding uses more or less bits per second, depending on the complexity of the signal. The encoder takes bits away from where they are needed least and puts them where they are needed most—in the more complex sections. This is like emptying the trash only when it's full. In general, VBR will produce significantly better sound quality than CBR at a similar rate.

With VBR, the file size will vary depending on the complexity of the music. A slow song consisting mostly of vocals and simple rhythms encoded with VBR will result in a smaller, yet higher quality file than if it was encoded at a comparable constant bit-rate. Rock, jazz or other more complex music usually requires more bits, which results in larger files. VBR also produces files with a more constant signal-to-noise ratio than CBR.

A disadvantage of VBR is that many portable players will not report song lengths and elapsed times properly. VBR is also difficult to stream over a network because most streaming protocols allocate fixed bandwidth for each channel. VBR uses slightly more processing power than CBR during both encoding and playback, but this should not be a problem on systems with G3 or Pentium II (or better) processors.

VBR can be set to produce several levels of quality ranging from low to high. Naturally, the higher settings also produce larger files. AudioCatalyst and MusicMatch use different terms to describe their settings for VBR. MusicMatch provides settings from 1 to 100 and AudioCatalyst provides five settings ranging from Low to High. Table 24 shows similar VBR settings for both programs, along with comparable constant bit-rates.

Table 24 - VBR Settings

AudioCatalyst VBR Setting	Music Match VBR Setting	Comparable Constant Bit-rate
Low	25	96
Normal/Low	40	112
Normal	50	128
Normal/High	75	160
High	100	192

* Average bit-rates for VBR will vary according to the type of music.

Selecting the Best Bit-rate

Even though the optimum bit-rate depends on many factors, the generalizations below will help new users better understand the options. Advanced users should experiment with different rates to find what works best for them.

With MP3, fair quality sound can usually be achieved with VBR set to **normal**, or with CBR at 128 kbps. Music with complex passages and wide stereo separation will benefit from higher rates. All types of music will benefit from VBR. Rock music usually sounds fine with CBR at 128 kbps, or with VBR set to **normal**. For jazz or classical music, it's better to use a CBR of at least 192 kbps or VBR set to **normal/high**.

If you listen to a lot of classical or complex music, you should use even higher bit-rates. For critical listening, or archiving music with MP3, I recommend using either a CBR of at least 256 kbps or VBR set to high quality. For AAC, I recommend using a bit-rate of 128 kbps with the "Main" profile. At these rates, most people can't tell the difference between the encoded file and the original source.

Lower bit-rates make sense if you will be listening to your music on a portable player. Because the earphones and speakers on most portable units limit the quality of the sound, bit-rates much higher than 96 kbps would be wasted. I personally use VBR set to normal/high for home listening and VBR set to low for portable players. MusicMatch and RealJukebox both allow you to easily convert your MP3 files to a lower rate for use with a portable player.

Table 25 shows how many four-minute songs would fit on various types of media at different bit-rates.

Table 25 - Bit-rates vs. Capacity of Common Storage Media

Bit-rate	4-min. Songs/ 32MB RAM	4-min. Songs/ 64MB RAM	4-min. Songs/ CD (650MB)	Hours/CD (650MB)	4-min. Songs/ Gigabyte
64 kbps	17	34	355	24	546
80 kbps	14	28	284	19	437
96 kbps	11	22	237	16	364
128 kbps	9	18	177	12	273
160 kbps	7	14	142	9	218
192 kbps	6	12	118	8	182
256 kbps	4	8	89	6	137

Some programs can export the files listed in a playlist to a portable player in one batch process. MusicMatch can export playlists to the Rio and has an option to convert the files to a lower bit-rate before they are exported. This feature is handy because you don't have to maintain two versions of the same song at different bit-rates.

Verifying the Results

It's important to listen to the first couple of songs after they are encoded before you take the time to process your entire music collection. If the MP3 file doesn't sound right, rip the same track to a WAV file and listen to it. If the WAV file sounds okay, the problem most likely happened during the encoding process. If the WAV file sounds funny, then you may need to adjust the jitter correction settings in the ripping software.

A/B Comparisons

The best way compare sound quality of the original and the encoded file is to do an A/B comparison, where you can play both simultaneously, and quickly switch back and forth.

An A/B comparison between a computer and external stereo system works well because you can sync up the two sources and rapidly switch back and forth. This is important because the "acoustic memory" of most people is very short lived—especially for subtle differences in sound. Another good test is to compare the sound of the WAV file to the MP3 file and switch back and forth by using two instances of Winamp or one of the DJ mixer programs listed in Chapter 7, *Choosing the Right Software*.

Some inexpensive CD-ROM drives use poor quality D/A converters and can cause a CD to actually sound worse than MP3 files encoded from it. If the source is a CD, it's best to play it on an audio CD player and listen to it and the MP3 file through a good set of headphones or stereo speakers, and use an A/B switch to change between the two sources.

Table 26 lists a few of the more popular MP3 encoders. Check out the MP3 sites listed in Appendix A, *Interesting Web Sites*, for information on other encoders.

Table 26 - MP3 Encoders

Encoder	Developer	Web Site
BladeEnc	Tord Janssen	www.bladeenc.mp3.no
MP3 Producer	Fraunhofer/Opticom	www.opticom.de
MPecker (Mac)	Rafael Luebbert	www.anime.net/~go/mpeckers.html
Lame	N/A (Open-Source)	www.sulaco.org/mp3
Xing	Xing Technologies	www.xingtech.com

Chapter 17

Editing Sound Files

Some WAV files will benefit from a bit of clean-up before they are encoded. The most common forms of clean-up are trimming silence from the ends of songs, removing unwanted noise and normalizing the volume so all songs will play at similar levels. More sophisticated users may want to add fades, equalization or dynamic range compression. These effects change the nature of the music, so they should be used sparingly unless you are mixing a recording of your own music.

Files must be uncompressed (PCM WAV or AIFF format) before they can be edited. If the song is already in MP3 format, you can convert it to WAV format, edit it, and then convert it back to MP3. Each time you do this you will lose fidelity. Files encoded at higher (192 kbps+) bit-rates will lose less fidelity during the decoding/re-encoding cycle than those encoded at lower bit-rates.

Note: A few programs, such as MP3 Trim, allow you to edit MP3 files directly. These programs are typically limited to just trimming silence and normalizing the volume.

Sound Editing Software

Cool Edit and Sound Forge are popular programs that can record and edit sound files. Both programs are available in professional and "lite" versions. The lite versions include the basic features for trimming silence, adding fades, normalizing the volume and removing noise. The professional versions offer high-end capabilities for recording engineers and are overkill for most users.

AudioCatalyst and MusicMatch can normalize the volume automatically when the file is ripped. AudioCatalyst can also automatically trim silence from the ends of each track, and MusicMatch can automatically apply fade-ins and fade-outs. For more extensive editing, you should use specialized sound editing software, such as CoolEdit or Sound Forge.

Normalization

Many CDs do not use the full 96 dB dynamic range that's available. This can result in songs from some CDs playing much louder than others, even at the same volume setting. Normalization corrects this by scanning the uncompressed audio file to determine the peak or average level and proportionally increasing or reducing the levels throughout the file to obtain the desired volume level.

Prerecorded CDs that were digitally remastered from analog tapes are more likely to require normalization than CDs that were originally digitally mastered, but there is no hard and fast rule. Normalization is often needed for WAV files created from records and tapes.

Some rippers and most sound editing programs include a normalization feature. The Audiograbber ripper has the most flexible normalization feature of all the programs I've used, although some people might find it too complicated. The normalization features in Sound Forge XP and Cool Edit 2000 are very basic and require working with each file individually. The professional versions of Sound Forge and Cool Edit are much better, but they are expensive and neither is as flexible as Audiograbber.

AudioCatalyst, which is based on Audiograbber, has a simple normalization feature that allows you to normalize all files to a set level, or to normalize only the files where the peak level is lower or higher than the thresholds you specify. MusicMatch Version 4 has a very limited normalization feature that adjusts all tracks to a single level.

Most normalizers allow you to specify a percentage of the maximum possible level for the highest peak. The maximum level may be referred to as 1, 100% or 0 dB, depending on the software. A setting of 50% (or .5) would be the same as -6 dB, because each doubling or halving of the signal level represents a change of 6 dB. A value of 100% (0 dB) will normalize the volume so it covers the full dynamic range, so the highest peak will be at the maximum level. Values above 100% should not be used because this will cause clipping wherever the level exceeds 0 dB.

Generally, all songs on a prerecorded CD will be recorded at about the same level, so you can assume that if the level needs to be adjusted for one song, the same adjustment will be needed for all the songs.

Normalization Settings in AudioCatalyst

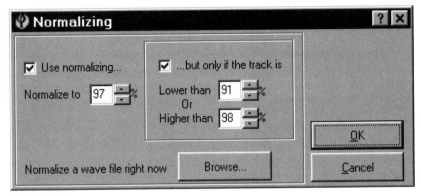

If you have a CD collection that contains a variety of music, there's a good chance that some songs will sound louder than others even when normalized to the same level. This occurs because the average volume may be different even though the peak levels are similar. Other factors such as differences in frequency content (especially with higher frequencies) and recorded distortion (electric guitar effects, synthesizers, etc.) will affect the apparent loudness of a song.

Listening is the best way to judge the appropriate level, but it takes time to listen to every song and normalize each one individually. An approach that works for most CDs is to normalize all songs lower than 91% or higher than 98% to a 97% level. Table 27 shows the results of normalizing four songs using these settings.

Table 27 - Results of Normalization

	Old Peak Level	New Peak Level
Song 1	96	Unchanged
Song 2	85	97
Song 3	100	97
Song 4	93	Unchanged

If you want more control over normalization, Audiograbber provides advanced settings based on either average or peak levels, along with an option for dynamic range compression. Normalizing based on average levels will make the playback levels more consistent. However, raising the average level can easily cause clipping.

Audiograbber can be set to automatically apply dynamic range compression all of the time, or only when it's needed to avoid clipping. Audiograbber can also be set to not compress songs that are already highly compressed. (See Chapter 11, *A Digital Audio Primer*, for an explanation of the difference between dynamic range compression and "compaction" type compression.)

If you have MP3 files that have not been normalized, you can use a player like Winamp and a plug-in like AudioStocker or RockSteady. These plug-ins adjust the level automatically for each song when it's is played. It's still better to normalize the WAV file before you encode it, because most portable and dual/mode CD players can't compensate for individual songs recorded at different levels.

Transitions Between Songs

Professional DJs and anyone who records tapes for their own listening pleasure understand the importance of having a smooth flow of music. Playlists eliminate the need to swap records and CDs, but the problem of transitions between songs still exists.

Transitions between some types of songs need to be handled differently. For background music it's OK to have a few seconds of silence between songs, but for dance music it's usually better to crossfade between songs with no silence in between.

Trimming Silence

Many songs have a few seconds of silence at either end. Trimming off this silence will make the files smaller and allow for a more continuous flow of music. In most cases, you should leave anywhere from ¼ to ½ second of silence at the end of each song, unless you are making a continuous mix of dance music, in which case you'll want no silence.

Many songs have excessively long intros or trailing sections of music or vocals that can be removed. If you remove one of these sections you should add a fade-in or fade-out so the song does not start or stop abruptly.

Fades

It usually sounds bad to have one song end abruptly and the next one start immediately, except for dance mixes where the songs have the same number of beats per minute. Fade-ins and fade-outs can be applied to the ends of the songs to provide a smoother transition, similar to the way a DJ would use a mixer with a crossfade control.

DC Bias

A condition known as DC offset (also called DC bias) can occur in sound files that were recorded with improperly grounded sound cards. This problem is more common with low-end sound cards. DC offset forces the baseline of the audio signal to be offset from the centerline. You can determine if this is a problem on your system by recording a few seconds of silence and zooming in on the signal and checking to see if it's centered. Most sound editing programs have filters that can fix this condition. Cool Edit's normalization function can also be used to correct a DC offset.

Fades can be created with sound editing programs, but it's important to remember that these will be permanently stored in the file. There are several crossfade plug-ins for Sonique and Winamp that work without modifying the file. This approach works well if you play most of your music on a computer, but if you use a portable or dual-mode CD player, you would need to create the fades by editing the WAV files. (See the tutorial for Cool Edit in Chapter 20, for instructions on trimming silence and adding fades to a WAV file.)

Playing a song that slowly fades in immediately after a song that slowly fades out may result in too long of a lull in the music. One way to avoid the lull is to steepen the fade-in and fade-out slopes. Most editors give you several ways to control the "envelope" of the slope. Usually, you select the section of the file where the fade is needed, then graphically adjust the slope of the fade, or specify the starting and ending volume levels. Many sound editors include preset fade envelopes and the ability to save custom envelopes.

Another approach to crossfading would be to play the music using Winamp with a cross-fade plug-in and record the output using Cool Edit; or use Winamp with the Nullsoft Disk Writer plug-in and save the output directly to a WAV file. You could then break the WAV file into the individual songs at the transition points. This approach also works great if you want to record pre-crossfaded music to a cassette tape or even a CD-R.

If you splice files together to make a continuous dance mix, you may have a hard time getting the beats to match exactly. One way around this is to use a sound editor to reduce or increase the tempo of one file to match the other and then splice them together so the beats match. The tempo adjustment feature stretches or compresses the length of a song, which effectively changes the tempo. DJ mixer programs like PC-DJ by VisioSonic have built-in features for matching tempos of songs.

Optimizing Audio for the Web

Sound editing software can also be used to convert digital audio to different formats and to optimize audio files for use on the Web as downloadable music or streaming audio.

Internet access is slow for many people. Currently, most people connect to the Internet via a 33.6 kbps or slower analog modem. Even with a 56k modem, users are lucky to achieve connection speeds of more than 48 kbps. If you want the broadest possible audience for your Web site, it's best to assume a "lowest common denominator" connection speed of 28.8 kbps.

Downloadable Formats

Compressed formats like MP3 are a good choice for just about any type of downloadable music. Uncompressed formats can be used for very short clips but should not be used for full-length songs. The advantage of using an uncompressed format like PCM Wave is that most Web browsers will be able to play it without special software.

You can choose from many different formats when adding downloadable music to your Web site, but you should stick with popular formats as much as possible. Otherwise, you risk losing users who may not want to install yet another player to support some proprietary format. Table 28 lists some of the more common formats for downloadable music.

Small Is Beautiful

Your goal with Web audio is to create the highest quality sound file, at the smallest possible size, in the most commonly readable format. You can reduce file sizes (and bandwidth requirements) of both compressed and

Table 28 - Common Downloadable Music Formats

Type	Extensions	Format
MP3	.mp3	MPEG Audio Layer-III
Windows Media Audio	.wma	Proprietary (Microsoft)
QuickTime	.qt	Proprietary (Apple Computer)
RealAudio	.ra, .ram	Proprietary (Real Networks)
WAV	.wav	PCM*

*WAV files can use other formats besides PCM.

194

uncompressed audio. Even if you plan on using a compressed format like MP3, it still makes sense to tweak the uncompressed audio file to make it smaller before it is encoded. This will result in a smaller encoded file as well.

The type of material and desired sound quality are the two main factors to consider in optimizing an audio file. For example, for sound effects and voice, the sampling rate (which determines the frequency response) and resolution don't need to be as high as required for music. Table 29 shows different combinations of sampling rates, resolution and channels that are appropriate for various types of uncompressed audio.

Stereo or Mono?

Is stereo necessary for the type of audio you are using? Certainly it is, if you are working with CD-quality music. For short clips and voice, using mono will cut the file size in half. Mono is also fine for many sound effects and background music.

16 Bits or 8 Bits?

You can reduce the resolution from 16 to 8 bits and cut the file size in half again, but the signal will have more distortion from quantization errors (because it cannot be recorded as precisely with fewer bits). The difference between 8-bit and 16-bit resolution will be more noticeable in complex music with a wide dynamic range. For voice and sound effects, 8-bit resolution is usually adequate.

Sampling Rate

CD audio is sampled at 44.1 kHz and can reproduce frequencies up to 20 kHz. Most people can't hear frequencies above 16 kHz. For music on the

Table 29 - Web Audio Optimization

Type of Audio	Sampling Rate	Resolution	Channels	File Size of 1-Minute Clip
CD Quality	44.1 kHz	16 Bits	Stereo	10.3MB
Music Clips	22.5 kHz	16 Bits	Mono	2.5MB
Sound Effects	22.5 kHz	8 Bits	Mono	1.25MB
Voice	11.25 kHz	8 Bits	Mono	630KB

Web, you could use a sampling rate of 22.5 kHz, and many people will not notice any difference when using typical computer speakers. For higher quality music, a 32 kHz sampling rate can be used in place of 44.1 kHz and many people will not be able to tell the difference, even with a good speaker system. For voice, you can reduce the sampling rate to 11.25 kHz and it will usually sound fine.

Streaming Audio

Streaming audio is optimized by the streaming server and is usually compressed to deliver a higher bit-rate over slow Internet connections. Some streaming systems, such as RealNetwork's SureStream technology, automatically optimize the bit-rate of each stream to the speed of the user's connection. Other systems may need to use a different streaming server for each bit-rate.

For streaming audio to work well, the speed of your Internet connection must be greater than the bit-rate of the sound file. The Internet is designed to send data in scattered bursts. Good audio playback requires audio data to be delivered continuously, at a constant rate.

To allow for network congestion, the bit-rate should be no more than two thirds the available bandwidth. For instance, 128 kbps is considered the minimum bit-rate for good quality MP3 files, but this is much higher than the bandwidth that any analog modem can deliver. A bit-rate of 15 to 20 Kbps would be more appropriate for a 28.8 or 33.6 modem.

To listen to streaming audio at 128 Kbps, even a dual channel ISDN connection would be just barely enough. A higher speed connection like a cable modem or an ADSL (Asynchronous Digital Subscriber Line) connection would be required.

Table 30 - Streaming Media Systems

Type	Primary Format	Developer
Windows Media Technologies	Active Streaming Format (ASF)	Microsoft
Icecast (open source)	MP3	The Icecast Team
QuickTime	QuickTime	Apple Computer
RealSystem	RealAudio	RealNetworks
SHOUTcast	MP3	Nullsoft

> ### Modem Speed
>
> A modem's speed does not equal how fast you can move data over the Internet. Some of the capacity is used by communications overhead and error correction. Variable telephone line quality also has a big impact on actual upload and download speeds. It's not unusual to achieve speeds of less than 80 percent of an analog modem's rated capacity. High-speed connection technologies like ISDN and ASDL can operate closer to their rated speeds because they have much less overhead than analog modems.

For short promotional clips of music, you should consider offering more than one format so your site will appeal to a wider group of users. It is becoming more common to find sites offering audio clips in multiple formats, such as WMA, RealAudio and streaming MP3.

The major streaming media systems support multiple formats, including MP3. But if you only offer streaming audio in a proprietary format like RealAudio or ASF, you risk losing users who may prefer to use a player like Winamp to listen to streaming audio. Table 30 lists some of the more common streaming media systems.

For more information on integrating audio into a Web site check out the book *Audio on the Web* by Jeff Patterson and Ryan Melcher, listed in Appendix C, *Recommended Reading*.

Sound Editing Utilities

Following are descriptions of several programs for directly editing MP3 files, processing WAV files and creating HTML interfaces for MP3 CDs.

MP3Cutter

MP3Cutter (*http://members.xoom.com/videoripper/mp3cutter*) by the VideoRipper is freeware that allows you to cut, paste and splice sections of MP3 files, and edit ID3 tags. A special function can split MP3 files into equal size parts and remove unnecessary information (WAV headers, etc.) from the file.

MP3 Trim and Wave Trim

MP3 Trim and Wave Trim (*www.logiccell.com/~mp3trim*) by Jean Nicolle are handy for editing large batches of MP3 and WAV files. Both programs are available in shareware and professional versions.

MP3 Trim allows you to edit MP3 files without decoding them to WAV format. It can detect and remove digital silence and truncated frames to recover wasted space. Without MP3 Trim, you would have to decode the MP3 file to WAV format, trim the silence with a program like CoolEdit, and then convert it back to MP3.

Wave Trim scans the first and last 10 seconds of a WAV file and removes the digital silence and any bits of audio left over from other tracks. Wave Trim also can normalize the volume, and accept command-line parameters for batch processing. Batch processing allows you to process a lot of songs without opening and editing individual WAV files.

Audio Prepare

MP3 Prepare (*http://aryhma.pspt.fi/audioprepare*) is a program for making HTML-based user interfaces for MP3 CDs It can automatically create an HTML page that lists all albums on the CD and a playlist that includes all the songs. MP3 Prepare can also create separate HTML pages for each album, and include cover art, song titles and play times. MP3 Prepare features a range of fully customizable graphics and HTML templates, and includes MP3 Browser, which is an Explorer-like interface for browsing MP3 files on your hard disk. MP3 Browser can also display and edit ID3 information and generate playlists.

Ray Gun

Ray Gun from Arboretum Systems (*www.arboretum.com*) is a shareware program for removing noise from WAV files and adjusting signal levels. It can also be used to record audio. Ray Gun is available in both Windows and Macintosh versions and can be used as a plug-in for recording programs like CoolEdit and Sound Forge that support DirectX.

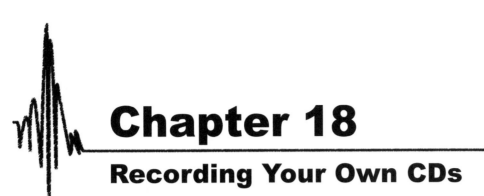

Chapter 18

Recording Your Own CDs

It's great to have hundreds of hours of music stored on your PC, but how do you take all that music on a trip? And what happens if the 17 gigabyte hard drive holding your entire MP3 collection crashes? You could use a tape drive to backup your MP3 files and make them portable, but tape is a linear media—which is very slow for accessing individual files. A better solution is to use a CD Recorder and "burn" your own CDs.

CDs are a good solution for storing MP3 files and backing-up moderate amounts of data. CDs are more portable than tapes and support random access, so any file can be accessed quickly regardless of where it's located on the CD. Another advantage is that CDs can be read by virtually any CD-ROM drive, unlike tapes, which come in dozens of incompatible formats.

A popular use of CD recorders is to record audio CDs with compilations of songs from different albums. CD-R's are much cheaper than blank cassette tapes and it only takes about 20 minutes to record an hour of music with a 4X CD-R drive, compared to a minimum of one hour for a cassette tape.

CD Construction

Prerecorded CDs are created by a pressing process similar to the process used to create vinyl records. A pattern of pits and lands (raised areas) that correspond to the 1s and 0s of binary data is pressed into the disc. The difference in reflectivity between the pits and the lands is sensed by the laser in the audio CD player or CD-ROM drive and converted to a digital signal.

Recordable CDs

Recordable CDs (CD-Rs) are "burned" with a CD recorder (also called a CD writer). A blank CD-R disc contains a pre-grooved spiral track that guides the recorder's laser as it burns a microscopic series of holes called pits in a layer of organic dye. The pattern of pits and lands (the unburned part) encodes the information in the same manner as the pattern stamped on a prerecorded CD. Once recorded, data on a CD-R disc can't be erased.

Figure 37 - CD-R Construction

Label (optional)
Scratch-resistant or printable coating (optional)
UV-cured lacquer
Reflective layer of 24K gold or silver colored alloy
Recording layer
Clear plastic polycarbonate substrate

Rewritable CDs

Rewritable CDs (CD-RWs) are similar to CD-Rs but can be erased and re-recorded thousands of times. Most audio CD players and many older CD-ROM drives can't read CD-RWs. This is because the amount of laser light reflected from the recording layer of a CD-RW is much lower than that of a CD-R.

Instead of burning a pit in the recording layer like a CD-R, the recording laser in a CD-RW recorder causes a phase change (from crystalline to amorphous state) in the recording layer. The different states act as the pits and lands do on a CD-R disc and are detected by the difference in the way they refract light.

CD-RW drives cost slightly more than CD-R drives but can also burn CD-R discs. As of this writing, you can purchase a 4X CD-R drive for under $100 and a 2X CD-RW drive for under $150.

Figure 38 - CD-RW Construction

Label (optional)
Scratch-resistant or printable coating (optional)
UV-cured lacquer
Reflective layer
Upper dielectric layer
Recording layer
Lower dielectric layer
Clear plastic polycarbonate substrate

CD Recorders

CDs can be created on computers with CD-R or CD-RW drives, on dedicated CD recorders that are designed to work with home audio equipment, and with stand-alone recorders designed for mass duplication. CD-R and CD-RW drives used with computers can also function as CD-ROM drives, although they tend to be slower because of the heavier laser mechanism required for recording.

> **Why Record Your Own CDs?**
>
> CD recording is a convenient way to create standard audio CDs or MP3 CDs with custom mixes of music. If you're in a band, CD recorders provide a low-cost way to create demo CDs of your songs.

Write Speeds

The write speed of a CD recorder determines the time it will take to record a CD. Write speeds are measured in the same "X" units (2X, 4X, 8X, etc.) that are used to measure a CD-ROM drive's read speeds.

The combined read/write speed of CD-R recorders is specified by the read speed, followed by the write speed, for example, 12X/4X. CD-RW recorders often have different write speeds for CD-RW and CD-R discs. The speed of a CD-RW drive is specified by [CD-ROM read speed]/[CD-R write speed]/[CD-RW write speed], for example, 20X/4X/2X.

Recording a full audio CD at 1X speed takes at least 74 minutes plus the time required to locate files on the hard drive and about 2 minutes to write the table of contents. Recording a CD at 2X takes at least 37 minutes, 4X takes at least 18 minutes, and 8X takes at least 9 minutes.

CD Standards and File Systems

Standards define the way different types of information, such as audio, video or data, are stored on a CD. Currently, there are more than 10 different standards for CDs. Many of these, such as CD-I (Compact Disc-Interactive), were designed for use with proprietary players that combined audio and text or graphics data, and never caught on. The three main formats currently used for audio and data CDs are named for the color of the standards books that describe them.

Red Book Audio

The *Red Book* standard was the original format developed for storing music on CDs. This standard is also referred to as CD-DA (Compact Disc-Digital Audio). Audio CDs have the advantage of being playable almost anywhere, though the capacity is limited to 74 minutes of music (approximately 18 four-minute songs).

Most audio CDs contain only the digital data for the music, plus a table of contents (TOC) with the track numbers and the starting position and lengths of each track. The TOC does not contain any information about the artist, album or song titles, although this information can be obtained from the CDDB. (See Chapter 9, *Organizing and Playing Music*.) Some newer audio CDs support the CD Text extension to the Red Book format, which allows information, such as song titles and artists names to be stored on the CD, although many CD players are not capable of reading this information.

Data CDs

The Yellow Book standard defines how data is stored on prerecorded CD-ROMS. The *Orange Book* standard is similar to the *Yellow Book* and defines the format for CD-Rs and CD-RWs. MP3 files and other compressed audio formats are simply data files, so they are stored on *Yellow Book* (pre-recorded) or *Orange Book* (CD-R and CD-RW) CDs.

Data CDs are limited to 650MB, due to the overhead of increased error correction. When used with a compressed format such as MP3, data CDs can hold many times more audio than *Red Book* CDs. These MP3/data CDs can only be played on PCs with CD-ROM drives or special dual-mode CD players with built-in MP3 decoders, such as the AudioReQuest (see Chapter 8, *Choosing the Right Hardware*).

CD File Systems

File systems describe how data files are stored and retrieved by different computer operating systems. The most common CD file systems are ISO-9660, Joliet, and HFS. ISO-9660 only supports file names up to eight characters long, plus an optional one to three character extension (filename.ext). ISO-9660 can be read by computers running DOS, Macintosh, OS-2, UNIX and all versions of Windows. Joliet (developed by Microsoft) supports file names up to 64 characters, but is only supported by Windows 95/98/NT and recent versions of Linux. HFS is only supported by the Macintosh.

Table 31 - Common CD Standards and File Systems

Standard	File System	Capacity	Systems	Long File Names
Red Book	Audio (CD-DA)	74 min	Audio Players	N/A
Yellow/Orange Book	ISO-9660	650MB	PC, Mac, UNIX	No
Yellow/Orange Book	Joliet	650MB	Windows	Yes
Yellow/Orange Book	HFS	650MB	Mac	Yes

A number of other CD-ROM and file systems standards exist that are beyond the scope of this book. For more information, consult the resources listed at the end of this chapter.

CD Media

Blank CD-R and CD-RW discs are available from many different manufacturers. Depending on the type of dye and reflecting layer, each brand will be some combination of gold, silver, green and blue. Different brands are certified for 2X, 4X and 8X recording.

Many CD recorders will work better with some brands of media than others, and some audio CD players and CD-ROM drives will read some brands but not others. It's a good idea to try several brands in both your recorder and player before buying large quantities.

Both CD-R and CD-RW discs are more sensitive to heat, humidity and direct sunlight than pre-recorded CDs, so don't leave them in a hot car. The data on any type of CD is closer to the metal side of a CD than the plastic side, so be careful when labeling not to scratch it. Use a permanent felt-tipped pen or a circular CD label to avoid damaging the CD.

A good product for removing scratches from CDs is Wipeout (*www.cdrepair.com*). If the CD is scratched but sounds OK, the error correction is working. Be careful when polishing a CD, because polishing can actually introduce more errors if performed improperly.

Media Cost

CD-RW discs are more expensive than CD-R discs, but not by much if you shop around. CD-R discs can be purchased for anywhere from 25 cents to $2 each, and CD-RW discs can be purchased for anywhere from $1.50 to $7.50. Prices vary widely depending on the quality, quantity and whether or not jewel cases are included. Higher cost does not necessarily equate with higher quality. I've had just as good luck with lower-cost brands as I've had with more expensive brands.

Audio vs. Data CD-R Media

Two kinds of blank CD-R media are available. One type is intended for data, the other for audio. The discs for audio cost more than discs for data. The Audio Home Recording Act specifies that royalties must be paid on blank CDs marketed for home audio recording. These royalties are placed into a pool to compensate for the loss of royalties from illegal CD duplicating.

Many standalone CD recorders check for a special code present on blank audio CDs and will refuse to work with data CDs. CD recorders used on PCs aren't required to look for this special code and can use the lower cost data CDs for audio as well as data. Blank CD-R discs labeled for audio usually cost $4 or more each.

CD Recording Software

Two types of programs can be used to record CDs: stand-alone programs, such as Adaptec's Easy CD Creator (for PCs) or Toast (for Macs), and packet writing programs, such as Adaptec's Direct CD program. Many all-in-one programs, such as EarJam and MusicMatch, support burning CDs directly from the MP3 files contained in a playlist.

With stand-alone CD recording software, all setup, layout creation and recording is done through the program's interface. Packet writing software is more like a driver that makes your CD recorder act like a floppy drive. This allows you to copy files or drag and drop them to the drive from Windows Explorer or Finder (Mac).

A packet-written disc can only be read on the system on which it was created until it is finalized. Even then, some CD-ROM drives have problems reading packet-written discs. Packet writing can waste up to several hundred MB of the capacity of a disc, and is most useful with CD-RW discs used for data backup.

Before You Record

Successfully recording a CD requires a constant, uninterrupted stream of high-speed data. CD recording software places the data to be written in a small area of memory called a buffer. The CD recorder can draw data from this buffer at a constant rate while the software is busy reading files from the hard drive.

Mouse movement, network and Internet activity, virus scanners, screen savers, or anything that requires the processor's attention can interfere with keeping the buffer full of data. A buffer underrun occurs if the CD recorder empties the buffer before it's finished writing a track. This ruins the disc, creating what is called a "coaster." A smoothly running system is essential to keeping the buffer filled.

Update Your Software, Drivers and Firmware

Check the Web site of the manufacturer of your CD recording software for downloadable updates or patches. A patch contains only changes to the software and will update the software without the need to reinstall it.

Also check the Web site of the manufacturer of your CD recorder to make sure you have the latest firmware. Firmware is the internal program that controls the CD recorder hardware. You'll need a special program and instructions on how to upload the firmware to the recorder. If you have a SCSI CD recorder, check the Web site of the manufacturer of your SCSI controller to make sure you have the most current drivers.

Stabilize Your System

Before you attempt to record a CD, clean up your system by following the steps listed below.

- Delete any unnecessary files, empty the recycle bin and defragment (defrag) your hard disk. Also, make sure you have plenty of free space on your hard disk for temporary files.

- Disable auto insert notification for your CD recorder by right clicking on it in the Windows Device Manager, under the CDROM folder, and then clear the check box for Auto Insert Notification under the settings tab. (See Chapter 15, *Digital Audio Extraction*, for instructions on disabling auto insert notification.)

- Exit all other programs and disable virus scanners and screen savers. Remove any non-essential programs from your Startup folder, and restart your computer.

If you performed the steps listed above and still have trouble recording, you may need to disable other programs or background processes. If you have a network card, you may need to temporarily disable it in the Windows Device Manager (see the Easy CD Creator tutorial in Chapter 20, *Software Tutorials*).

To see if any other programs are running in the background, press **Ctrl-Alt-Del** to start the Task Manager. If any programs other than Explorer and Systray are listed, you can terminate them by highlighting each one and selecting **End Task.** (You may need to do this twice for some programs.) You can also disable these programs using the Msconfig program that is included with Windows 98.

Test Your Hardware

After installing the CD recording software, be sure to run the system tests to characterize the performance of your hard disk and CD recorder. This helps the software optimize the data flow from the hard disk to the CD writer and determines the maximum write speed.

Recording Options

The following examples are taken from Adaptec's Easy CD Creator program. Although the information applies to all CD recording software, some of the terms may vary. (See the Easy CD Creator tutorial in Chapter 20 for step-by-step instructions on burning a CD.)

A layout describes which data or audio tracks are to be recorded on the blank CD, and in what order. When you start recording, the recording software searches your hard drive and reads the data as it is writing to the CD. This only requires a small (less than 50MB) amount of temporary space on your hard drive but can cause problems if your hard drive is slow or fragmented.

An image file contains all of the data that will be recorded on the CD, exactly as it will be written, in one large file. This makes for more reliable recording, especially at high speeds, but requires as much free space on your hard drive as the CD you are recording (up to 750MB). Using an image file can significantly increase your success in creating CDs, especially at higher speeds.

To make an image file, create your layout and select **Create CD Image File** rather than **Record CD.** Although this adds an extra step, the extra time is minimal because the data files specified in the layout have to be read anyway. If you create multiple copies from an image file, the overall time will be less because the second and subsequent copies don't have the overhead of gathering the data.

Multi-Session CDs

CDs can be multi-session, which allows you to mix audio and data on the same CD. This way you can have the CD audio and MP3 versions of your songs on the same CD. The audio tracks must be stored in the first session. To allow this, choose **Close Session and Leave Disc Open** when recording. Then you can record a second session with MP3 files.

You can record more than one data session on a CD, but normally you can view only the files added in the last session, unless you specifically select another session to be active. A better way to access data recorded in multiple sessions is to import the previous session into each new session when recording. To do this, right-click on the icon for the CD in the lower-left quadrant of the Data CD Layout screen and select **Properties**. In the **Data Settings** tab of the CD Layout Properties screen, select **Automatically import previous session**. To finalize a CD, choose **Close Disc** when you record the last session.

Be aware that making a multi-session disc takes about 23MB extra for the first session, and 16MB for each additional session. Take this into account when calculating how many files you'll be able to fit on a CD.

Track-at-Once vs. Disc-at-Once Recording

Track-at-once allows the CD recorder to write one track at a time and turn off its laser while reading data for the next track. This allows the recording software as much time as it needs to read the data for the next track and can be more forgiving than disc-at-once recording. When recording audio CDs, track-at-once places a two second gap between each song.

Disc-at-once keeps the laser on for the entire recording and eliminates the requirement for the two second gap between audio tracks. Disc-at-once is also more demanding of your system because of the need for uninterrupted data. Some plants that perform CD duplication services require disc-at-once masters.

Test Writes

Most CD recording software can perform a test write to determine if the recording process is likely to succeed. This test goes through the entire process of locating, reading and sending data to the CD recorder, with the recording laser turned off. A test write takes the same amount of time as actually recording the disc. If the test write fails, you can troubleshoot the problem without wasting a disc.

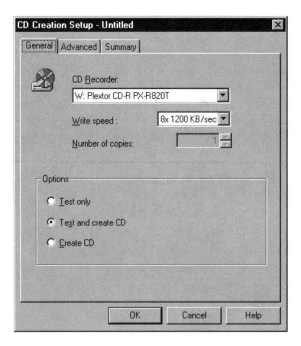

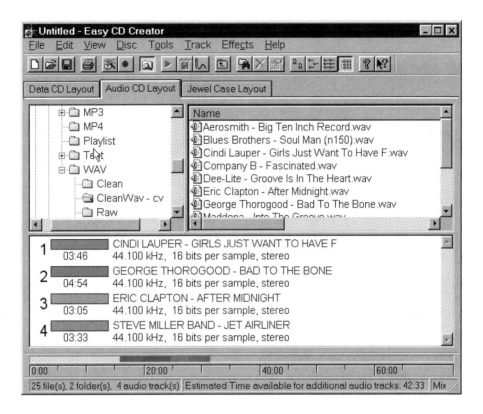

It's a good idea to do a test write the first few times you record, especially at higher recording speeds. Prior to recording, you'll usually have a choice of **Test Only**, **Test and Create**, and **Create**. Test and Create will automatically start recording the CD if the test phase is successful. Later, you can select **Create** when you are sure of your system's performance.

Recording Audio CDs

If you want to play your custom CD in a standard audio CD player, you must create a Red Book format CD. Each song needs to be in a 16-bit, stereo, 44.1 kHz uncompressed WAV format. If you only have MP3 files, many programs, such as MusicMatch and Winamp, have an option to decode them into WAV files (see the MusicMatch and Winamp tutorials in Chapter 20).

Don't Touch

Once you start recording, don't touch your system or attempt to run any other programs. This is a good time to take a break and get away from your computer.

Once you have the songs in WAV format, select the Audio tab of the CD layout. Browse for the WAV files in the upper pane of the window, then drag and drop them on to the lower pane. After you have added all of the files, you can rename or reorder them. Make sure to select the option to close the session or to close the disc. Otherwise, the CD will only be playable in the CD recorder and not in audio CD players.

Figure 39 - Recording Audio CDs from MP3 Files

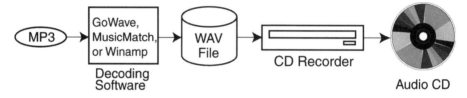

Recording MP3 CDs

MP3 files are just data files as far as a CD recorder is concerned, so you will need to record them to a data format CD. Before you record the CD, your songs must already be encoded as MP3 files. (See Chapter 16, *Making Your Own MP3 Files*.)

To begin, select the **Data** tab of the CD layout window, then select **File**, then **CD Layout Properties**, then select the **Data Settings** tab. If the CD will only be used on Windows 95/98/NT machines, choose the Joliet format to allow long filenames. If you want to use the CD on a Mac or other system, choose the ISO-9660 format.

Figure 40 - Recording MP3 CDs

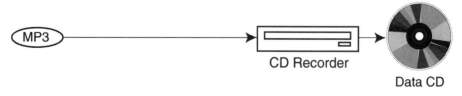

MP3 CDs and Standard Audio CD Players

Audio CD players can't play CDs with MP3 files. If you want to play music on one of these, you'll need to convert your MP3 files to WAV format and create a Red Book audio CD. Another option is to purchase a dual-mode MP3/audio CD player like the AudioReQuest.

If you choose the ISO-9660 format and you have used any long filenames for your MP3 files, the CD recording software will truncate the names to conform to the 8+3 character limitation of ISO-9660. Sometimes this creates names that are difficult to decipher. To avoid this problem, rename the files before burning the CD.

Add your MP3 files using the explorer-like interface by dragging and dropping them into the lower pane of the window. Rename and reorder the files as needed, and click on the **Record** button. Since these are data CDs, you don't need to close the CD to use it. On the **Advanced** tab of the CD Creation Setup screen, choose **Close Session and Leave Disc Open** if you want to add more files later. Otherwise, choose **Close Disc** to finalize the CD.

Duplicating CDs

There are varying opinions on the legality of making CD-R copies of prere-corded music. The RIAA maintains that it's illegal to burn copies of a prere-corded CD, even for your own noncommercial use. However, the Doctrine of Fair Use (see Chapter 5, *Digital Music and Copyright Law*) can be inter-preted as to allow it. In any case, it's illegal to sell or give away CDs contain-ing copyrighted material without authorization.

The Adaptec Easy CD Creator program includes a utility called *CD Copier Deluxe* for duplicating an entire CD. The files or audio tracks are read the same as if you were creating a CD layout manually. This requires a large amount of temporary file space on your hard drive and may not work with some CDs.

If you have a Plextor drive, you can use the Discdupe utility to quickly copy CDs. Discdupe copies the entire CD "bit by bit" and can duplicate any type of CD, even non-PC formats. If your system is fast enough, the "on the fly" option doesn't require much hard disk space and works faster. This option is more sensitive other processes running at the same time, so avoid the tempta-tion to do anything else on the system while the CD is recording.

Additional Resources

Web Sites

Organization	URL
CD Media World	*www.cdmediaworld.com*
Andy McFadden's CD-Recordable FAQ	*www.fadden.com/cdrfaq*

Books

Title	Date	Author	ISBN
The Compact Disc Handbook, 2nd edition	1992	Ken Pohlmann	0-89579-300-8

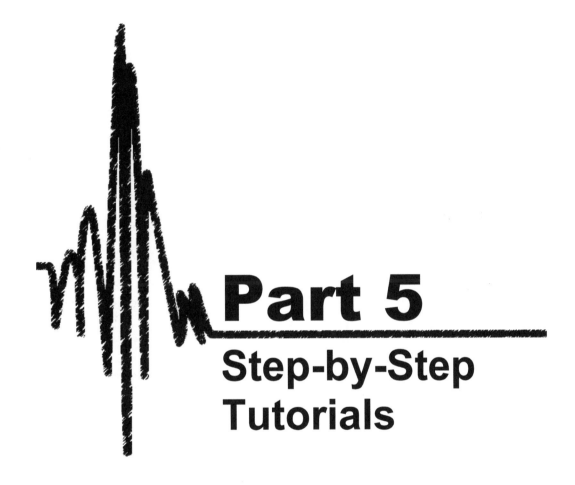

Part 5

Step-by-Step
Tutorials

Chapter 19

Basic Tasks

Installing Software

Software can be downloaded and installed in several different ways, depending on the program. Often this is a multi-step process where you first must download a file, then execute it to run a setup program.

Have a Good Backup

The most important thing to remember before installing any new software is to have a complete backup of your system in case anything goes wrong.

It is not uncommon for a system that is functioning perfectly fine to become unstable and develop all sorts of problems after new software is installed. One reason for this is that many programs rely on shared files, and often installation programs will replace some of these files with different versions that are not compatible with the existing software.

The best type of backup is a disk image on a CD or another hard disk partition. This is generally better than a tape backup because it restores your system exactly the way it was, eliminating the need to reinstall the operating system and other software or data.

Most CD-R drives include backup software that can be used in this manner. I use a product by PowerQuest called Drive Image for this purpose because it can create the image file on any type of media: CDs, hard disks, Zip disks, etc.

Downloading Software

To download a program, point your Internet browser to the Web site and find the download link for the file. Right-click on the link and choose **Save Target As** in the dialogue box that appears. You then need to specify the folder where you want the file to be stored. If you click on the download link instead of right-clicking, the file may automatically download to a temporary folder, or you may have to specify the folder, depending on how the link is defined and your system configuration.

Once you install a downloaded program, you can delete the installation files from the download directory. Some people prefer to keep the downloaded install files so they can avoid downloading them again in case they need to reinstall the program.

It's a good idea to create a separate download directory on your hard disk with subdirectories for each type of file you download. Figure 41 shows two simple directory structures for storing downloaded files. The first example works well if you do not plan on keeping the installation files.

Figure 41 - Organizing Downloaded Files

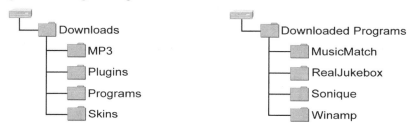

Zipped Files

Most downloadable software is compressed (zipped) to shorten download time. These files will have a .ZIP or .EXE extension. MP3 files are already compressed so they are usually not zipped. To extract files from a .ZIP file, you need a program, such as WinZip (*www.winzip.com*). The following steps outline this process using WinZip.

1. Download the zip file, and save it to your hard drive. It helps keep things organized if you first create a directory for the program that you are downloading and unzip everything there.

2. Right-click on the zip file and select **Extract to folder ....** The unzipping program will extract the files to the same folder as the Zip file.

3. Look for the executable program called Setup or Install, and double-click on it to begin the actual installation.

4. The program should bring up an installation wizard and guide you through installing the software on your computer.

Nullsoft Winamp Setup: Install Files ☒

This program will install Winamp 2.23 for Windows 95/98/NT (Intel) on your system.

Winamp is shareware, and if you use it beyond the 14 day evaluation period you must register. For more information on registering Winamp, see the about box in the program once you've finished the installation.

Select a directory to install Winamp in:

`C:\PROGRAM FILES\WINAMP`   Browse...

`C:\PROGRAM FILES\WINAMP\Plugins\in_mod.dll`

Cancel   Next>

Self Extracting EXE Files

Some programs are packaged in self-extracting executable files. These will have an EXE extension. Download the executable file into a designated directory, and double-click on it. The program will self-extract and usually run setup automatically. If not, find the setup (usually setup.exe) program that has been extracted, and double-click it. It should run automatically and guide you through the setup process using an installation wizard to take you step by step.

Direct Internet Install

Some programs can be installed without needing to be downloaded, by executing the installation software over the Internet. If a window comes up asking you to **Run this program from its current location** or **Save this program to disk**, you can choose to run the program and it will install the program onto your computer with the aid of an installation wizard. If you choose **Save the program to disk**, the program will be downloaded to your system and you will need to launch the executable file for its setup routine.

Downloading MP3 Files

To download a file from MP3.com, go to *http://www.mp3.com* and click on the Music link at the top of the page. A new page will display with links that allow you to search for MP3 files and browse files by music genre. Click in a link for a genre and you'll find dozens of songs by a variety of emerging artists.

If you want to know more about the artist, click on a link to a song, and a page for the artist(s) will appear with related information and a list of the artist's albums and promotional songs available in MP3 format. You can download these promotional MP3 files for free or click on a button to buy the album on CD.

> **Tip**
>
> Create separate folders for your MP3 files to keep them separate from programs and other digital audio file types. This makes it easier to keep them organized so you can quickly find the files you need.

To download an MP3 file, click on the Get MP3 link. You may be prompted to register if this is your first download. Register, if you haven't already, and then click Continue Download.

If you have a default MP3 player installed, the song may download to a temporary folder and begin playing automatically. If you want to save the file so you can listen to it later, right-click on it and choose Save Target As to download it to your hard disk.

Play or Enqueue MP3 Files from Explorer

MP3s can be played by double-clicking on them from Windows Explorer. You can also right-click on the file and a pop-up menu will appear. You should see choices for Play and Enqueue. Select Play and the file will begin playing immediately. Select Enqueue to just add the file to the playlist. You can also highlight a selection of files and drag and drop them on top of the playlist.

Modifying File Type Associations

When many player programs are initially installed, they can alter the file type associations to make themselves the default player for MP3 files. The following procedure shows you how to change the default player for the .MP3 file type to a specific program. See Chapter 9, *Organizing and Playing Music*, for more information on file type associations.

1. Launch Windows Explorer or double click the **My Computer** icon.

2. Select the **View menu** and then scroll down and select **Folder Options**.

3. Click the **File Types** tab at the top of the window. Scroll down to the file type for MP3, then click the **Edit** button.

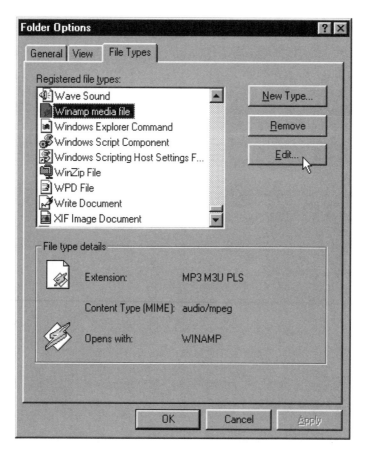

Edit File Type

Change Icon...

Description of type: Winamp media file

Content Type (MIME): audio/aac

Default Extension for Content Type: .mp3

Actions:
Enqueue
open
Play

New... Edit... Remove Set Default

☐ Enable Quick View ☑ Confirm open after download
☑ Always show extension ☐ Browse in same window

OK Cancel

Note: The file type for MP3 might be called Winamp Media, MPEG Audio or some other name depending on which players you have installed, but at least one of the extensions for it will be .MP3.

4. Under **Actions:**, highlight **Play** and click on the **Edit** button.

5. Type the full path to the player executable enclosed in double quotes, or click the **Browse** button to find the location of the player program (FreeAMP, Sonique, MusicMatch, etc.) you want to use. Look for the executable file (file with .EXE extension) in the directory of the player.

Editing action for type: Winamp media file

Action:
Play

OK

Cancel

Application used to perform action:
"C:\Program Files\FreeAMP\freeamp.exe" "%1"

Browse...

☐ Use DDE

Note: Make sure to add **"%1"** after the name of the executable file.

6. Click **OK,** and then click **OK** again to save the changes.

Note: Winamp and Sonique can associate themselves with audio file types through their configuration menus. See the Winamp tutorial for instructions on how to accomplish this with Winamp.

Creating a New File Type

If you have multiple players, a neat trick is to create a single file type with actions defined for each player program. This way, when you right-click on an MP3 file, you can choose which player to launch from the menu. To do this for MP3 files, either modify the existing MP3 file type, or delete it and add a new one.

1. To add a new file type, select **New Type** from the **File Type** tab of the folder Options Window.

2. Enter **.MP3** for the **Associated extension** and select **audio/basic** for the **Content_Type**.

3. Select **New** to define an action for this file type.

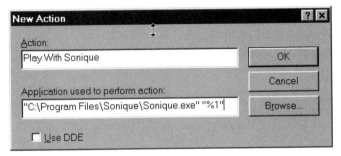

4. Enter the name of the player for the action and the full path to the player executable, followed by **"%1"**.

5. Click **OK** to save the action.

6. Repeat steps 2–5 for each additional player.

7. Highlight one of the actions and select **Set Default.**

8. Click **OK** to save the file type.

Note: It is possible to have duplicate file types defined. If you define or modify a file type association and it does not work properly, check and see if there is a duplicate definition of that file type. Deleting the duplicate definition should correct the problem.

Chapter 20

Software Tutorials

AudioCatalyst

The following procedure outlines the process of configuring AudioCatalyst and then ripping a track and encoding it in MP3. The settings recommended in this procedure should produce good quality files for most types of music. Once you are more familiar with the software, you may want to experiment with other settings.

Configure AudioCatalyst

1. From the Main window, select **Settings,** then **General**.

2. Select **ASPI** for the CD-ROM access method.

3. Click the **Browse** button, and then select the directory to store files.

Select Directory
d:\Music
d:\
Music
MP3
Playlist
Test
WAV
d: [scsi]

OK

Cancel

4. Set the Rip method as follows:

- The Rip Method controls the amount of jitter correction. On Plextor and any other drives with built-in jitter correction, you should set this to **Unbuffered Burst Copy**.

- For other drives, start with the rip method set to **Dynamic Sync width**. This varies the amount of overlap as needed. If this works and the file sounds OK, then you could try one of the **Unbuffered Burst Mode** to see if it increases the speed without introducing any errors.

- If **Dynamic Sync width** doesn't work or generates any errors, then try **Fixed sync width** with progressively higher values until one works. The higher values slow things down. If you set the sync width higher than 3 or 4 and still have problems, you should consider purchasing a new CD-ROM drive with better seeking accuracy.

5. On the **Naming** tab, select **Artist name** and **Track name**.

6. On the **Silence** tab, select **Leading silence** and **Trailing silence**, and enter **0.2** for each.

7. On the **Rip Offset** tab, select **Spin up disc before reading starts** and **Shorten last track by 10 frames**. Make sure all values are set to 0.

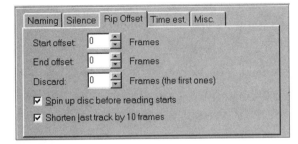

Note: The **Shorten last track by 10 frames** setting helps prevent seeking errors at the end of the outermost track. If your CD reader has problems finding the exact start and stop points of tracks, you may need to set a start or end offset. If your CD drive produces a click at the beginning of each track, set Discard Frames to 1 or 2 and see if that helps.

8. The default values on the **Time est.** tab should be OK.

9. On the **Misc.** tab, make sure that use **cdplayer.ini** and **Autosave CDDB queries** are the only options selected.

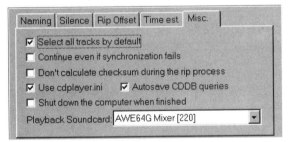

10. Select OK to exit to the main screen.

Configure MP3 Settings

11. Select the **MP3** button.

12. In the **Grab to** section, select one of the following:

- Select **MP3 file** to convert the tracks to MP3 without keeping the WAV files.

- Select **Wav file** if you want to edit the WAV file before encoding it.

- Select **Both** if you want to create an MP3 file and keep a copy of the WAV file.

13. Select **Use intermediate wave file** if you want to normalize the volume or if you are having trouble ripping at higher speeds.

14. Select **Use ID3 tag**.

15. Select the bit-rate in the Encoder Settings section.

- **Variable Bitrate** at the **Normal** setting will produce sound quality that is good for most types of music, with a compression ratio of about 10=1.

- **Variable Bitrate** at the **High** setting will produce the best sound quality, with a compression ratio of about 7=1.

- The **Normal/High** setting is a good compromise between file size and sound quality.

16. Select **OK** to exit to the main screen.

```
┌─ XingMP3 Encoder Settings ───────────────── [?] [X] ─┐
│  ┌─ Grab to: ─────────────────────────┐              │
│  │  ⊙ MP3 file    ○ Wav file   ○ Both │              │
│  └────────────────────────────────────┘              │
│                                                       │
│   ☑ Use intermediate wave file        Create an MP3 now│
│                                                       │
│   ☑ Use ID3 Tag          [Edit ID3 tag...]  [Browse...]│
│  ┌─ Encoder Settings ──────────────────────────────┐ │
│  │   ⊙ Variable Bitrate      ○ Constant Bitrate    │ │
│  │                                                 │ │
│  │      ├──────────────────▼──────────┤            │ │
│  │    Low   Normal/Low  Normal  Normal/High  High  │ │
│  │                                                 │ │
│  │   Description  Archival Quality-For high-end stereos │
│  │    Algorithm   MPEG-1                            │ │
│  │    Channels    Default (Joint Stereo)  [Advanced...] │
│  └─────────────────────────────────────────────────┘ │
│         [  OK  ]      [ Cancel ]      [ Help ]        │
└───────────────────────────────────────────────────────┘
```

Configure Normalization Settings

17. Select the **Norm.** button.

18. Select **Use normalizing**.

19. Set **Normalize to** to 97.

20. Check **...but only if the track is.** Set **Lower than** to 91 and set **Higher than** to 98.

21. Click **OK** to exit to the main screen.

Rip and Encode

1. Begin by inserting a CD, then launch AudioCatalyst. If this is the first time you have used the CD with AudioCatalyst, the main window should display a list of tracks.

2. If the track names are not displayed, select the **CDDB** button. Audio-Catalyst will attempt to connect to the CDDB via your Internet connection and obtain the song titles. Once AudioCatalyst has obtained the song titles, it will display them in place of the track numbers.

3. Select the tracks to rip by placing checkmarks in the boxes next to them.

4. Select **Grab**. This starts the ripping process. Do not use any other programs until the processing is complete.

Note: If ripping fails you may need to change the sync settings.

5. Listen to the tracks and compare the sound to the original CD.

The best test is to play the CD on an audio CD player or listen to the MP3 and WAV files. Some low-end CD-ROM drives use cheap 12-bit digital-to-analog converters, and the CD may sound worse when played on the computer's CD-ROM drive than on an audio CD player.

Cool Edit

The following procedures outline recording, trimming silence, removing noise and normalizing volume levels with Cool Edit.

Recording from a Record or Tape

1. Start by selecting **File**, then **New** from the main window. You will be prompted for the sampling rate, number of channels and resolution. For CD-quality audio, choose **44,100**, **Stereo** and **16-bit**.

2. Launch the Volume Control applet by clicking on the speaker icon located on the Windows system tray or the level slider icon on the task bar. If you can't find either of these, you can access the Volume Control program from the Windows Start menu by selecting **Programs**, **Accessories**, and then **Volume Control**.

3. Click on **Options** on the menu bar at the top. Then click on **Properties**. Make sure you have the proper sound card highlighted in the Mixer Device pull down menu. Then click on **Recording**. You want to make sure you also have a check in the box next to Line In.

4. In the Recording Control window, make sure that Line-in is the only control selected and set the slider about three quarters of the way up.

Note: What you hear from the speakers is the level of playback signal, not the level that will be recorded. It is a good idea to zero the sliders for the other volume controls because noise may leak in from other devices.

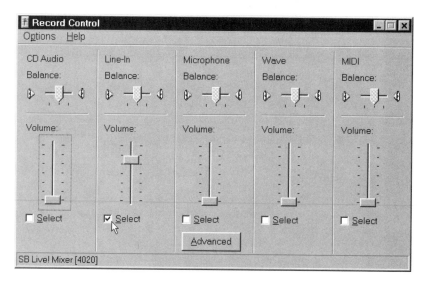

5.   Queue up the song you plan to record, and record a short test clip from the loudest portions of the song. Adjust the Line-in level so the signal peaks average around -6 dB, but do not exceed -3 dB. This will provide a good signal-to-noise ratio and prevent distortion caused by clipping.

6. Once the levels are set, close the test file, create a new file and queue up the beginning of the song again.

Note: You can avoid the step of closing and creating a new file by clicking the far right border of the main window. This will reset the start marker to the beginning and allow you to record over the previous clip.

7. When you are ready to record, in quick succession, hit the **Record** button located at the bottom of the main window of Cool Edit, and then press **Play** on the cassette deck, or lower the arm of the turntable. You should see the level meters at the bottom of the main window moving with the music. Any leading or trailing silence can be trimmed from the file later.

8. Click **Stop** once the song is finished playing. A waveform should appear in the main window.

9. Select **Save As** from the file pull-down menu to save the file to your hard disk. Choose Windows PCM WAV when prompted for the format.

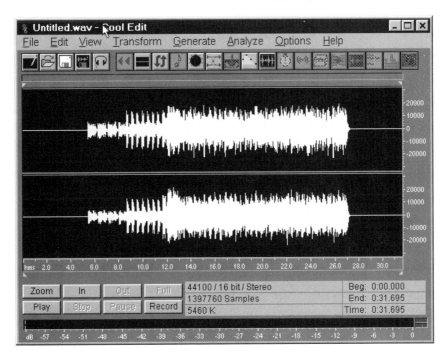

Trimming Silence from a WAV File

Cool Edit lets you view the full WAV file and trim off leading and training silence. Silence is easily identified by a flat line, whereas the song and other recorded noises will show up as sharp peaks.

1. Begin by highlighting the section of the WAV file that you wish to keep. Do this by clicking just before the start of the music and then drag the indicator to just past the end of the music. This should highlight the main portion of the WAV file.

2. Once you are satisfied with your selection, select **Edit** from the pull-down menu, and then click **Trim**. The highlighted section will remain and anything outside will be removed.

3. Once again, save your WAV file.

Filtering Noise From a WAV File

When recording from a cassette or from an LP, you can pick up a lot of background noise or hissing. This is due to the wearing away of bits of vinyl or magnetic oxide that the analog signal is recorded on. This noise can be filtered out using Cool Edit.

1. To remove noise from a WAV file, open the file in Cool Edit.

2. Highlight a section with just background noise and no music. A small one or two-second section should be enough.

3. Select the **Transform** pull-down menu, then select **Noise Reduction**. A dialogue box will display with parameters for noise reduction.

4. Click **Get Noise Selection from Profile**. It may take a few seconds, but this will analyze the noise in the selection. Then click on the **Close** button to return to the main window.

5. Highlight the entire song, or however much you want to filter, and then go back to the **Noise Reduction** window and click the **OK** button. This will filter noise from the selected section using the parameters from the noise profile you just created.

Normalize a WAV File

Cool Edit can normalize WAV files to adjust the volume. Many songs are recorded louder or quieter than others. Normalization can be used to adjust them to the same loudness.

1. Begin by selecting the entire WAV file.

2. Select **Transform**, then **Amplitude**, and then **Normalize**.

3. Enter a value of around 97%, which gives a little bit of leeway to help avoid clipping from further processing.

4. Click **OK** and Cool Edit will normalize the file. To ensure consistent levels from song to song, normalize all WAV files before you burn them to CD-Rs or encode them to MP3.

Cool Edit's normalization feature can also be used to correct a DC offset (bias) by entering the percentage of adjustment required.

Easy CD Creator

The following procedure outlines the steps for burning a custom MP3 CD with Adaptec Easy CD Creator.

1. Before you begin, close any open programs. The CD writer requires a continuous flow of data while writing each track. Other programs running while burning a CD can interrupt the data flow to the CD writer, creating a condition called a "Buffer Underrun." The CD burning will stop with an error message creating a "coaster."

2. If your system has a network card, you may need to temporarily disable it. This process does not require a reboot. Double-click on the **System** icon in the control panel to open the System Properties window, and select the **Device Manager** tab. Click on the **+** sign next to Network Adapters, and double-click on the icon for your network card to bring up the properties screen.

3. Check the box labeled **Disable** in this hardware profile, click **OK** to close the properties window, and click **OK** again to close System Properties. Your system will appear to hang for a few seconds while the card is disabled. Reverse this process to re-enable your network card after you finish burning the CD.

4. Start the Easy CD Creator program by clicking on the **Start** button, then choose **Programs,** then **Adaptec Easy CD Creator,** and then **Easy CD Creator**. The main Easy CD Creator window will appear. Cancel the Wizard if it appears.

5. If this is the first time you have run Easy CD Creator, select **Tools**, then **System Tests** and run the Transfer Rate and CD Recorder tests. This will determine the maximum writing speed that your system can support and configure other internal settings necessary for reliable CD writing.

6. Select **File**, then **CD Layout propertie**s. Click on the **Data Settings** tab, and make sure that the File System is set to Joliet to support long file names.

7. Click on **OK** to return to the main window. Make sure the **Data CD Layout** tab is selected.

8. Select the drive and folder that contains your MP3 files using the Windows Explorer style display in the top left pane of the Easy CD Creator window.

9. Select the files you want to include, and drag them to either of the lower panes of the window. Select multiple files by holding down the **Ctrl** key while clicking on them. If you drag a folder to the layout, the entire contents of the folder will be added to the layout.

10. As you add files to the layout, the status line at the bottom of the window shows a bar graph of space used, the number of files, total size and free space remaining on the CD.

11. Save the layout of the CD by selecting **File**, then **Save**. This will allow you to modify or recreate the layout in the future.

12. Place a blank CDR media in your CD recorder.

13. Select **File**, then **Create CD** or click on the round red button on the toolbar. The CD Creation Setup window will appear.

14. Select your CD writer's maximum speed. The first few times select **Test and Create CD** (the default). This will process all of the selected files and simulate recording the CD with the laser turned off before actually recording the CD to make sure your system can access the data fast enough to keep up with the selected recording speed. After you have successfully created a few CDs, you can select **Create CD** instead, which will save a few minutes.

15. On the **Advanced** tab of the CD Creation Setup screen, choose **Close Session and Leave Disc Open** if you want to add more files later. Otherwise, choose **Close Disc** to finalize the CD.

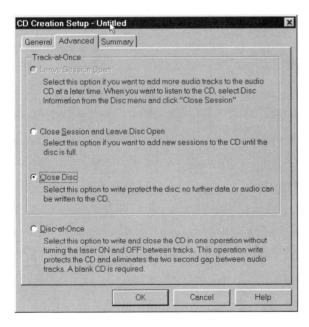

16. Click on **OK** to begin burning the CD. A status window will appear
    showing the writing progress. Click on the **Details** button to see more in-

formation. Don't run any other programs or move the mouse while writing a CD.

17. The message "CD created successfully" will appear, and the drive will eject the CD.

18. Use a felt tip permanent marker to label the CD. You can also use a laser or inkjet a stick-on label or use the Jewel Case Layout tab to create and print an insert for the jewel case.

If an error occurs, try creating a CD image file, then burn the CD from the image. This gathers all of the data and formats it into one large file and requires as much free hard drive space as the amount of the data you will be writing to the CD (up to 650MB).

This doesn't add too much time to the process since the data collection has to be done anyway, and the majority of the time required is for writing the CD tracks. If you still have problems, try successively slower writing speeds until you find one that works consistently.

MusicMatch Jukebox

The following procedures outline the basic uses of MusicMatch Jukebox. The MusicMatch interface consists of separate panels for a player, playlist manager, track information, and a music library. MusicMatch supports both ripping CDs and analog recording from multiple inputs.

Figure 42 - MusicMatch Jukebox Interface

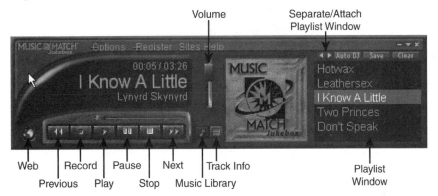

Configuring MusicMatch

The first time you run MusicMatch, it will auto-configure itself, based on the capabilities of your computer and your CD-ROM drive. It's a good idea to specify the default location of files and the recording (encoding) quality at this point.

1. Select **Options**, then **Settings**, and click on the **Recorder** tab.

2. Set the recording quality as follows:

• Use a constant bit-rate if you need predictable file sizes. A rate of 160 kbps is needed to approach CD-quality. **Custom Quality/VBR** (variable bit-rate) will generally produce better quality files.

• VBR with the 50% setting will produce sound quality that is good for most types of music, with a compression ratio of about 11=1.

• VBR with the 100% setting will produce the best sound quality but will take up more disk space, with a compression ratio of about 7=1.

• VBR with a 75% setting is a good compromise between file size and sound quality.

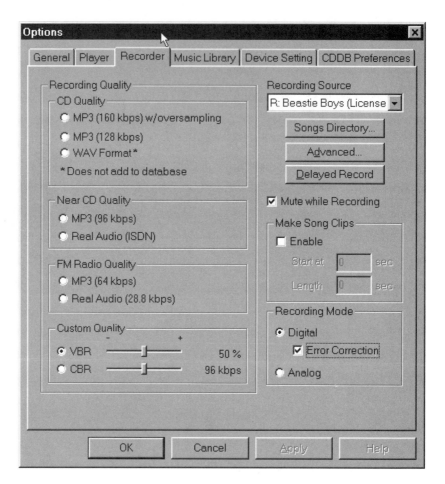

3. Click **Songs Directory** and specify the directory for MusicMatch to store new files. Uncheck **Artist** and **Album** under **Make Sub-Path using** if you want to prevent MusicMatch from automatically creating folders.

4. Under **Name Song file using:** select **Track Name** and **Artist** and use a hyphen as a separator. This will give your MP3 files meaningful names when they are recording.

5. Under the **Advanced** tab, you can set parameters for fades and normalization. Two or three seconds for **Fade-ins** and **Fade-outs** and a setting of **97** for **Normalization** should work OK for most songs. If you use the Winamp player with MusicMatch, you can install its crossfade plug-in to add the fades at the time the songs are played.

Ripping and Encoding MP3 Files

MusicMatch defaults to ripping and encoding simultaneously. It can also be configured to rip directly to WAV files, and it can be used for analog recording. The following procedure covers ripping from a CD.

1. Begin by inserting the CD in the CD-ROM drive, then click the **Record** button on the main interface. This will bring up the Recorder window. MusicMatch will read the CD and display the track names if you have a connection to the CDDB. Otherwise, it will display only the track numbers and lengths.

2. Place checkmarks in the boxes next to the tracks that you wish to record.

3. Click the **Play** button at the bottom of the Recorder window. Mu-sicMatch will automatically rip and encode the tracks you have checked and add them to its Music Library. Color-coded indicators are used for each track to identify any problems. Green means there were no errors, yellow means there were a few errors, and red means there were too many errors for the track to be processed.

Working With Playlists

The MusicMatch playlist is located at the right end of the player window. Songs can be added to the playlist by double-clicking on them or dragging and dropping them from the Music Library. The order of songs can be changed by dragging them up or down the playlist.

Once you have created a playlist, you can save it for later access.

1. Click on the **Save** button at the top, and you will be prompted to name your playlist. If you want to use that playlist later, just click on its name in the saved playlists window.

2. To play music in a continuous loop, go to the options menu at the top of the player and select **Player**, **Play Cycle**, then **Repeat**.

3. To play songs in a random order, go to the options menu and select **Player**, **Play Order**, and then **Shuffled Order**.

Using the Music Library and Auto DJ

The Music Library keeps track of all MP3 files in MusicMatch's database, even if they are not on any playlists. You can sort your music by Title, Artist, Album and six other categories ranging from Tempo to Mood by clicking at the top of the column. Many of these categories are automatically entered from the ID3 tags, but some will have to be entered manually. You can edit the predefined entries for Mood, Preference, Tempo and Situation by editing the file BRAVADJ.CAT in the folder where MusicMatch is installed.

Note: MP3 files must be imported into the Music Library before they can be played with MusicMatch.

1. To add files to the Music Library, click on the **Add** button at the top of the window.

2. A browse window will pop up and ask you to locate music files on your hard disk. Once you have selected the files, MusicMatch will add them to its database so they are one click away from being added to the playlist.

3. Once you have populated the Music Library, you can use the Auto DJ to automatically compile playlists based on criteria from the ID3 tags.

4. Click the **Auto DJ** button at the top of the playlist.

5. Enter the length of time for your playlist and select the criteria to be used in creating it. You can choose up to three selection criteria and multiple choices for each one.

6. Click the **Preview** button, and MusicMatch will create a new playlist based on your choices.

Converting MP3 Files to WAV Format

MusicMatch can convert MP3 files to WAV format, which is useful if you want to burn a standard audio CD.

1. From the **Options** pull-down menu, select **File**, then **Convert**. A window will pop up with two sets of directories; one is the source of the MP3 files, and the other is the destination of the converted WAV files.

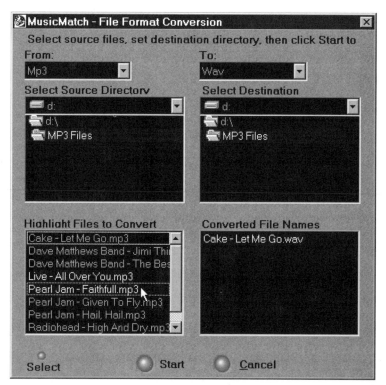

2. At the bottom of the window, change the **Source Data Type** to **MP3** and change the **Destination Data Type** to **WAV**.

3. Highlight the MP3 files you want to convert, then hit **Start**. MusicMatch will convert the selected files to WAV format, and they will be ready to be burned onto a CD-R.

Using Winamp as the Default Player

1. MusicMatch has the option of using Winamp in place of its built-in player, while you merely organize all your files with MusicMatch.

2. In the player window, select the **Options** pull-down.

3. Select **Player**, then **Use Winamp Player**. You may have to specify the location of Winamp executable. Normally, this would be **C:\Program Files\Winamp\winamp.exe**.

Exporting a Playlist to the Rio

A popular way to take your MP3 files with you is to use a portable player like Rio. MusicMatch can export songs directly from a playlist and download them to the Rio.

1. Begin by connecting the Rio player to your computer through the included adapter.

2. From the **Options** pull-down menu, select **Device Settings**. This will take you to the **Device Settings** tab of the **Settings** menu. Here you can choose the conversion rate of MP3s downloaded to the Rio. The lower the bit-rate, the more songs that will fit in the Rio's memory. Usually a bit-rate of 80 kbps will produce quality good enough for most people.

3. Click **OK**. Then from the **Options** menu, select **Send to Device,** and then select **Send Playlist to Rio**. The Rio software should start and receive the songs from the playlist you have created. This process will take longer if you have chosen bit-rate conversion.

RealJukebox

The following procedures are for recording MP3 files from CDs and working with playlists using RealJukebox. The RealJukebox interface is based on Windows Explorer and supports multiple levels of folders for organizing files. The music library records are stored in an MS Access database.

When you launch RealJukebox, it defaults to the **get music** window. Here you can access a number of popular Web sites for downloadable music. You can download music from these sites directly to the RealJukebox music library. Figure 43 shows the RealJukebox interface in both normal and compact modes.

Figure 43 - RealJukebox Interface

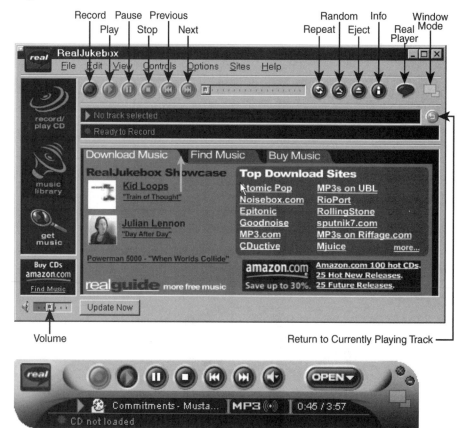

Configuring RealJukebox

Before you use RealJukebox to record MP3s files, you need to make sure it is properly configured.

1. From the **Options** menu, highlight **Preferences**.

2. Select **Recording Options,** then select the **Encoding Options** tab. Make sure **MP3 (Popular Format for CD Recording)** is highlighted in the format window.

3. Choose the quality level for your MP3s. The MP3 files will sound better at a higher bit-rate, but will take up more hard drive space. The shareware version of RealJukebox is limited to a maximum bit-rate of 96 kbps. This is well below CD quality. To create files at higher bit-rate, you will need to purchase the full version of RealJukebox.

4. If RealJukebox is your default media player, you can secure your MP3 files by selecting **Secure my Music Files when encoding**. This will create files that can only be played by RealJukebox. It is recommended that you do not secure files. Otherwise, you will not be able to play them on other players like Winamp or Sonique or on portable players like the Rio.

5. Click **File Storage** and specify the default directory for RealJukebox to store your recorded and downloaded audio files. You can also specify that any audio files RealJukebox finds on your system be automatically moved to the default files directory by selecting **Yes automatically move files**. If you do this, any standard playlist files that reference the old file locations will no longer work.

Recording MP3 Files

1. To record (actually, rip and encode) a track from a CD, click on the **record/play a CD** icon on the left side of the main window. Then insert your audio CD into the CD-ROM drive.

2. A track listing will appear containing track numbers and lengths. To get the song titles and artist names for each track, from the CDDB, click the **Track Info** button located at the top next to the **Eject** button.

3. Place checkmarks in the boxes next to the tracks you want to record.

4. Click the record button, and RealJukebox will automatically rip and convert the CD tracks to MP3 files in the folder you specified earlier.

Working With Playlists

Playlists can be created in RealJukebox with a few simple mouse clicks.

1. To create a new playlist, click the **music library** icon on the left side of the window, just under the **record/play CD** icon.

2. Near the bottom of the window, click the **New Playlist** button, then enter a name for your playlist.

3. Click the **Add Tracks** to add MP3s to your playlist. Highlight the tracks you wish to add and then click the **Add >>** button at the bottom of the window.

4. Hit the **Play** button at the top and enjoy your music.

Playlists can also be created by selecting files from the music library and dragging and dropping them on a playlist folder. Click on the top of any column in the music library to sort by that field. You can also "drill down" through files grouped by ID3 tag fields by clicking on the folders under Master Library in the left-hand pane of the music library window.

Winamp

The following section describes the Winamp interface and procedures for using the basic features of Winamp.

The Winamp interface consists of separate panels for a player, equalizer/preamp, playlist manager and mini browser. Each panel can be toggled on or off from the Winamp menu, and the equalizer and playlist panels can also be toggled on and off by buttons on the player. Additional commands and settings can be accessed via keyboard shortcuts and pop-up menus.

The Winamp menu can be accessed by right-clicking when the mouse pointer is over the middle of the player or by clicking on the sine wave symbol at the upper left corner of the player. Figure 44 identifies the controls on the Winamp player. The buttons for each control may look very different in other skins, but they always are in the same location, regardless of the skin.

Figure 44 - Winamp Player Interface

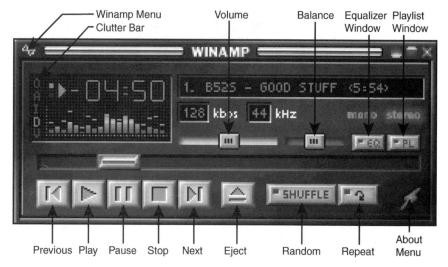

Winamp Menu and Minibrowser

Nullsoft Winamp...	
Play File...	L
Play Location...	Ctrl+L
View File Info	Alt+3
✓ Main Window	Alt+W
Playlist Editor	Alt+E
✓ Equalizer	Alt+G
Minibrowser	Alt+T
Options	▸
Playback	▸
Visualization	▸
Exit	

WINAMP BROWSER

WINAMP minibrowser

Welcome to the Winamp Minibrowser.
Find artist information while listening with the Nullsoft Winamp Minibrowser.

- Free Music, Live MP3 Radio - Tune into SHOUTcast
- Visit Winamp.com for News, Winamp Skins and Plug-ins
- Buy CDs from Amazon.com
- Artist Photos, Bios and Reviews on Rollingstone.com

Copyright © 1999, Nullsoft, Inc.

file:///C:/Program Files/Winamp/winampmb.htm

Configuring File Types

Winamp can be associated with MP3 files, playlists, WAV files and other file types as the default player that is launched when you double-click on one of these files in Windows Explorer. Installing other players may change these associations, but it's fairly simple to change them back.

1. Bring up the Winamp menu by clicking on the sine wave symbol at the upper left corner of the player, highlight **Options,** and then select **Preferences**.

2. Select **File Types** under **Setup**, then highlight the file types that you want to associate with Winamp.

3. Select **Close**. Winamp will now be the default player for those file types when you double-click on them in Explorer.

Working With Playlists

The Winamp playlist queues up the MP3 files to play. It can also be used to create and edit standard text (.M3U & .PLS) playlist files.

1. Bring up the playlist window by clicking the small button labeled **PL** on the right hand side of the player.

The buttons at the bottom of the playlist bring up pop-up menus with buttons for additional choices. You select a choice by pressing and holding on the first button and, while keeping the mouse button depressed, move the cursor

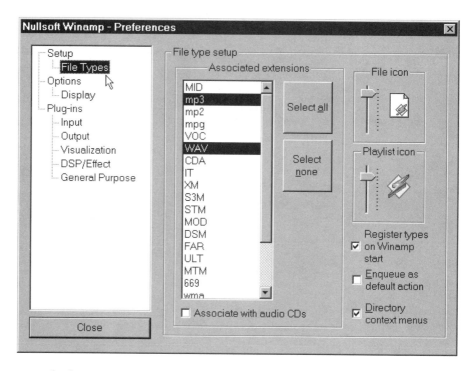

up to the button you want and release the mouse button. (This method of selecting buttons is not very intuitive.)

2.   Add a few songs to the playlist by either clicking the box in the lower left hand corner marked **+ file** or dragging and dropping the files onto the playlist window. The order of songs can be changed by dragging them up and down the playlist.

3. To sort the playlist, click on the **Misc. Opts** button, and drag the mouse pointer over the **Sort List** button, then let go of the button.

4. To save the playlist to a file, click on the **Load List** button, and drag the mouse pointer over the **Save List** button, then release it.

5. To play a song, double-click on it in the playlist window.

Note: Songs that are selected will be highlighted. The song title in reverse color is the one that is currently playing.

Equalizer Presets

Winamp's 10-band equalizer allows you to modify the frequency response and preamp gain. You can create and store standard equalization settings, and you can create settings for specific songs that can be automatically retrieved whenever the song is played. This is an extremely useful feature, especially if you have songs that vary widely in volume level.

1. To display the equalizer, click the **EQ** button on the Winamp player.

2. Turn the equalizer on by clicking the **On** button in the upper left corner of the EQ window.

3. Adjust each slider to equalize the sound. Lower frequencies (60-310 Hz) are predominately the bass drums and bass guitars. Midrange frequencies (600-6k Hz) are mostly keyboards, vocals, and guitar riffs. Higher frequencies (12k-16k Hz) are mainly cymbals.

4. The preamp gain can be adjusted to increase or decrease the volume level. The preamp gain setting is stored along with the equalization settings. Avoid setting very high levels because this will cause clipping.

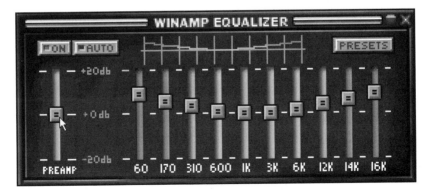

Load ▸		Auto-Load Preset	▏
Save ▸	Preset...		
Delete ▸	Auto-load preset... ▸	vid Lee Roth - Sensible Shoes.mp3	
	Default	nna Summer - Bad Girls.mp3	
	To EQF...	ney Drippers - Rockin' at Midnight.mp3	

David Lee Roth - Sensible Shoes.mp3
nna Summer - Bad Girls.mp3
ney Drippers - Rockin' at Midnight.mp3
pellerheads - History Repeating.mp3
Talking Heads - Swamp.mp3
Van Morrison - Brown Eyed Girl.mp3

Cure - Lovesong.mp3

Save   Cancel

5. To save an equalization setting for a specific song, click the **Presets** button, then select **Save,** then **Auto-load preset**. Then select **Save** to use the name of the MP3 file as the name of the preset, so it can be automatically loaded whenever that song is played.

6. To save a preset that can be manually loaded, click **Presets,** then **Save,** and then **Preset.** Enter the name for the preset, then click **Save.**

7. To manually load a preset, click the **Presets** button, then **Load,** then select either **Preset** or **Auto-load preset,** and select the desired preset from the list.

Installing a Skin

Selecting a different "skin" can change the look of Winamp. Winamp skins are bit map (.BMP) files that overlay the Winamp interface. These skins can be created or edited with many of the graphics programs currently on the market.

1. To use a different skin, you must first download it from the Internet or copy it from a disk or CD to the Winamp skins directory (usually **c:\Program Files\Winamp\Skins**).

Note: Some skins are downloaded in a ZIP file. They do not need to be un-zipped to be used.

2. With Winamp running, move the pointer over the main part of Winamp, and right-click to bring up the Winamp pop-up menu.

3. Press **Alt-S,** or select **Options**, then **Skin browser**, and either select the new skin, or click **Download skins**, which will take you directly to the Winamp homepage where you can find thousands of interesting skins.

Installing and Configuring Plug-ins

Plug-ins are small programs (usually DLL files) that can be used to add features to Winamp, such as visualization and sound effects and support for additional audio formats. Winamp plug-ins are grouped in categories, by function. Names for the DLL files begin with a code for the category followed by an underscore and the rest of the file name. Names for output plug-ins begin with **OUT_** and names for visualization plug-ins begin with **VIS_**.

1. To install a plug-in, unzip it (if necessary) and copy the DLL files to the plug-ins folder below the Winamp program directory (typically **C:\Program Files\Winamp\Plugins**).

2. To configure a plug-in, click the hourglass on the upper left corner of the Winamp player to bring up the **Winamp Menu,** then select **Options,** then **Preferences**, and select the plug-in category under **Plug-ins**.

3. Select the plug-in and then click the **Configure** button.

The Winamp Visualization plug-in menu can be accessed by right-clicking when the mouse pointer is over the visualization window of the player, or access it from the Winamp menu by selecting **Visualization.** The menu allows you to configure the built-in visualization effects and to **Sele**ct or **Stop/Start** a Vis plug-in or **Configure** the active plug-in.

Winamp Visualization Menu

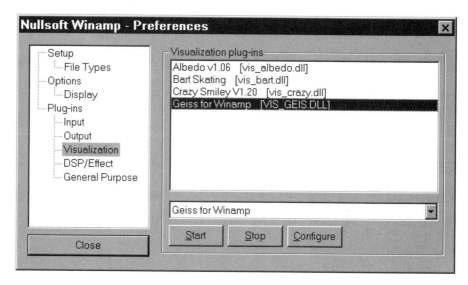

Converting MP3 Files to WAV Format

One of Winamp's Plug-ins is Disk Writer, which converts MP3s to WAV files. This is especially useful when burning CDs so you can create WAV files to burn onto a CD-R.

1. From the Winamp menu, highlight **Options**, select **Preferences**, then select the **Output** folder under **Plug-ins**.

2. Highlight the **Nullsoft Disk Writer Plug-in,** then click the **Configure** button at the bottom of the window.

3. Select the directory in which you wish to store the WAV files. (Note: Most CD-R media can only hold 650 MB, or 74 minutes, of music.)

Nullsoft Winamp - Preferences [X]

Setup
└─ File Types
Options
└─ Display
Plug-ins
├─ Input
├─ Output
├─ Visualization
├─ DSP/Effect
└─ General Purpose

Output plug-ins
Nullsoft waveOut plug-in v2.01 (x86) [out_wave.dll]
Nullsoft Disk Writer plug-in v1.0 (x86) [out_disk.dll]
Nullsoft DirectSound plug-in v0.96 [out_ds.dll]
Nullsoft WMA Output plug-in v0.90 (x86) [out_wm.dll]
Nullsoft Crossfading Output v0.91b (x86) (experimental)

[Configure] [About]

[Close]

4. Create a playlist with the songs you wish to convert to WAV format, then hit **Play** with the **Repeat** button toggled on.

5. You will not be able to hear the audio from the song, and the song timer will run very fast. However, once the songs have been processed, there will be a WAV file for each song in the designated directory.

6. Once you have finished converting the MP3s to WAV files, change the Nullsoft Disk Writer Plug-in back to Nullsoft WaveOut Plug-in or the original Plug-in that was in use before the conversion. To do this, go back to the output plug-ins folder and highlight **Nullsoft WaveOut Plug-in,** then click **Close.**

Nullsoft Winamp - Preferences [X]

Setup
└─ File Types
Options
└─ Display
Plug-ins
├─ Input
├─ Output
├─ Visualization
├─ DSP/Effect
└─ General Purpose

Output plug-ins
Nullsoft waveOut plug-in v2.01 (x86) [out_wave.dll]
Nullsoft Disk Writer plug-in v1.0 (x86) [out_disk.dll]
Nullsoft DirectSound plug-in v0.96 [out_ds.dll]
Nullsoft WMA Output plug-in v0.90 (x86) [out_wm.dll]
Nullsoft Crossfading Output v0.91b (x86) (experimental)

[Configure] [About]

[Close]

Winamp Shortcut Keys

Winamp can be controlled via shortcut keys. These keys can be mapped to remote control with an infrared receiver like the Irman. The table below lists some of the more useful shortcut keys that can be used with Winamp.

Table 32 - Useful Winamp Shortcut Keys

Key	Function
Ctrl+D	Toggle Doublesize mode
Ctrl+T	Toggle Time Display mode
Alt+W	Switch to Main screen (player)
Alt+E	Switch to Playlist Editor
Alt+G	Switch to Equalizer
Alt+T	Switch to Minibrowser
Alt+S	Load a skin
Ctrl+P	Go to Preferences screen
R	Toggle Repeat (loop) play mode
S	Toggle Shuffle (random) play mode
X (or numeric keypad 5)	Play
V	Stop
Shift+V	Stop with fadeout
C	Pause/unpause
B (or numeric keypad 6)	Skip forward to next track
Z (or numeric keypad 4)	Skip back to previous track
Up arrow	Increase volume
Down arrow	Reduce volume
Playlist Only	
L (or numeric keypad 0)	Add a file
Insert	Add a directory
Ctrl+N	New playlist
Ctrl+O	Open playlist
Ctrl+S	Save playlist
Home	Jump to beginning of playlist
End	Jump to end of playlist
Ctrl+Shift+1	Sort playlist by song title
Ctrl+Shift+R	Randomize playlist

Appendix A.

Interesting Web Sites

The Web sites listed in this section are ones I like or otherwise consider to be a good resource. This appendix is not intended to be an all-inclusive listing—there are thousands of other music-related Web sites that range from very good to very bad. See the MP3Handbook.com Web site for updated listings. If you know of any good sites that have been omitted, please e-mail the information to *feedback@mp3handbook.com*. Please note that, while the sites are grouped in categories, there is a lot of overlap between categories due to the flexible nature of Web businesses.

The following codes are used to indicate my personal recommendations:

^R   = Recommended
^{HR} = Highly recommended

Online Music Stores

Amazon.com ^R

www.amazon.com—Huge selection of CDs and downloadable music, books, videos, e-cards and more. Independent labels and artists can join the Amazon Advantage program and sell their music on consignment.

Audio Explosion

www.mjuice.com—Offers a wide selection of CD-quality MP3 downloads. Despite the promise of finding your "favorite songs," most of the music here is by independent artists. But who's to say the Bunion Peelers won't become one of your favorite groups?

CD Baby ^{HR}

www.cdbaby.com—One of the best selections of independent music on the Web. Worth a visit just to see the CD Baby logo. Shopping is easy and prices are lower than retail. On the last page of this book is a coupon for a CD with over 140 songs in MP3 format, courtesy of CD Baby.

CDNOW [R]

www.cdnow.com—Popular online music store. Includes music reviews and interviews, as well as thousands of music titles for sale on CDs, MiniDiscs, records, tapes and downloadable formats. Check the bargain bin for sales and special offers. CDNOW's Cosmic Music Network also provides resources for new and emerging artists.

CDuctive

www.cductive.com—Create a custom CD with cuts from your favorite cutting-edge artists. Or browse CDuctive's online store to sample new music from thousands of artists. CDuctive has licensing agreements with over 200 U.S. and European record labels.

City Music

www.citymusic.com—Online home of The Virtual Music Store. Download songs in MP3 format or purchase albums and CDs. The site has a nice interface for browsing through different categories of music.

CustomDisc.com

www.customdisc.com—One of the largest collections of downloadable music available for creating custom CDs. At this site, you can choose up to 25 tracks (or about 70 minutes of music), pick your cover art, create a title for the CD and send a gift message. Features like "Billboard Hits" make it easy for fans to find their favorite songs from the 50's, 60's, 70's and 80's.

Grand Royal Records

www.grandroyal.com—A complete online music store. Purchase music in CD and LP formats. Listen to Grand Royal artists 24 hours a day on Grand Royal radio. Read about the artists, and visit the Grand Royal online store for t-shirts, hats and other merchandise plus concert tour information.

Listen.com [R]

www.listen.com—A comprehensive directory for downloadable music. This site features a search engine enabling users to find music by artist or genre and direct links to music on downloadable music sites all over the Internet. Listen to music of independent bands, learn about today's top artists, and post feedback through their members' forum.

MCY.com

www.mcy.com—An extensive source of all genres of music, housing over 200,000 tracks. This site is devoted to tracking downloads to calculate and report royalty payments. Listen to samples and create your own mix to play on MCY.com's portable NETrax ™ player, which makes it easy for music fans to purchase music without using a credit card.

MusicMaker

www.musicmaker.com—Choose from many well-known artists and order custom CDs for a lot less than it would cost to buy a regular CD. A search engine helps you find your favorite artists. Now you can forget about buying a whole CD when all you really want is one or two songs.

Nordic Downloadable Music Site

www.nordicdms.com—An impressive collection of vinyl albums and downloadable music. The site also has links to over 100 radio stations offering more than 35 different genres, including holiday music, Spanish, Portuguese, techno, comedy, talk radio, tejano, hip hop and more.

Songs.com R

www.songs.com—A great site for independent music. The site has profiles on emerging artists, plus links so you can learn more about artists or purchase their CDs if they interest you. Songs.com also includes downloadable music in MP3 format and a database of independent artists so you can quickly find bands.

Ultimate Band List R

www.ubl.com—Great source of music from famous and not-so-famous bands. UBL.com is primarily a music shopping and sampling site. Your shopping cart will be full in no time when you browse through UBL's selection of compilations, movie soundtracks and boxsets. This site has the stuff you can never find in music stores.

Internet Radio Sites

Broadcast.com

www.broadcast.com/radio—The leading aggregator and broadcaster of streaming media programming on the Web. The Broadcast.com Web sites offer a large selection of music, sports, news and talk programming, plus Web TV, special events, music on demand and full-length audio books.

iCAST R

www.icast.com—A new breed of entertainment company that puts entertainment in the hands of the users, icast.com includes a mix of original, user-generated and syndicated audio and video content. Artists can have their songs added to iCAST streams with features to help them sell music.

Live365.com [HR]

www.live365.com—Live365 lets you create your own Internet radio station and listen to thousands of stations created by others. The EasyCast service allows you to upload MP3 files and playlists and have Live365 broadcast them for you. The LiveCast service allows you create a live broadcast from your own computer. There is no charge for either service, but you must comply with the webcasting rules set forth by the Digital Millennium Copyright Act (see Chapter 5, *Digital Music and Copyright Law*).

Music Radio

www.musicradio.com—Features college stations, commercial stations from the United States, Canada, Europe and dozens of other countries. Where else can you link to radio stations being broadcast in Antarctica and Mongolia? This site also features a music search engine and Billboard chart lists.

NetRadio Network

www.netradio.com—A good source of music whether you want to listen now or purchase for ongoing listening pleasure. Choose from over 120 music channels to listen to while you surf the Internet. If you're in the mood to buy, you can search through NetRadio's extensive collection of downloads.

Radio Moi

www.musicmusicmusic.com—All-request music in MP3 format. Create your own station with the artists and tunes of your choice or tune in to one of Radio Moi's preselected stations. This site has a vast music library that includes lyrics and interesting factoids for hundreds of songs.

Radio Sonicnet [HR]

www.radio.sonicnet.com—A dream come true! Create your own personal radio station with your choice of genres and/or artists. You and your friends (and the rest of the world) can tune in anytime, but only you can update your station with new selections. Don't feel like playing DJ? Check out one of Radio Sonicnet's own stations or critique other stations in the chat area.

RadioWave.com

www.radiowave.com—RadioWave.com creates and distributes streaming content on the Internet. RadioWave.com's products and services facilitate e-commerce, community building and advertising opportunities for clients.

Rolling Stone Radio [R]

www.rollingstone.com—Rolling Stone Magazine's Internet radio site. Features the David Bowie Radio Network (DBRN)—David Bowie's personalized favorites playlist. The site also offers more than a dozen other stations, complete with lists of the featured artists.

Spinner.com [HR]

www.spinner.com—Over 100 stations and 150,000 songs to choose from. Once the free Spinner player is downloaded, the music is just a click away. You can rate any song that's played, access artist information, and, if you want, purchase the CD.

Talk Radio News Service

www.talkradionews.com—Online version of the Talk Radio News Service, which provides insider news and scoops from Washington, DC and daily news from the White House and Congress for business and health talk shows.

Virtually Canadian

www.virtuallycanadian.com—Twenty-four hour radio with dozens of programs to choose from. If you miss a live broadcast, replay it in the archive section. Event listings and artist interviews will keep you up-to-date on your favorite artists and bands.

Yesterday USA

www.yesterdayusa.com—For fans of radio's "good old days." Yesterday USA broadcasts actual radio shows from the 1920s through 1950s, including vintage music, serial programs and westerns.

Internet Record Labels & Artist Resources

AMP3.com

www.amp3.com—An Internet record label that sells downloadable music and pays the artists up to 50 cents every time one of their songs is downloaded. Sponsors pay anywhere from 10 to 20 cents per download to place ads at the beginning of songs. Consumers have the option of downloading songs for free or purchasing the songs without the ads.

AMPCAST.com

www.ampcast.com—A site dedicated to introducing new musicians and bands, as well as providing a forum for the promotion of more established musical artists. AMPCAST offers a large archive of downloadable music (mostly in MP3 format). A search engine allows visitors to quickly search the musical archives by band name, music genre, artist location, instruments, musical influences and a variety of other criteria.

Amplified.com

www.amplified.com—A business-to-business music retail site with licensing for over 100,000 downloads in 17 music genres, plus thousands of songs available for purchase. Many music retail sites offering downloads and customized CDs get their music from amplified.com. For consumers, the site provides links to retail affiliates, such as Tower Records.

ARTISTdirect [R]

www.artistdirect.com—Put you one step closer to hanging out with your favorite band. The ARTISTdirect site links to the official Web sites for hundreds of major artists, ranging from the Back Street Boys to John Denver to the Rolling Stones. You can sample and purchase new music, read the latest reviews, and shop for t-shirts, posters and other band merchandise. You can also provide your own reviews and feedback in band-specific chat rooms.

Astrojams

www.astrojams.com—An organization created by bands that support free music. These bands allow their fans to record and distribute their music without worrying about copyright issues. The site offers both live and studio recordings. Astrojams also provides news on the latest digital music technologies.

Band Register [R]

www.bandreg.com—A Web site devoted to helping bands find their soon to be world-famous names, without taking someone else's. At this site, you can register your band name, and you can search the archives to make sure that no one has a name similar to yours. Best of all, this service is free.

EMusic.com [R]

www.emusic.com—One of the better known Internet record labels and music distributors. Through relationships with artists and license agreements with leading independent record labels, EMusic.com (formerly GoodNoise.com) offers a wide variety of downloadable music in MP3 format. EMusic also offers other music sites a percentage of sales that result from customers using their link to the emusic.com Web site.

Epitonic

www.epitonic.com—It's this type of site that makes me love the Internet. A carefully crafted site by a group of people in San Francisco, offering under-a-buck downloads of some pretty heinous independent music. There's plenty of attitude here along with a good selection of garage music, but the site is clean and easy-to-use. What's not to like?

GarageBand.com [HR]

www.garageband.com—A true Internet record label and great site for fans of independent music. Download MP3 files, listen to streaming audio, find out which bands are playing locally and collect award points that you can redeem for various products. Garageband.com is one of the few sites that actually signs bands to recording contracts. Contracts are typically worth $250,000 and are awarded based on the input of site visitors.

Internet Under Ground Music Archive (IUMA) [R]

www.iuma.com—A hip site providing interactive access to over 1,000 independent bands with sound bytes and music downloads, e-mail access to most of the artists, music reviews and discussion groups. This site gives independent artists an affordable, yet controlled distribution alternative to traditional record labels. IUMA Radio provides Internet radio with an attitude, and Liquid Audio downloads for just 99 cents.

J-Bird Records

www.j-birdrecords.com—Downloads by independent artists in a variety of music genres. Hear samples before buying and read up on your favorite artists and garage bands. The Tour Lounge allows you to search by month, specific date or state to find artists touring near you. The site also includes the J-Bird on-line radio station, along with Web pages and on-line sound stations for each artist.

LaserTrax.com

www.lasertrax.com—An independent label. This unique site has information on its featured artists, along with the latest news about the digital music industry. The site contains a "pre-owned" CD store with a large selection of low-cost CDs to choose from, along with MP3 downloads from independent artists and labels.

MP3.com [R]

www.mp3.com—MP3.com's Digital Automatic Music (D.A.M.) system lets any artist sign up to have their record produced and sold by MP3.com.

MP3.com offers the artists exposure to over 6 million listeners per month, with no sign-up cost or monthly fee. The artist simply receives 50% of the sale price of every CD sold. If the artist gets a record deal with a label, they can cancel the contract with MP3.com without obligation.

Riffage.com [R]

www.riffage.com —An elaborate site offering a large selection of free and purchasable downloadable music. For new bands, the site offers many services including distribution, direct marketing, and opportunities for self-promotion. The site offers plenty of links to top artists and current events, bringing together fans and musicians very effectively.

SpinRecords.com [R]

www.spinrecords.com—A great resource for emerging artists and their fans. The site is dedicated to the independent and underground music scene and provides all types of services as an independent label to unsigned artists and bands. Visitors can download music in MP3 and other audio formats, share information on the message boards and purchase products from the spinstore. There is also a section for local music, with information on clubs and concerts in major cities.

MP3 and General Music Resources

AudioGalaxy [R]

www.audiogalaxy.com—Provides reviews of independent artists, and free Web site hosting for musicians. The site includes an MP3 search engine, and it supports an MP3 streaming audio broadcast of the Top 40 Countdown. The site offers musicians 25MB of free space for uploaded music and Web pages and has a featured artist section and a chat room where you can talk with other music lovers.

Daily MP3

www.dailymp3.com—Download the latest and greatest versions of MP3 software. The site is updated daily as new versions become available. Music downloads and links to other MP3 sites are also featured.

Digital Music Australia

www.digitalmusic.com.au—A daily news site that uses MP3s and Real Audio for its downloadable music. This site offers links to hardware and software as well as general links to similar pages. There is a section where aspiring artists can sign up to put their music out on the Web. This site also offers a help section for people new to MP3 world.

Dimension Music

www.dimensionmusic.com—Features music from emerging artists and includes intros and music samples from several new bands each week. Headline news from the music industry is available, along with links to other MP3-related sites. For MP3 beginners, Dimension Music's online academy provides free, information on working with MP3 files, Internet Relay Chat and FTP. The forum and chat areas provide site visitors with the opportunity to give their own reviews on bands, software and more.

eatsleepmusic

www.eatsleepmusic.com—Especially useful for karaoke fans, the site offers downloadable music and music reviews. Look for free downloads of MP3 software, an online music club and music quizzes with chances to earn bonus points for free music and merchandise. A good selection of karaoke and children's sing-a-long music is available here.

Free-Music

www.free-music.com—Designed to help propagate the idea that great music can be produced without the need for corporate involvement. This site promotes the idea of free music and supports artists who distribute their music free over the Web. The site offers downloadable music from the artists who support the site and provides links to similar music sites.

Loud Factory

www.loudfactory.com—Showcases independent artists worldwide. The site broadcasts music 24 hours a day, and the music they feature is available in MP3 format. While you listen, download Winamp skins or check out the latest Winamp plug-ins. If your software is already up-to-date, read up on your favorite independent artists and have your say in the Loud Factory chat room.

MP3.com [R]

www.mp3.com—One of the most comprehensive sources of MP3-related information, industry news and music downloads. The site offers short tutorials on ripping CDs and creating MP3 files, plus a brief overview of MP3 technology and related legal guidelines. MP3.com provides reviews and downloads for dozens of MP3 players, encoders, playlist software, rippers and other utilities, plus tons of downloadable music. MP3.com also has bulletin boards for artists, programmers and end-users to share information and advice. For more information, see the listing for MP3.com under *Internet Record Labels and Artist Resources*.

MP3.com.au ᴿ

www.mp3.com.au—A popular Australian MP3 site. This site offers downloads of the latest music in MP3 format, along with news, music reviews and chat rooms. It also provides a directory on where to purchase the software and hardware you need for digital music.

MP3-2000

www.mp3-2000.com—Has links to basically everything you need to get up and running with MP3. Whether it's software and hardware listings (players, encoders, rippers, etc.), new bands, skins and plug-ins or basic information on MP3s, it's all here. This site includes news and reviews on the latest digital music. It also has price listings for the latest software and hardware plus a search engine for finding MP3s.

MP3now.com

www.mp3now.com—Need an "Intro to MP3" class? MP3now.com is the place for you, with brief tutorials on downloading, making and playing MP3 files. This site also includes reviews and downloads of MP3 players, encoders, decoders, rippers and other utilities; MP3 industry and music news; and a chat area.

MP3 Place

www.mp3place.com—Provides links to MP3 software, hardware and MP3 downloads. This site posts the latest news and reviews in the world of digital music and lists upcoming MP3 forums. It also has links on how to create, record, encode/decode and use MP3s.

MusicSearch.com

www.musicsearch.com—If you're looking for a Rickenbacker 12-string and don't know where to turn, try musicsearch.com. A music-only search engine with thousands of links to sites for artists, music events, industry news, music reviews, radio stations and music publishers.

Nordic Downloadable Music Site

www.nordicdms.com—Sample and download free and inexpensive music; download MP3 players; link to independent labels, recording studios and talent agencies; and listen to Internet radio sites from around the world.

Rioport.com

www.rioport.com—Created by Diamond Multimedia, makers of the popular Rio portable MP3 player, Rioport.com promotes new music and features "spotlight" artists. The site provides downloadable music and information on MP3 software and hardware, including the features of the Rio family of players. Rioport.com also provides links to the latest music and MP3 news.

Music News

Billboard

www.billboard.com—Daily online version of *Billboard* magazine, with tons of tidbits on current music topics and past chart-toppers. You could spend hours surfing through this busy site which features artist-of-the-day and album reviews, "this day in music" trivia, Internet-specific music updates, artist interviews, a reader question-and-answer section, and the Billboard challenge, a game in which your picks for the newest hot groups compete with those of other players for chances to win CDs and books. Of course, the famous Billboard charts are all here too, for singles and albums in every music category you can imagine.

dotmusic

www.dotmusic.com—Focuses on mainstream music that you hear on the radio. You can check out the latest in music news, see who's on top in the song charts, or download previews of the newest songs on the radio. This site also has an online CD store in case you find a song or group you like and want to buy the CD.

Localmusic.com

www.localmusic.com—Offers a new way to see what's going on in the world of music in a specific area. This site provides listings of who and what is playing in your area as well as reviews of the bands that recently played. Their search engine for live music lets you enter the type of music, band name, neighborhood, or even a specific club, and it will produce a list of shows that match your criteria. The site also lists local broadcast radio stations so you don't have to channel surf to find the type of music you like.

Mix Magazine Online

www.mixonline.com—Includes the latest news on digital recording technologies and reviews of equipment for professional DJs and recording engineers. The site also has a comprehensive directory of links to other audio related resources.

MP3 Critic

www.mp3critic.com—Devoted to reviewing music from new, independent artists. MP3 Critic offers thumbnail reviews—if you like what you read, you can bring up the entire review. If you want to learn more about a band, you can click on a link to go to their Web site.

Music Global Network

www.musicglobalnetwork.com—A daily news network to help you keep up with the digital music world. This site has links to MP3 software and hardware, as well as links to sites with similar content. The site also offers a downloadable MP3 section and has a top ten listing of independent artists. Another section lets you find new bands by genre and click on links to the band's Web site.

MusicDish [R]

www.musicdish.com—An award-winning & authoritative music industry magazine. MusicDish showcases cutting-edge artists & labels and provides career tips from industry experts, along with music reviews, the OMI (Online Music Industry) Award, and the Music Industry Survey.

NewMediaMusic [HR]

www.newmediamusic.com—A comprehensive resource center for artists, labels and consumers. The site offers special reports, editorials and interviews with new artists and producers, along with information on new products and services, special events and music industry press releases.

RollingStone.com [HR]

www.rollingstone.com—Part of the tunes.com network of music sites. Offers MP3 downloads as wells as videos, music news, reviews, streaming samples, Webcasts and an abbreviated version of the printed magazine. Artists can upload music and post their bios, photos, lyrics and tour schedules and track the number of downloads their music receives. You can also subscribe to the magazine here.

Tunes.com [HR]

www.tunes.com—A single source for everything related to music. The site offers more than a million song clips from 350,000 albums, over 1,000 music videos, profiles on 85,000 artists and bands, exclusive concert photos, daily music news, reviews and nightly live and archived performance webcasts. The site also includes the online archives of Rolling Stone, The Source and Down Beat magazines.

Webnoize [R]

www.webnoize.com—An in-depth news site devoted to the digital music world. The site supports streaming audio for its original programming, and it has an online guide for special events it hosts. Webnoize's research covers the entertainment and new media industries to keep you up-to-date on what's happening in the digital music scene.

MP3 Technical Information

Fraunhofer IIS

www.iis.fhg.de/amm/techinf—A techy site hosted by the Fraunhofer Institute for Integrated Circuits IIS-A, a European engineering research firm that develops microelectronics circuits and systems. Fraunhofer has developed major audio encoding schemes and contributes to MPEG standardization and research. This site focuses on audio and multimedia technology and includes information on licensing and industry news.

ID3.org

www.id3.org—Everything you wanted to know about the ID3 tag standard. Information is divided into low-tech, mid-tech and in-depth descriptions of the ID3 tag specification.

MP3Handbook.com

www.mp3handbook.com—The official site of *The MP3 and Internet Audio Handbook*. This site has detailed information on encoding, ripping, editing and playing MP3s. It includes content directly from the book to teach you everything you need to know about MP3 and digital audio technology. MP3Handbook.com also includes product reviews and links to other Web resources for MP3 and digital music.

MP3Tech [HR]

www.mp3tech.org—A good resource for those who want to learn more details of MP3 technology. This site explains MPEG-1 and MPEG-2 audio and also covers TwinVQ and Dolby AC-3 audio formats. MP3Tech provides a download page for MPEG Audio source code and discusses patent and license issues related to MP3. The site also offers downloads for MP3 players and encoders for different operating systems and a glossary and message board for people to learn more about MP3.

mpeg.org [R]

www.mpeg.org—A well-organized index to MPEG resources on the Web, with links to software, hardware, search engines, newsgroups and organizations related to MPEG standards. If you have a question about MPEG or MP3, you'll probably find the answer, or links to the answer, here. Please note that mpeg.org is *not* the official MPEG committee site. The address of the official MPEG site is *http://drogo.cselt.stet.it/mpeg*.

Home Recording & Pro Audio

Absolute Sound

www.theabsolutesound.com—Promotional site for The Absolute Sound, the high-end Journal of Audio and Music. Review sample articles from past issues to see if the journal is for you. If so, you can subscribe online, purchase back issues and even order Absolute Sound t-shirts and posters. You can also browse through an online audio classified section.

Audio Café ᴿ

www.audiocafe.com—An online reference for audio equipment manufacturers and products related to home stereo and theater, car sound systems and more. Win audio equipment and music in Audio Cafe's monthly quizzes. This easy-to-use site features equipment reviews, audio news highlights, directories of manufacturers, classified ads and a buyer's guide for audio equipment, and the Music Cafe bulletin board.

Audio Revolution

www.audiorevolution.com—An online publication for the AV world with reviews on audio equipment, music and current release movies as well as those available in DVD. The AudioVideo Marketplace is a great place to shop for new and used AV equipment from hundreds of dealers.

Audio Web

www.audioweb.com—An audio auction and classified site. Buy or sell just about anything related to the audio and video world. Write and post your own reviews on equipment, music and videos.

AudioWorld

www.audioworld.com—A Web page devoted to news about the digital music world. This site has articles on digital music products, the latest music industry news. The site also has a chat room where you can discuss the news with fellow music lovers and an event calendar so you can see what's happening in the digital music world. A media guide helps you find other sites related to your interests.

HomeRecording.com [R]

www.homerecording.com—Resources for people who record and mix their own music at home. The site has information on how to create recordings in MP3 format and how to record various types of digital music on CDs or hard disks. This site also includes equipment reviews, as well as instructions on how to make your own audio equipment and instruments. A mailing list is included for those who want to swap their music and tips with each other. A tutorial for beginners is also included.

Music Licensing

American Society of Composers, Authors and Publishers (ASCAP)

www.ascap.com—ASCAP is a performing rights organization committed to safeguarding the rights of its members by licensing and paying royalties for the public performances of their copyrighted works. This site features current and archived issues of ASCAP's *Playback* magazine, as well as the Art and Commerce Cafe, with a full menu of music news, reviews and interviews.

Broadcast Music, Inc (BMI)

www.bmi.com—BMI represents songwriters. Like ASCAP, BMI offers licenses for the public performance and broadcast of music published by its members and pays royalties to those members. This site features current and back issues of BMI's *MusicWorld* magazine and Planet Stereo, which offers sound bytes and reviews of new music. The BMI Store offers visitors all sorts of interesting items with the BMI logo.

Kohn on Music Licensing [R]

www.kohnmusic.com—A great resource for anyone who has questions about Copyright Law and Music Licensing on the World Wide Web. The site also has information on the leading book on music licensing, *Kohn On Music Licensing,* by Bob Kohn (Aspen Law & Business 1999). The site offers dozens of links to copyright organizations, music rights clearance organizations and other music industry resources.

National Music Publishers' Association, Inc. and Harry Fox Agency

www.nmpa.org—Site of the National Music Publisher's Association (NMPA), which protects the interests of its members through interpretation of copyright law and through education about music licensing. The site outlines licensing requirements for specific broadcast and performance situations and features links to sites related to music publishing, music rights, copyright law and other resources. The NMPA site also serves as a doorway to the Harry Fox Agency (*www.nmpa.org/hfa.html*), one of the United State's largest music licensing organizations.

SESAC, Inc.

www.sesac.com—SESAC, Inc. is the second-oldest performance rights organization in the U.S. Their site features sample audio clips with extensive artist profiles as well as plenty of interesting articles in their online magazine, *Focus on SESAC*. (SESAC used to stand for Society of European Stage Authors and Composers, although they no longer use that name and just call themselves SESAC.)

Associations

American Federation of Musicians

www.afm.org—Online home of the American Federation of Musicians, a union organized to promote and protect professional musicians. This site includes information on how to hire musicians, lists of member groups, booking agents, member benefits and an extensive history of the organization, which dates back to the 1890s.

Association for Independent Music

www.afim.org—The Association for Independent Music (AFIM) is an independent music association. Formerly called NAIRD, AFIM was founded by independent labels and distributors. AFIM's mission is to educate their members on how to succeed in the music industry without signing with a major record label.

Audio Engineering Society

www.aes.org—Online home of the Audio Engineering Society (AES), a professional society devoted to audio technology. Through conventions and publications, including the *AES Journal*, the group encourages and shares new developments in the world of audio technology. The site includes a list of member benefits, plus information on how to join.

Consumer Electronics Manufacturers Association

www.cemacity.com—The Consumer Electronics Manufacturers Association works to help shape industry legislation to benefit manufacturers of consumer electronics products. Their Web site includes information on trade shows and conventions for the consumer electronics industry.

Digital Future Coalition

www.dfc.org—Online home of the Digital Future Coalition, a 42-member group formed in 1995 to ensure a fair balance between protecting intellectual property and affording public access to it. The group formed in response to the Clinton administration's release of a white paper, which recommended altering copyright law for better protection of rights for motion picture creators and other intellectual property owners.

Electronic Frontier Foundation [R]

www.eff.org—The Electronic Frontier Foundation promotes the rights of free speech on the Internet. They have the latest news about the rights of free speech and how they are trying to protect and promote it. You can join their movement by signing up online.

European Imaging and Sound Association

http://eisa.techlink.gr—Online home of European Imaging and Sound Association (EISA), the largest editorial multimedia organization in Europe. The group includes 40 European audio, video and photo magazines. Members meet annually to bestow EISA awards on top manufacturers of audio, video and photo equipment.

Guild of International Songwriters and Composers

www.songwriters-guild.com—Online home of the Guild of International Songwriters and Composers. This organization offers members services in obtaining copyrights, assessing songs, recording demos, publishing and more. Members include songwriters, lyricists, publishers, musicians and other artists.

Home Recording Rights Coalition (HRRC)

www.hrrc.org—Online home of the Home Recording Rights Coalition (HRRC), an advocacy group that strives to protect the right of noncommercial use of VCRs, audio recorders and computers, i.e., protecting your right to download MP3 files from the Internet. The site includes a chronology of events in home recording rights, digital audio recording rights and legislation, and back issues of recent HRRC newsletters. The site also includes links to other sites related to legislation affecting use of recordings for noncommercial purposes.

International Standards Organization (ISO)

www.iso.ch—Online home of the International Standards Organization (ISO), a worldwide non-government federation of national standards bodies from 130 countries. The group works to create and publish standards in most technical areas. The site includes a list of ISO members, ISO criteria and a catalog of standards publications.

Moving Picture Experts Group

www.cselt.it/mpeg—Online home of MPEG, the group in charge of developing standards for compression, decompression, processing and coded representation of moving pictures and audio. You'll find overviews, as well as in-depth technical information describing each standard. The FAQ page is a good place to start if you have MPEG-related questions. The site also includes press releases, a schedule of upcoming MPEG meetings, plus tips on submitting an MPEG contribution.

MusicMaker Relief Foundation [R]

www.musicmaker.org—For serious blues fans. This is the online home of the Music Maker Relief Foundation, a non-profit charitable organization dedicated to helping the pioneers of traditional Southern music. Recipients of the group's donations must be rooted in the Southern music tradition, must be 55 years or older and must have an annual income of $18,000 or less. The site includes biographies and photos of pioneer Southern artists, plus sample music downloads.

Recording Industry Association of America

www.riaa.com—Online home of the Recording Industry Association of America (RIAA), a trade group formed to support fair legislation for U.S. copyright owners. This site includes information on legislation affecting use of recorded music, as well as information on Web licensing, piracy issues, censorship, record sales statistics and more.

Secure Digital Music Initiative

www.sdmi.org—Online home of the Secure Digital Music Initiative (SDMI), a group dedicated to developing technical specifications for securing music across all digital delivery platforms. Companies active in developing digital security systems are welcome to join SDMI; eligibility requirements and requirements to join are listed on the site. The site also features press releases on recent SDMI activity, a schedule of upcoming SDMI meetings and "members only" areas.

Appendix B.

What and Where to Buy

The products listed in this section were selected based on my own experience and research. Many other good products are available, but the goal here is not to present any product as the best, rather to give you a sampling of good, reasonably priced products that will get the job done. Prices in bold type are retail prices as of August 2000. All other prices are advertised prices from various retailers, also as of August 2000. The following codes are used to indicate my personal recommendations:

R = Recommended, HR = Highly recommended

Software

Product	Price	Manufacturer	Where to Purchase
PLAYERS			
FreeAmp	Free	Open Source	www.freeamp.org
Hum (Windows CE)	**$19.95**	Utopiasoft	www.utopiasoft.com
MACAST	**$24.95**	@soft	www.macast.com
Sonique R	Free	Mediascience	www.sonique.com
Wplay	**$10.00**	Xaudio	www.xaudio.com/wplay
Winamp HR	Free	Nullsoft	www.winamp.com
Xmms (Linux/Unix)	Free	Xmms Project	www.xmms.org
Xaudio MP3 Player (multiplatform)	**$10.00**	Xaudio	www.xaudio.com
ALL-IN-ONE			
Earjam	**$29.00**	Earjam	www.earjam.com
MusicMatch Jukebox HR (Mac and PCs)	**$19.99**	MusicMatch	www.musicmatch.com
RealJukebox R	**$29.99**	RealNetworks	www.real.com
SoundJam (Mac) HR	*$39.99	Cassidy & Greene	www.soundjam.com

* Downloadable price

Product	Price	Manufacturer	Where to Purchase
DJ SOFTWARE			
Party DJ [R]	*$15.00	DC Software	http://fon.fon.bg.ac.yu/~dcolak
Virtual Turntables	$42.00	Carrot Systems	www.carrot.prohosting.com
PCDJ [R]	Free	VisioSonic	www.visiosonic.com
PCDJ Digital 1000sl	$49.00	VisioSonic	www.visiosonic.com
PCDJ Digital 1200sl [R]	$199.00	VisioSonic	www.visiosonic.com
RIPPERS & ENCODERS			
AudioCatalyst [R]	$29.95	Xing Technologies	www.xingtech.com
Xing MP3 Encoder	$19.95	Xing Technologies	www.xingtech.com
MP3 Producer Professional	$199.00	Opticom	www.opticom.de
RECORDING AND SOUND EDITING			
Cool Edit 2000 [HR]	$69.00	Syntrillium	www.syntrillium.com
Easy CD Creator Deluxe	$69.96	Adaptec	www.egghead.com
GoldWave [R]	$40.00	GoldWave	www.goldwave.com
Peak LE (Mac)	$99.00	Bias, Inc.	www.biasinc.com
SoundEdit 16 (Mac)	$221.95	Macromedia	www.buy.com
Sound Forge XP	$59.95	Sonic Foundry	www.sonicfoundry.com
Total Recorder [R]	$11.95	High Criteria	www.highcriteria.com
UTILITIES			
RadioSpy	*$20.00	Game Spy Industries	www.radiospy.com
MP3 Explorer [R]	*$20.00	Pierre Levy	www.mp3-explorer.com
Audio Prepare	Free	Petri Damstén	http://aryhma.pspt.fi/audioprepare
MP3 Trim	Free	Jean Nicolle	www.logiccell.com/~mp3trim
MP3 Trim Pro	$99.00	Jean Nicolle	www.logiccell.com/~mp3trim
Ray Gun	$99.00	Arboretum Systems	www.arboretum.com
Wave Trim	Free	Jean Nicolle	www.logiccell.com/~mp3trim
Wave Trim Pro	$99.00	Jean Nicolle	www.logiccell.com/~mp3trim

* Shareware

Hardware

Product	Price	Manufacturer	Where to Purchase
CD-R/CD-RW DRIVES			
Sony Spressa CRX100E/X2 (USB)	$244.95	Sony	www.buy.com
PlexWriter HR 12/10/32A (IDE)	$258.95	Plextor	www.buy.com
PlexWriter HR PX-W12432TI/SW (SCSI)	$318.95	Plextor	www.buy.com
PORTABLE PLAYERS			
PJB-100	$695.00	HanGo	www.mp3factorydirect.com
NOMAD II	$249.95	Creative Labs	www.buy.com
Lyra	*$149.99	RCA	www.rca.com
Rave MP 2200 R	$260.99	Sensory Science	www.hardwarestreet.com
Rave MP 2300	$279.99	Sensory Science	www.hardwarestreet.com
Rio 500 HR	$199.00	S3	www.buy.com
Rio 600	$165.99	S3	www.buy.com
CAR PLAYERS			
Aiwa CDC-MP3 R	$299.95	Aiwa	www.crutchfield.com
empeg-car (6GB)	**$1,099.00**	Empeg	www.empeg.com
eXcelon Z919	**$750.00**	Kenwood	www.crutchfield.com
MP-ROM	**$200.00**	Jeremy Briggs	www.carplayer.com
DUAL MODE MP3/CD PLAYERS			
AudioReQuest HR	**$799.95**	ReQuest	www.audiorequest.com
Brujo	$229.99	netDrives	www.netdrives.com
D'Music SM-200C	$199.95	Pine	www.outpost.com
SOUND CARDS			
Montego II Quadzilla	$47.94	Voyetra Turtle Beach	www.buy.com
Sound Blaster Live! Platinum R	$155.95	Creative Labs	www.buy.com
Sound Blaster Live! MP3+ HR	$77.95	Creative Labs	www.buy.com

* 32MB model (RD2201). $229.99 for 64MB model with car kit (RD 2203)

Speakers, Cables & Audio Interfaces

Product	Price	Manufacturer	Where to Purchase
SPEAKERS			
ACS48 Powercube Plus	$87.95	Altec Lansing	*www.buy.com*
SoundWorks	$69.99	Cambridge Sound	*www.hifi.com*
MicroWorks **HR**	$129.99	Cambridge Sound	*www.hifi.com*
Accoustimass	$334.95	Bose	*www.buy.com*
USB SPEAKERS			
A305	$136.95	Altec Lansing	*www.buy.com*
Yamaha 80 watt USB (YSTMS55DW)	$133.95	Yamaha	*www.buy.com*
MA-150U **R**	**$188.00**	Roland	*www.ubstuff.com*
REMOTE CONTROLS			
Irman	**$35.00**	Evation	*www.evation.com*
USB AUDIO INTERFACES			
UA-30 **HR**	$245.00	Roland	*www.computersandmusic.com*
UA-100 Audio Canvas	$398.00	Roland	*www.computersandmusic.com*
CABLES			
100' 1/8" mini-phone to dual RCA (male/male) **R**	**$29.99**	MusicMatch	*www.musicmatch.com*
300' 1/8" mini-phone to dual RCA (male/male)	**$49.99**	MusicMatch	*www.musicmatch.com*
20' 1/8" mini-phone to dual RCA (male/male) **R**	**$19.95**	Monster	*www.jandr.com*
4' 1/8" mini-phone to dual RCA (male/male)	**$14.99**	Radio Shack	Radio Shack
ADAPTERS			
Sony mini-phone stereo to cassette adapter **HR**	14.96	Sony	Wal-Mart
RCA to RCA (female/female)	**$2.49**	Radio Shack	Radio Shack (P/N# 274-1553)
1/8" mini phone to mini phone (female/female)	**$2.49**	Radio Shack	Radio Shack (P/N # 274-155)
S/PDIF Toslink (optical) to Coax (RCA) adapter	**$69.00**	Midiman CO2	*www.computersandmusic.com*

Product	Price	Manufacturer	Where to Purchase
WIRELESS DEVICES			
MP3 Anywhere [HR]	$79.99	X10	*www.x10.com*
LeapFrog WaveMaster [R]	**$99.99**	Terk	*www.starlink-dss.com*
iRhythm Remote Tuner	**$99.95**	Sonicbox	*www.sonicbox.com*
WAVECOM Sr. 2.4 gHz wireless A/V system [R]	$99.95	RF-Link Technology	*www.rflinktech.com*

Additional Resources

For more information on MP3-specific products, visit the hardware and software sections of MP3.com. For more information on general computer products, visit the product review section of ZDNET.com.

Appendix C.

Recommended Reading

The following books are recommended for readers who want a deeper understanding of the topics covered in this book.

An Introduction to Digital Audio

John Watkinson
Focal Press, 1994. Paperback—$42.95
This book is more technical than the title implies, and is more suitable for sound system engineers and electronics designers. It provides in-depth coverage of the principles of audio, digital to analog conversion, digital electronics, digital signal processing, recording and editing digital audio, and digital recording hardware.

Audio on the Web

Jeff Patterson & Ryan Melcher
Peachpit Press, 1998. Paperback—$34.95
This is a good book for anyone who wants to incorporate downloadable music or streaming audio into a Web site. It explains the basics of digital audio, working with downloadable music and working with streaming audio. It also covers various digital audio file and streaming formats, and streaming audio software from several major vendors.

The Compact Disc Handbook

Ken Pohlmann
A-R Editions, 1992. Paperback—$34.95
This book provides a comprehensive introduction to compact disc technology. It covers the basics of digital audio processing, error correction, coding modulation for CDs and just about everything else related to CD technology.

Getting into Digital Recording: Digital Audio, Basics, Operations, Applications

Paul Lehrman

Hal Leonard Publishing, 1996. Paperback—$9.95

This is a good book for anyone who wants a basic understanding of digital recording technology. It covers the basics of digital audio, digital-to-analog conversion, encoding methods, error correction, popular formats and techniques for digital recording and mixing.

Making Music with Digital Audio: Direct to Disk Recording on the PC

Ian Waugh

PC Publishing, 1997. Paperback—$17.95

This is an excellent book for musicians and anyone else who wants to record and mix music on a PC. It covers the basic principles of sound and digital audio, computer hardware, software for editing and mixing, working with MIDI devices and software, and troubleshooting.

Poor Richard's Web Site

Peter Kent

Top Floor Publishing, 1998. Paperback—$37.95

This is a straightforward book, full of practical advice for anyone who needs to set up a Web site and keep costs down. Even if money is not an issue, this book is extremely useful for the novice Web designer or Webmaster and anyone whose business depends on a Web site.

Internet and World Wide Web Simplified

maranGraphics

IDG Books, 1998. Paperback—$24.99

This is a great book for anyone new to the Internet. It covers the basics of Web browsers, e-mail, chat, searching, downloading and more. Dozens of step-by-step procedures and 3D color illustrations are included.

Tim Sweeney's Guide to Releasing Independent Records

Tim Sweeney & Mark Geller

T.S.A. Books, 1996. Paperback—$24.95

This short, easy-to-read book is geared to musicians who want to learn about releasing their own records.

288

Glossary

a2b—AT&T's a2b music distribution system.

AAC—Advanced Audio Coding (part of MPEG–2).

AARC—Alliance of Artists and Recording Companies.

ADC—Analog-to-digital converter.

ADPCM—Adaptive Differential Pulse Code Modulation; a type of digital audio compression that predicts the values of upcoming samples.

analog audio—Audio represented by a signal that continuously varies.

AIFF—A common audio format for the Macintosh; normally uncompressed.

ASPI—A method of accessing a CD-ROM drive. Originally developed for SCSI, ASPI often works well with IDE drives via the ATAPI protocol.

ASCAP—American Society of Composers, Authors and Publishers; a performing rights organization that provides blanket licensing on behalf of music copyright holders.

ATAPI—A protocol used to communicate with non-hard drive IDE devices like CD-ROMs.

AU—An audio format commonly found on Sun and NeXT computers.

bandwidth—The transmission capacity of a network, or other communications medium.

broadcasting—A method of transmitting information that indiscriminately sends the same information to all systems.

bit—A binary digit (either a 1 or a 0).

bit-rate—The number of bits (1s and 0s) used each second to represent a digital signal.

BMI—Broadcast Music, Inc.; A performing rights organization that provides blanket licensing on behalf of music copyright holders.

byte—A sequence of eight bits.

buffer—A place for temporary storage of data.

CAV—Constant Angular Velocity.

CBR—Constant bit-rate.

CCIR—Centre for Communications Research.

CDDA—Compact Disc-Digital Audio.

CDDB—Compact Disc Database; a free Web site (*www.cddb.com*) with a database that contains information, including artist names and song titles, for over 300,000 music CDs.

CD—Compact disc.

CD-ROM—Compact Disc-Read Only Memory; generally used to refer to a pre-recorded data CD.

CD-R—Compact Disc-Recordable; a CD that can be recorded only once.

CD-RW—Compact Disc-Rewritable; a CD that can be recorded and erased multiple times.

checksum—A unique number generated by applying a formula to the contents of a data file. Checksums can be used to determine if a file has been modified or if two files are identical, without directly comparing the files.

clipping—The truncating (or flattening) of a waveform peak when it reaches the maximum possible level.

CLV—Constant Linear Velocity.

codec—An algorithm for encoding and decoding digital information.

CompactFlash—A small solid-state memory card with an onboard controller that emulates a hard disk.

crossfade—A way of using a mixer to overlap the beginning of one song with the end of another and vary the levels to create a smooth transition.

DAC—Digital-to-analog converter.

DAE—Digital audio extraction.

DAT—Digital Audio Tape.

dB—Decibel; a relative unit measurement for sound.

digital audio—Audio represented by numbers—usually in binary format (1s and 0s).

digital audio extraction—The process of copying audio data directly from a CD (also referred to as ripping).

dithering—A method of adding random noise to a digital audio signal to minimize the effect of quantization distortion.

Doctrine of Fair Use—Part of copyright law that allows copies to be made without permission of the copyright holder under limited circumstances.

DVD—Digital Versatile Disc; a high-density media, similar to a CD, with a capacity of up to 18.8 GB.

dynamic range—The range of signal levels an audio system or piece of audio equipment is capable of handling.

EMF—Electro-Magnetic Frequency.

encoder—Software or hardware that encodes information.

encoding—The processing of converting uncompressed audio into a compressed format.

enqueue—Queue, or place, in a list of items to be processed.

EPAC—A perceptual audio encoding scheme based on PAC—developed by Bell Labs, the research and development arm of Lucent Technologies.

equalization—Adjusting the relative levels of bands of frequencies to modify the frequency response of an audio signal or file (usually to make it smoother).

firmware—Computer programs that are stored on a piece of hardware.

First Sale Doctrine—Part of copyright law that permits consumers to resell pre-recorded music they already own, provided they do not retain any copies.

frame—A small chunk of data. (Sectors on audio CDs are sometimes referred to as frames.)

freeware—Software that is free.

FTP—File Transfer Protocol; a protocol used to transfer files across the Internet.

GB—Gigabyte. 2^{30} (1,073,741,824) bytes.

genre—A category of music; e.g., blues, jazz, rock, etc.

gHz—One billion cycles per second.

Hertz (Hz)—Cycles per second; used as a measurement of frequency.

HTML—Hypertext Markup Language.

HTTP—Hypertext Transfer Protocol.

Huffman Encoding—A method of data compression that uses shorter codes to represent patterns that are more common.

ID3 Tag—A method for storing data inside an MP3 file.

IDE—Integrated Drive Electronics.

ISA—Industry Standard Architecture; an older type of PC interface (bus) for plug-in cards.

ISDN—Integrated Services Digital Network; a type of digital telephone line capable of transmitting combinations of voice and data at up to 128 kbps.

ISO—International Standards Organization.

ITU—International Telecommunications Union.

jack—A generic term for plug-in connectors on audio equipment.

jitter—Errors introduced into a digital signal due to the seeking inaccuracy of many CD–ROM drives.

jitter correction—A method of reading overlapping blocks of data from CD-ROMs to eliminate jitter.

JPEG—Joint Photographic Experts Group; A group of experts nominated by national standards groups to develop standards for image compression.

k—1,000.

K—2^{10} (1,024).

KB—Kilobyte 2^{10} (1,024 bytes).

kHz—Thousands of cycles per second.

kbps—Kilobits (bits x 1,000) per second.

Kb/sec—Kilobytes (bytes x 1024) per second.

line-level—A range of levels (higher than phono or mic levels but lower than speaker levels) found on inputs and outputs of audio equipment.

line-in jack—An input jack designed to accept the output from a line-level output.

line-out jack—An output jack that bypasses the amplifier of a piece of audio equipment.

lossless compression—Compression that always reproduces an exact copy of the original data.

lossy compression—Compression that removes irrelevant or redundant information and is incapable of reproducing an exact copy of the original data.

MB—Megabyte 2^{20} (1,048,576) bytes.

memory card—Non-volatile, solid-state memory, such as Compact Flash and SmartMedia.

microdrive—A miniature hard disk made by IBM that's about the size of a matchbook.

MIDI—Musical Instrument Digital Interface.

mHz—One million cycles per second.

MiniDisc—A small rewritable optical disc designed by Sony Corporation for recording and playing audio, similar to a CD.

MPEG—Moving Pictures Experts Group.

MP2—MPEG Audio Layer-II.

MP3—MPEG Audio Layer-III.

MP4—MPEG AAC.

WMA—A proprietary audio encoding scheme developed by Microsoft.

multicasting—A method of transmitting information that allows multiple users or systems to subscribe to the same stream (or channel).

musical work—A term used in copyright law that refers to the actual notes and lyrics used in a song.

NBC—Not backwards compatible.

normalization—The process of adjusting the level of a digital audio file so all songs play at the same volume.

Nyquist Theorem—A theory that states that the sampling rate of a signal must be at least twice the highest frequency that needs to be produced.

OS—Operating system.

octave—The interval between any frequency and another frequency twice as high.

patch—A file that updates a program by modifying or replacing only the portions of the program that have changed.

PCI—Peripheral Component Interface; a newer type of PC interface (bus) for plug-in cards.

PCM—Pulse code modulation.

PCMCIA—Personal Computer Memory Card Industry Association.

PCMCIA card—A small plug-in card typically used on notebook computers to added features like modems, network interfaces and external drives.

playlist—A list of songs that can be played in succession, automatically.

plug-in—A software module that adds functions to a program.

preamp—A device that sets the level of an audio signal before it is sent to the main amplifier.

psycho-acoustic encoding—A lossy digital audio compression based on the properties of human hearing.

public domain—Intellectual property (music, text, etc.) that may be freely copied and distributed. Intellectual property becomes public domain when the copyright expires or the copyright owner explicitly declares that the property is in the public domain.

pulse code modulation (PCM)—A common format for uncompressed digital audio that uses fixed length pulses to represent binary data.

quantization—Rounding of voltage sample values to the nearest integer.

QuickTime—An audio and video encoding and streaming media system developed by Apple Computer.

RAM—Random access memory.

RealAudio—A proprietary audio encoding and streaming format developed by RealNetworks.

Red Book audio—The standard format for audio CDs.

resolution—The number of bits used to represent each sample in an uncompressed digital audio signal (typically, 4, 8, 16 or 20 bits).

RIAA—Recording Industry Association of America.

ripping—See digital audio extraction.

SCMS—Serial Copy Management System.

SCSI—Small Computer System Interface.

SDMI—Secure Digital Music Initiative.

sector—A pie-shaped section of a disc that holds a fixed amount of data. Sectors on CDs are often referred to as frames.

SESAC—A performing rights organization that provides blanket licensing on behalf of music copyright holders. (Formerly the Society of European Stage Authors and Composers.)

shareware—Software that can be freely distributed and evaluated but must be purchased if used beyond a certain period.

SHOUTcast—A streaming MP3 system developed by Nullsoft.

skin—A file that controls the appearance of a program's user interface.

SmartMedia—A type of memory card with no onboard controller.

sound recording—A term used in copyright law that refers to the artist's interpretation of a musical work and the actual recording.

S/PDIF—Sony/Phillips Digital Interface.

SPL—Sound Pressure Level; a measure of sound intensity.

statutory license—A license, provided for by law that is automatically granted to parties that meet certain conditions.

streaming—Information (usually audio or video) that can be heard or viewed as it is being transmitted.

streaming media—A term that encompasses streaming audio, video and text.

synchronization—The process of synchronizing overlapping blocks of sectors to eliminate jitter.

THD—Total harmonic distortion.

track—An entire song.

TwinVQ—Transform-domain Weighted Interleave Vector Quantization—an audio encoding scheme developed by the NTT Human Interface Lab.

unicasting—A method of transmitting information that uses independent streams (or channels) to send the same information to multiple users.

USB—Universal Serial Bus; a high-speed interface for personal computers that supports multiple devices and doesn't tie up interrupts.

VBR—Variable bit-rate

VQF—File extension for TwinVQ.

watermarking—A method of transparently embedding data in a file to identify the copyright holder.

WAV—A common type of audio file, usually uncompressed; pronounced "wave."

Index

About the Authors

Bruce Fries is a writer, technology consultant and entrepreneur who lives in Silver Spring, Maryland. He entertains frequently and is an associate of the Audio Engineering Society and the founder of several high-tech companies.

Marty Fries is a technology consultant, audio engineer, blues pianist and teacher of the Alexander Technique, in Laurel, Maryland. He has designed and built studio equipment and is the founder of Imagimedia (*www.imagimedia.net*), a CAD and network services company.

Other Books from TeamCom

TeamCom is an innovative new media publishing company that produces high quality how-to books, Web content and related products to help people improve and enrich their lives. Below are some of our other books.

Succeeding in America: Lessons from Immigrants Who Achieved the American Dream

By Leticia Gallares-Japzon; February 2000; $16.95
Succeeding in America is a how-to/success book that focuses on the principles and techniques used by immigrants to overcome all manner of obstacles and become highly successful citizens of the United States.

The Retired Person's Guide to Computers and the Internet

By Dirk Lammers; October 2001; $19.95
The Retired Person's Guide to Computers and the Internet contains practical advice and information of interest to retired persons and senior citizens. It covers basic information on using computers and the Internet, including information about software and Web sites of particular interest to seniors.

Free Music CD

As a purchaser of this book, you are entitled to a free CD, with approximately 100 full-length songs from more than 40 different music genres, courtesy of CDbaby.com—"the best little record store on the Web."

These songs are not "filler"—CD Baby's founder Derek Sivers has personally selected each one. The CD also includes a shareware version of MusicMatch Jukebox and a nice HTML interface.

To get the CD as soon as possible, send an e-mail with your name and address to *FreeCD@TeamComBooks.com* and we'll send you the CD right away. You can also write to TeamCom Books at P.O. Box 1251, Burtonsville, MD 20866. Include a note with the words "Free CD" along with your name and address.